ID640506

The South and the Nation

PAT WATTERS

The South and the Nation

E 70

VINTAGE BOOKS
A Division of Random House, New York

Copyright © 1969 by Pat Watters

All rights reserved under International and Pan-American Copyright Conventions. Published in the United States by Random House, Inc., New York, and simultaneously in Canada by Random House of Canada Limited, Toronto. Originally published by Pantheon Books in 1969.

ISBN 394-71160-2
Library of Congress Catalog Card Number: 69-15475
Manufactured in the United States of America

First Vintage Books Edition, September 1971

Cover photographs by Al Clayton and courtesy of
Southern Regional Council

TO

Ellen Watters and Patrick Watters

Acknowledgments

I AM INDEBTED to all those Southerners, too numerous to name, who provided information and insights for my specific research for this book, and all those others who over the years have similarly contributed to my feeling for the South.

I am indebted to fellow staff members at the Southern Regional Council, the people of the Councils on Human Relations across the South, and the workers in other organizations devoted to building a just society in the region. I am grateful for the suggestions and criticisms of Dr. Robert Coles of Harvard University Health Services, Dr. Samuel DuBois Cook of Duke University, and Leslie W. Dunbar, executive director of the Field Foundation.

I gratefully acknowledge a grant from the Rockefeller Foundation's program in imaginative writing and literary scholarship, which enabled me to complete this book.

The quotations from "The Annealing of the South," by Leslie W. Dunbar, the *Virginia Quarterly Review*, copyright 1961, are reprinted with permission of the *Virginia Quarterly Review*.

Introduction

I STARTED out to write about the South as it has usually been done, treating the region as a separate entity with its own distinctive culture, economy, problems, and romantic image in the consciousness of Americans. I would begin by stating my own version of what always has to be an arbitrary definition of the region, saying that for our purposes it is the Old Confederacy—the eleven states of Alabama, Arkansas, Florida, Georgia, Louisiana, Mississippi, North Carolina, South Carolina, Tennessee, Texas, and Virginia —but then adding that, in considering general and specific statements about the region, the reader would have to make the kind of mental adjustments most Southerners make when they use the term. This would entail knowing that Texas probably no more belongs in the definition than, say, Kentucky or Maryland and knowing all the differences within and between the eleven states—of mountain country, piedmont, piney woods, and coastal plain—or knowing the essential difference between Deep South and upper and border states and most of all knowing the difference between Black Belt (a trailing of rich black soil through parts of the Deep South where most of the plantations were and where the Negro population remains highest) and non-Black Belt country.

Then, within the limits of the definition, I would attempt to assess the great changes that had occurred in the region, their effect on a self-contained Southern society or, if you will, Southern civilization. But it soon became clear

that the main effect of the most basic of these changes had
been to end forever whatever there remained (or ever had
been) of self-containment, of separateness in the South
from the rest of the nation.

This was striking in the great economic changes, the
shift from an agricultural to a semi-industrial base with a
corresponding shift of the population from predominantly
rural to some kind of urban setting. This shift ended
Southern separatism in ways not immediately obvious, for
it was not merely a matter of moving away from an
agrarian base. After all, much of the rest of America had
all along had and still kept such a base. But in the South,
the shift was from an agriculture radically different from
that in the rest of the country and of the essence of Southern separateness, an agriculture of antiquated methods and
equipment and system of labor. Where agriculture remained in the South, it had also shifted away from the old,
one-crop, feudalistic, mule-powered sharecropping to modern, mechanized agribusiness of the national norm. In like
manner, industrialization came not as the logical growth of
the old manufacture, for that, too, had been an important
part of Southern separateness. It had consisted of an extension and adaptation of the plantation system to most of the
few existing units of industry, cotton mills most in-
famously but other sweatshop and brute-labor situations as
well. Their owners thought that profits and success depended on discouraging all other industry, on maintaining
such an overabundance of labor that wages and working
conditions were entirely controllable and jobs were an instrument of social and political control, most notoriously
used to prevent the poor of the two races from joining
together as a social and political force. If the South had
been a colony because of these old conditions (a colony in
the classical economic sense, producing raw materials, buy-
ing factors, not in that strained and metaphorical sense
that seeks to superimpose African and Asian reality not
merely on Southern but also on Northern racial relations),

it was a self-willed colony. National requirements of World War II prevailed over the masters of the old system and started the South toward a different kind of industrialization, ending colonial status and forging the region to the national economy as a working component of it. (The war was, of course, a catalyst; the conditions for change had been building through the twentieth century, World War I and the Depression having their own stimulus. George B. Tindall has chronicled the impetus for change, the battling against negative forces during the period 1913 to 1945, "the struggles for economic development: the drive for industry, farm programs, the labor movement . . . the struggles for cultural development . . . and above all, the growth of critical attitudes . . . the origins of a Second Reconstruction. . . ."[1]

The basic economic changes had been inevitable from the beginning. More than one writer traveling across early America saw this in the slave system (in its economic unfeasibility, in its cruelties, but also in that wryest of Southern racial jokes, its sense of slaves owning masters, dominating their lives); they noted the slaveholders' uneasy awareness that they were into something that was not only morally indefensible, but economically unworkable, something that couldn't last. Perhaps all of Southern history is summed up in the inevitability of the economic changes, and all its tragedy in the slowness with which they came, their delay by stubborn Southern resistance and irresolute acquiescence by the rest of the nation, to the irresponsible neglect of human victims. Certainly this was the sum of the Southern racial tragedy.

Of course, the even more fundamental changes in race relations were the beginning of the end of the South's most distinctive, most disturbing, most alienating characteristic of separation.

To anyone aware of all the racial injustice still rampant

[1] George B. Tindall, *The Emergence of the New South, 1913–1945* (Baton Rouge, Louisiana State University Press, 1967), pp. ix–x.

in the South of the late 1960s, it was an affront to hear, as one nearly always did at interracial gatherings, some white Southerner exclaim sanctimoniously how only a few years ago such a meeting couldn't be held, such a luncheon couldn't have happened, and so on. But this was, indeed, true and was quite often remarked with fervent approval by Negro Southerners, too. To appreciate fully how great an advance was entailed in the mere act of white and black sitting down together in public places to talk or to eat, was to realize how different the South had been from the rest of the nation, how far it had had to come before one could be angry about the kind of failure to achieve racial justice that was not exclusively Southern, was a national problem.

So almost at the outset it became obvious that I could not write about the South of the 1960s as a thing apart but had to attempt to see it in terms of its new ties to the nation. I came to realize this in early drafts of the material when almost invariably, after discussing some murky outrage or problem that once had seemed distinctively Southern, I would find myself compelled to add a qualifying sentence to the effect that a similar problem existed in the nation or that worse things were happening elsewhere. It became such an annoying mannerism in the writing that occasionally I would delete such comparisons, perhaps mistakenly. For example, after describing a small city businessman outraged because a national newspaper had not, in a story on his town, praised it one-sidedly, I deleted the afterthought of whether it wasn't the same in cities across the nation, and indeed at the seat of national power in Washington.

Other recent books on the South have, of course, acknowledged the interrelatedness with the rest of the nation. Two have centered on it and on the essential questions of race and regional flavor that I have struggled with. Frank Smith, a former Mississippian living in Tennessee, hailed the move into the political and economic main-

stream of America and questioned whether regional distinctiveness depended on retaining racism, and, not without regret, concluded that the distinctiveness would have
to be sacrificed if that were necessary to rid the region of
racism.[2] Howard Zinn, a Northerner who taught for a
time in the South, came closer to some of my own feeling
when he wrote that the South, far from being distinctive,
was merely the mirror image of the rest of America with
certain national defects, mainly racism, in exaggerated
perspective.[3]

My approach to all such previous writing about the
South—especially writing based on thought so penetrating
that it became accepted as truism on both the scholarly
and popular level—was to re-examine the ideas in the light
of new realities, along with the accepted myths and folklore faiths. As much as anything else, I sought to revivify
some of the old truths that had come to be accepted without much regard for their meaning or implications. If this
has resulted in a tendency to question the unquestionable
or even to seem smart-alecky in approach to hard-come-by
understandings of books and men I admire deeply, that
was the last thing I intended.

This is not a book built with painstaking, scholarly research in the accumulated findings of other people. Nor is
it a book built out of social science methodology or, for
that matter, one that puts much stock in statistics. It is
rather based on more than casual reading of all kinds
about the South (including its newspapers), on considerable
travel and reporting in the region, and on my work on the
staff of the Southern Regional Council, a biracial organization of Southerners working for equal opportunity in the
South. (Though it should be stated the book reflects my
own thought, not that of the Southern Regional Council.)

---

[2] Frank E. Smith, *Look Away From Dixie* (Baton Rouge, Louisiana
State University Press, 1965).

[3] Howard Zinn, *The Southern Mystique* (New York, Alfred A. Knopf,
1964).

To a great degree, its opinions and predictions are based on feeling and intuition more than on solid fact or certain knowledge. I offer this book with matter-of-fact awareness that the South cannot be fully captured by any writer, no matter what his method, and with the promise not of omniscience but only of honesty and respect for truth.

Of all that I learned about the new relationship of the South and the nation, one thing was so important that it became a unifying principle of this book. This was the realization that the central experience of the South's recent change, the anguished racial struggle, was an experience that seemed soon likely to consume all Americans.

What happened in the South was that its dominant majority, the majority of the white people, suddenly had the very core of their value system challenged on moral and legal grounds by a spirited and inspired minority, and, finally, overthrown.

In the South, the issue was race. In the rest of America, minorities had begun to raise a whole range of issues, such diverse matters as foreign policy, education, standards in politics and public administration, and conventional morality in sex, drugs, art, and what-have-you. Such skirmishes, largely led by the young, seemed inevitably to lead to an ultimate questioning of the economic, political, and moral systems by which the dominant majority of the nation lives.

Such challenge, as the South painfully knows, makes for a time of reckoning, a time when every old truth must be re-examined, when everything that has been accepted as right and proper must be reassessed. Not all Southerners on either side of the racial issue always behaved with honor or even dignity, though most of those who made the challenge and some of those who defended the old order did. Emerging from this ordeal, Southerners have not even approached full reconciliation of their differences or anything like a total restructuring of their society. A major purpose of mine in this book is to explain why there has not been more of each. The results of my study of this question are replete with the wisdom of Southern experience and its warnings for the nation as it enters a similar ordeal. For, in many ways, to see the South of the 1960s is to see what may happen to the nation or, better, what the nation might avoid.

To see the South clearly—to try to thread one's way through all the romantic and symbolic imagery in the Southern landscape—has always been difficult. In 1962 a white Northern civil rights worker wrote excitedly to headquarters about an old plantation house he had discovered in a little Deep South town. It was the real thing, he reported, with four Corinthian columns, one replaced by a conglomeration of two-by-fours, the others patched and peeling. The porch was sagging, and outside, a "mournful, overgrown arborway" was choked in underbrush. Behind the big house, where no one lived, stood old slave dwellings, apparently never renovated but occupied now by Negro families. Nearby, a new house had been built, and its owners were using one of the little slave cabins, with its swaying chimney, as a garage. "Thus," he concluded his report, "the new does not supplant the old. The new merely is superimposed on the old."

This had been true in the past, of course, of the many "new Souths" that have risen, glimmering, with romantic hope, only to fade finally into hopelessness. And while it was true in part of the South in the 1960s (for instance, in the building of cities with the people and memories of the rural past), it was not true at all of the fundamental changes in the way people made a living. Such a symbol as the old plantation house has its own, almost irresistible logic, easily obscuring reality and the appropriate new symbols. The South's languid, tropical climate has been to a great extent modified by air-conditioning, and cities are connected to the nation and world by standardized air terminals. The imagery and symbolism of reality has come to reside in the cities, no longer in the ghosts and dreams and pretenses of the past.

Nowadays another danger in writing about almost anything—but probably especially about the South because the South abounds in deplorable and outrageous situations—is that people have been so exposed to generalizations and statistical evidence about deplorable and outrageous situations that they have, in self-defense and in the name of sanity, become numbly immune to them. Most of the truth about the South of the 1960s, the definitive work, is contained in any recent year's edition of *The Statistical Abstract of the United States*. But it speaks a language no longer capable of reaching the spirit in Americans which moves them to correct deplorable and outrageous situations.

I have tried to overcome these and other difficulties by means of the oldest approach to writing about Americans: by assembling accounts of the specific and piecemeal reality I encountered in my travels through the South, drawing the reader emotionally along to conclusions from these. I have attempted to see the South first as the most casual traveler sees it, out the window of an automobile, traveling its roads, seeking a panoramic vision of its vastness and great contrasts of geography and modes of life, invoking as much as possible the important things that have been happening to the ways people live. Then after viewing the countryside in this random sort of way, I have regarded the big cities as a guide to the future, for these are the places where more and more people will live, which, in all unplanned likelihood, unfortunately will become bigger and bigger. But again, my approach to the cities is random, more specific than abstract, more impressionistic than statistical. In the same manner, I have tried to tell of the smaller cities and towns, in a time of their becoming something else, either to grow or to fade away; in them I have sought to understand what underlies the growth of the cities and to fathom the mind of the South that prevailed in the 1960s, a mind that was no longer agrarian and not yet a part of the urban culture. Once more, I tried to give the feel, the flavor, the spirit of these places of mighty influence.

After all this travel in the South, it seemed possible to present generalities, even statistics, conclusions, judgments, for I hoped that the reader, having come to know the flesh and very feel of the South, might respond appropriately, with outrage and compassion over outrageous situations and with recognition of the nation's coming plight in the South's continuing one.

In all of this, I have tried most of all to portray with respect and fairness the South's people. Nearly everything they have done, the worst of the evil, the most absurd of the cruelty, the best of the heritage, has been simply an anguished cry for dignity.

They are so eloquent in unconscious ways. Their talk and stories abound in metaphor, all unawares: "Now my daddy had to struggle for his education. He worked two jobs and drove twenty miles a day to town to college; he got himself a motorcycle and rode it on the railroad crossties as a shortcut, near to ruined himself. And then one day there in town, a damn nigger stepped out in front of his motorcycle and he hit him, nearly killed the nigger, and crippled my daddy, one leg shorter than the other, for life . . ."

The two old men, the white one and his "nigger paddler," as close in the relationship as two friends can ever be, go out to the boathouse in the gray of dawn. "Watch out for snakes," says the white one. "Aw, I can smell snakes," says the black one. And they step down into the boat and discover a moccasin coiled in the bottom, and both go over the side of the boat without a word, and, sputtering there in the cold water, the white one exclaims, "Hell, I thought you said you could smell snakes," and the black one without a pause says, "I never said I could smell 'em when they're sleeping." And both, black and white, pull themselves back into the boat, that same boat that they have been in together all their lives.

Finally, I hope that this book—deliberately loose and rambling because the South is so—will impart, to those who do not know the region, some sense, some sharing of the Southerner's fondness and exasperation and despair and joy in the land and its people and that, to those who already know the South, it will give a heightened sense of these feelings, withal new insights into reality. In both instances, this is an attempt to evoke that special feeling Southerners have for the South; ultimately, it may well be that the only distinctiveness of the South will be the place it occupies in the heart.

If any of this affords a better understanding of the South's people—black and white, good and evil—that can be carried over in understanding other Americans in other struggles, I will be satisfied.

Contents

PART ONE

A Change in the Mind of the South

CHAPTER 1

I

THE TREMENDOUS CHANGES in the South that have occurred since World War II have been for the most part structural: changes of things rather than people, changes of economics, demography, institutions, laws. The South is no longer predominantly rural or agricultural. While its economic situation is still worse than that in the rest of the nation, it has improved somewhat—though mostly for whites. Its institutional undergirding of segregation and legalized discrimination has been destroyed. Eventually these structural changes would inevitably cause changes in the people. This process has begun, but its outcome is by no means predictable. How would it change the minds of the people—the way they think and believe and feel and what they teach their children—and how would Southern civilization itself change?

Southerners, even in casual conversations and with varying degrees of awareness and approval or disapproval, raised the crucial questions: Would their civilization lose what was left of its distinctiveness? Would it rid itself at last of racism or retain it in new forms? Were the South's distinctiveness and racism so closely intertwined that eliminating the evil of one would mean losing the good of the other?

In olden times, before 1960, when writers attempted to deal with the South, most often they wrote about only the white South, as though the one-fourth of its population that was black did not exist. But this, too, has changed.

One of the main points that W. J. Cash made in his great book[1] was that the mind of the South was incapable of rational thought. He maintained that the South, consequently, was without rational leadership, and from this he inferred that by learning to think, the South could free itself of bad leadership. But Cash was writing largely about the white South, and things didn't happen that way.

Cash's chain of causality (the riddle of the chicken or the egg) was broken in 1960 by Negro Southerners who assumed leadership for a brief but crucial time, bypassing conventional political and social structures forbidden them and forcing change of these structures by direct action. This, rather than any widespread enlightenment among white Southerners, made possible the most important, most necessary change of all, the freeing of whites as well as blacks from the curse of racism. It also accounted for the continuing struggle, the state of flux into which the structural changes regarding race had plunged the South. A minority of the region's people had forced change of basic institutions against the will of the majority.

The lesser writers of the past who treated the South exclusively in terms of its white population were usually guilty of another dishonesty, described by Myrdal as a flaw of white Southern liberals: "The general public of the South is often spoken of by southern liberals as hopelessly backward, but at the same time it is flattered in the most extravagant terms of regional mythology. It is made a main point that the southern public must not be enraged into resistance."[2] One of the immediate effects of the great move toward leadership by Negroes was to free Southerners—many blacks as well as white liberals—from the grip of that old fear of enraging "common" whites into some holocaust of physical resistance. (This fear was not easily shed. To make interracial visits to restaurants or even

[1] *The Mind of the South* (New York, Alfred A. Knopf, 1941).

[2] Gunnar Myrdal, *An American Dilemma,* rev. ed. (New York and Evanston, Harper & Row, Publishers, Inc., 1962), p. 470.

homes in the first days of the new racial laws—and years afterward in some Deep South locales—was to encounter fearsome hostility, most of it real, but some of it only imagined. To receive an anonymous phone call, as often happened, after such an interracial adventure was to know terror even beyond the considerable amount appropriate in the circumstance.) But sit-in students, voter registration applicants in the most dangerous areas, even first-grade children entering white schools had proved that though the violence of resistance and reprisal was all too real, it was not all-consuming. It could be endured, even contained. All it really took, all it ever had taken, was a half-way competent police force doing its duty. Thus died one of the worst of the evil myths Lillian Smith had instructed the South to exorcise. Honest men could criticize and speak truth bluntly, and dishonest ones had lost their favorite rationalization. Such a gain does not come easily. As far along in the process of exorcism as the school desegregation in Grenada, Mississippi, in 1966, when grown men with chains and clubs attacked children, one Negro child told what it meant to her: "I know it's true that God is dead. Or He wouldn't let them do to us what they did." Hearing such things, a white judge kept repeating, "I had no idea. I had no idea it could be like this." Too much of the most brutal truth about the old order of Southern race relations was made clear to whites at the cost of physical pain to Negroes. And too few white Southerners ever confronted the truth. By the time of the disgrace at Grenada, the rest of the nation was able to turn its face away, too; in the same month, the Congress defeated a civil rights bill for the first time in many years. Its provisions would have made it a federal offense to intimidate and harm persons, like the children in Grenada, seeking civil rights. With the never-ending irony of Southern racial affairs, by the time such a law (frankly acknowledging the failure of Southern state and local law enforcement) was being considered in 1967, it was regarded as a kind of non-controver-

sial sop to throw to the dwindling number of "respectable"
Negro leaders. It was also considered a sort of nostalgic
return to the old Northern-conscience normalcy wherein
the South, and not the riot-torn North, was the villain in
racial matters. This legislation of 1967 was not then attached to a bill calling for housing desegregation, for this
was as unwanted in the North as in the South (it had
caused the defeat of the civil rights bill of 1966). Striking
at the heart of the North's *de facto* segregation, housing
legislation was no longer considered a possible national
legislative goal in 1967. It took the murder of Dr. Martin
Luther King, Jr., in 1968, to achieve passage of halfhearted
versions of both bills.

Irony becomes too delicate an instrument to deal with
some of America's racial outrages. In 1967, proposals were
afoot from the most respectable sources (including the
columnist C. L. Sulzberger of *The New York Times*) for
national legislation to curb spoken and written incitement
likely to result in race riot. After many millions of vicious
incitements by white racists over the years, after all that
freedom of demagogic speech, at last the cry had come to
curb it. Mr. Sulzberger said legislation would prevent the
spoiling of democracy by "black power fanatics, Ku Klux
Klanners, Nazi, and other minority groups." No wonder
that (without examining the desirability or for that matter
constitutionality of such legislation) black power fanatics
were indeed goaded to scream that all of white America
was most murderously intent upon the humiliation and
subjugation of all black people. After so many whites had
wallowed for years in every conceivable obscenity of racist
verbal violence (developed a generation ago into an art
form in the South) and related cruelties, Mr. Sulzberger
and others finally became alarmed—when Negroes developed their own versions. No wonder Negroes sometimes
seemed pathologically suspicious of white America: as in
the story about the man with an inferiority complex, they
had good cause for paranoia.

Much of the emotion behind black power was the dismay of young civil rights activists who had taken too much physical punishment and had seen how little white people heeded the existential truth that this revealed.

II

The effect of another version of enraged Southern resistance was even less easily ended. This was political. As Negro voter registration under the 1965 Voting Rights Act began to approach more than 50 percent of potential, a major question developed: Would this new voting strength be isolated and thus, in most locales (where it is a minority), powerless, or could it be combined with the moderate white vote to improve the quality of government? The answer seemed to be that the latter was possible only if Negro demands were muted and if appeals to Negro votes on purely civil rights or racial issues were avoided. Otherwise, the moderates might be "enraged into resistance," and enough of them might be pushed into the camp of the still-prowling racist candidates. The line between "moderate" and racist voters was that thin.

The lesson carried over into operation of the Southern state governments. Serving needs of Negroes could not go too far lest, once again, moderate support would be lost. Thus a blandness and caution, indeed a new brand of conservatism, began in the wake of the 1965 Voting Rights Act to develop as the pattern for the better state administrations and local governments in the South. Tokenism was the result of the basic demands of Negroes for the standard forms of desegregation. And in the South—as in the nation—this stopped short at the crucial point of housing.

De facto segregation never developed to a high degree in the pre-1960s South; law and custom kept public life separate while adjacent streets, the opposite sides or ends of a street, and even some entire streets were likely to be

nicely desegregated. In the general pattern sections of niggertown were scattered, rather than centralized in a single,
full-fledged ghetto. By the mid–1960s, however, municipalities across the South were beginning to build or to
consolidate their own niggertown versions of the Northern
ghetto by means of a kind of public policy not readily
apparent to the public, by planning boards, urban renewal, and the like. Atlanta, because it was larger, was
probably deeper into the process than most, but it could
be seen developing in any large city, and many of the small
ones.

Most of the South's municipalities were, of course, still
governed by whites and, in matters of self-interest, controlled by white business. Often these were whites who
publicly proclaimed progressive racial and social attitudes
and who, indeed, were genuinely striving for progress in
such matters as the upgrading of low-quality schools or the
development of the conventional symptom-alleviating
poverty programs.

For many years, a growing body of sophisticated whites—
mostly in the large cities—had flinched at the violent language of the Talmadges and Bilbos and Wallaces and had
derided such talk, just as they had long disavowed the Ku
Klux Klan. In encounters with Northerners over the years,
many a respectable white Southerner has been startled to
discover himself stereotyped as a barefoot, backward, avid
Klansman. Upon asserting the respectable white Southerner's contempt for the Klan in such circumstances, he
found himself hailed as a paragon of enlightenment out of
the benighted Southland. If he were smart, he would not
mention the rest of the respectable norm on race—which
was that it was not nice to question segregation any more
than it was nice to embarrass a colored person by calling
him "nigger" or, for that matter, "Negro."

But these sophisticates acquiesced to the "general public"—off somewhere ready to be enraged easily over race
and needing, apparently, constant doses of ranting—by ex-

cusing the Southern politicians' indulgence in demagoguery. "Oh, they have to do that to get elected." Similarly, the racist styles of office-seekers could be ignored by
sophisticates, accepted as a given, the candidates being eval-
uated on other qualities. Thus a county school superintendent from Alabama, obviously from his talk an earnest,
reasonably well-informed and well-intentioned worker for
the considerable improvement needed in his system, could
in the Mrs. Wallace campaign give an analytical rationale
for supporting her in the name of promised boons to education. If you should ask him about the danger of losing
federal aid from some future Wallace schoolhouse door
grandstanding, he would have the old, ironically correct
answer, "Oh, that's just talk; they have to do that."

Moderates showed a similar tendency to excuse politi-
ians who, counting the Negro vote, began to make code-
ord acquiescence to their Negro constituents—as long, of
rse, as this did not go too far. Rounding out this re-
arkable development of subtle political communication
as the aforementioned fact that Negro voters were forced
o accept less than their due of the long-awaited benefits
of the ballot. All in all, it was a continuation of a tradition
of muddled misdirection in politics, a Southern system.

Myrdal had noted the lack in the South, unique he said
in all time and all places, of understanding "that political
actions, which for the moment amount to little more than
mere demonstrations and which may actually cause a reaction in the individual case, in the long view may have been
tremendously important as powerful stimuli to progressive
thinking."[3] In their nonviolent demonstrations, particularly those pure, classical ones of the first years, 1960
through 1962, Negroes showed the keenest awareness of
this axiom (another mark of the superior quality of leadership asserted during the brief time when Negroes acted
in the streets, and the established white leadership merely
reacted and retreated). This had inspired hope that the

[3] Myrdal, p. 471.

process might carry over into the new politics of black voting.

But in the first years after Negro enfranchisement, the new politics was conducted by means of the more typically Southern, murky kind of communication just described, and once again the South seemed successful in avoiding the real political issues of all its history, involving such matters as economics and education. Increasingly, it became apparent that raw racism was still preferred as a campaign style by the majority who resided not in large cities, but in small cities and towns.

Of course, that "general public" (always lurking, likely to explode into violent racism, always so feared in the South) was the poor whites—like the Negroes, victims of the failure of the South ever to come to grips with its real social and economic problems. A few of the reasons some of these most-feared folk gave (informally to Julian Bond political workers) in 1966 for supporting the racist Maddox in Georgia are interesting to note.

An old lady with few teeth, sitting on a windowsill, spitting snuff into a tin fruit can: "Well, Lester's a good Christian man. All my people are going to vote for him. But you know how Lester feels about the colored. If he's elected, there's gonna be war. Now Callaway's got a better education. Lester really isn't smart enough to be governor. But Callaway doesn't need the money. He's got all those cotton mills. And Lester could use the money. I've been knowin' his family for years. Lester is a good Christian gentleman . . . Guess I'll vote for Lester."

A retired sailor: "Lester Maddox will keep the niggers down, so I'll vote for him." A woman: "Lester knows how to handle those niggers. He's a very religious man." A woman visiting her: "I'm for Maddox, too. But not because of civil rights. I'm a Democrat. I couldn't vote for a Republican."

Such Southern public opinion, seldom sought, seldom what you expected, sums up most of the mystery and muddle of Southern politics and helps explain why they defy analysis on the superficial social science level more often than the politics of the rest of the nation. One other Southern theme that is missing in these comments emerges in the remark of yet another old lady in the same set of interviews: "I don't vote any more. I'm on Social Security. I used to vote, but I don't any more. I just think God will take care of these things. I feel sure God will give us the best governor He can provide." ("God will make a way," was the comment of an elderly Negro lady in the Black Belt. "All we have to do is trust Him." She was quoted in a movement newspaper apropos her approval of the Northern Negro riots of 1967.) Another theme is associated more closely with Negroes, yet is more common than generally acknowledged among whites, and with them (one would swear upon encountering its obstinacy) dates back to feudal Europe. It was expressed by a young white woman who was asked about Lester Maddox: "I've never ted. I don't want to get in any trouble."

III

The increase in Negro voter registration (from 40.8 percent of potential in 1964 to 62 percent in 1968) meant that for the first time in its history, the South was on the way toward full self-government. The implications were great, indeed global. For the plight of the South (it had never changed: poverty and racial animosity) reflected in American terms the plight of more than half the world. If an emerging democracy in the South could find solutions to these problems, America from the experience might have a new wisdom in its dealings with the rest of the world, and new confidence based on real achievement rather than pretenses.

The political hope found expression in the benign myth that the masses of poor whites and poor Negroes—the poorest people in the richest nation of the world—might come together politically and force the meeting of their needs. This has, so the myth goes, always been prevented by the rich who served their own needs instead by pitting the poor of the two races against each other. Moreover, they did this in the cruelest way possible, declaring the black ones of them inhuman.

This explanation of irrationality in Southern politics has become so commonplace among intellectuals (Southern politicians and Southerners generally seem unaware of it) that its implications are glossed over. But consider them. Here were men capable of consciously and cold-bloodedly setting one part of the people of their land at war against the other part, instilling war's psychological justification of murder, dividing them to keep them conquered—all for personal monetary profit. It is a myth of monsterism as hideous as any the world has known. No wonder that a civilization with such a myth at its base drove so honest a student of it as Cash to destruction, and its greatest writer to drink.

The myth places all the blame the rich, old, ir tional leadership and holds ordinary hite people not re sponsible. They were simply caught in this diabolical scheme. Freed from this evil design, the spell cast upon him, the average white Southerner will, the myth implies, quickly find a more realistic base for his politics and soon show the world a better way for the races to dwell side by side in peace, prosperity, and love. A whole new set of myths has grown up around this hope.

Identifiable as a class, the Bourbons continued to exist, Southern, strongly entrenched up and down the lines of power from small towns to big cities, often prevailing amid all the new elements of power, from branch-office outposts of national big business to the representatives of the rising middle class. And the poor people, of course, continued to exist in larger proportions than elsewhere in the nation, still voting and acting against their own best interests more often than not. But does the dense and rich and complex reality of the South support the myth? How, we must ask, could the poor white of the South have been so easily gulled throughout history, so easily tricked into fighting his natural ally instead of his born enemy? And what of the monstrous rich man? Could there really have been, generation after generation, such unadulterated evil?

IV

For a better understanding of the dynamics of the interrelationships of these two classes of people, it becomes necessary to sort them out further sociologically. Rather than speak of a middle class (which the myth leaves out, anyway) let us divide the white South—as the South divided itself in the past and as it continues for the most part to do in the present—into "nice" people and those who are "common." The connotation of "common" is not that patronizing, benign one of "common people," but of a snobbish sneer. "She's common," Southern youngsters still were saying in the late 1960s and there was no question but of slur and distaste. "That's common."

The Bourbons would be mostly "nice" people, and the poor whites would be mostly "common." But not all "nice" people were rich, any more than all "common" ones were poor.

An often-noted trait of all these whites is their essential honesty: in dealings with their Negro brothers they lack the hypocrisy that marks such relationships in the rest of the country. White Southerners, particularly the "nice" ones, were learning this. "I have been for all that's happened so far, mind you," they have learned to say in preface to a racist harangue, "but I feel like now they have gone too far."

Hypocrisy is harder for the white Southerner. There were still in the late 1960s so many Negroes still living in such wretched conditions; they were not yet isolated even where there were ghettos but were all about, so that the

sham and shabbiness of the hypocrisy were too easy to se
The Negro poor remained a yardstick against which th
motorboats and backyard swimming pools of the ne
prosperity in the South after World War II were merc
lessly measured.

(This "new prosperity" must not be exaggerated: W
are not talking about the kind of affluent society that ex
isted in the rest of the country, even with its own dispara
ties along the scale from well-off to destitute. In 1966, a l
eleven Southern states had higher percentages of familie
making less than $3,000 a year than the country as a whol
had. Such statistics lumped whites and Negroes togethen
But taken separately, 42.5 percent of the Negro families in
the United States Census Bureau's definition of the South
made less than $3,000 in 1966, compared with 17.4 percen
of white families. The average for both nationally wa
14.3 percent. We are thus considering glaring dispari ty
between living standards of whites and blacks where nei
ther was as well off as in the rest of the country. An
though in 1965 per capita income in every South
was fewer percentage points behind the national
than in 1950, the gap in actual dollars earned was g
In 1950, the per capita income for the South was $1,096, or
73 percent of the national average. In 1965, it was $2,140
or 79 percent of the national average. But the difference
in money between the Southern and the national averages
was $400 in 1950 compared with $584 in 1965. In Miss—
issippi, the percentages were 50 percent in 1950 compared
with 57 percent in 1965, but the money gap was $741 in
1950 compared with $1,159 in 1965.[5] The South couldn't
win for losing. Finally, such statistics underlay an always
dangerous social situation, that of a small number of
people being very wealthy and a large number very poor,
with few in between. This was not the profile of the rest
of America.)

[4] Figures are from *Statistical Abstract of the United States*, 1968, p. 326.
[5] "New South Notes," *New South*, Vol. 24, No. 4, Winter, 1969, p. 1.

In the course of postwar prosperity in the South, large numbers of white Southerners have for the first time in history come to know a new kind of guilt about Negroes. Previously, all Southerners, black and white together, were in the same bad boat financially, the Negroes of course in the lowest depths of it. Even if there had been a will to do anything about the terrible Negro poverty of the past, whites could more or less justifiably cite an inability to do anything about it. "What could we have done back then?" a well-heeled white leader in a Southern town could say in the late 1960s, looking uneasily at the too-little, too-late efforts of the poverty program to forestall rioting or other uprising among a large, extraordinarily impoverished Negro population. He referred to his own family's experience of post-Civil War pennilessness, lack of education, boll weevil and agricultural depression disasters, and the hopelessness of the 1930s.

Too often, of course, what the white South did was to use the pitifully small monetary advantage it had over the Negro to exploit the Negro shamelessly. Even in the late 1960s in areas of almost universal poverty among whites and Negroes, Negro women (with families of their own) were being paid three dollars a day or less for long days of domestic servitude. Scales were a little better (eight dollars a day and carfare in Atlanta, for example) in more prosperous, urban climes. But even so, the new kind of guilt (that special American one of living opulently amidst a world of poor and hungry people) was creeping into the already guilt-burdened psyches of more and more white Southerners.

It may not be necessary to look much furthe r one reason why even "nice" white Southerners are y to shed the thought processes of dehumanization. Li ir counterparts in the rest of America, they have increasin in the 1960s felt impotent to do much of anything about conditions, and they weren't about to take on the burden of admitting the humanity of all those poor Negroes. And many whites, whether they were aware of it or not, had a vested interest in keeping Negroes poor.

But the most pitiful and profound thing about the white Southerner's honesty about race has been that he *believed* that the South's ordering of race relations was right.

He believed it in a special, crippling way. He believed it against his secret knowledge of the difference between good and evil, right and wrong. He learned at his mother's knee, along with dictums to be clean and Godly and to do unto others as he would have others do unto him, that he must be a white supremacist, too. Among the "nice" people, it was not, of course, put that way. But neither was it expressed in the way that the Negro mother (in the first step to freedom) came to put it to her children: "You must learn to survive with things as they are down here, but these things are not right." The white Southerners had inculcated in them with the force of childhood conditioning the belief that they were right. They were the way God had ordered the world.

The white Southerner hates nothing more than to be told he hates Negroes. "Why, we love our colored . . ." What he hates—and he never seems able to find a way to explain it—is for Negroes or Yankees or, worst of all, other white Southerners to act as if the ordering of race relations that he was brought up on has not been right, the way God meant it—"nice." For generally (though there were exceptions, more unconscious than conscious) he was not taught to hate. If he were "nice," he was taught the racial etiquette. A child learning to talk learned to call grownups "Mister" and "Mizzis," and to say "sir" and "ma'am." But should he with proper logic have so addressed the Negro maid in the kitchen or the yard man out back, he was gently corrected, perhaps even by the Negro. And there would be enough force of emotion in the episode to make a lasting impression. If his parents were "common," perhaps he was slapped down for the offense.

What such children were taught (and this would include all the generations of adults in the late 1960s) con-
tradicted all the good of America and the South and Western civilization that they might have gleaned from their
schools, from reading, radio, television, newspapers,
movies, and their various religions. This latter could not
have but penetrated the consciousness of even the worst
schooled of the "common" whites and, as Myrdal noted,
was a staunch creed among the "nice" people. So they were
burdened with the impossibility of believing both, racism
and its contradictions, or knowing that their upbringing
betrayed them. George Orwell's description of compartmentalization of such conflicting ideology often comes to
mind in contemplating the South.

So this has been the white Southerner's tragedy, his
dilemma. "I know," said the beseiged official of a little
town to Negro leaders making their demands, "that everything you ask is right. But you have to remember that
every time I make a concession to you, I have to go against
my raising."

The consequences of the cultural conflict within the
traditional dutiful and right-thinking white Southerner
were all about him in Gothic towerings. If Cash erred in
his assessment of the mind of the white South, it was in a
typical way: by putting into apposition the ability to think
and the ability to feel. "From first to last, and whether he
was Virginian or *nouveau*, he [the white Southerner] did
not (typically speaking) think; he felt; and discharging his
feelings immediately, he developed no need or desire for
intellectual culture in its own right—none, at least, powerful enough to drive him past his taboos to its actual
achievement."[6]

Yet who can say of any white Southerner, common or
nice, who has seen a sharecropper cabin, a city's niggertown slum, a nursemaid tending one white child all day
(at less wages than will support her own black brood run-

[6] Cash, p. 99.

ning loose and ragged in the slum alleys), has seen a television film of attacks on Negro demonstrators, has read
history, has looked into the eyes of a Negro child, that this
white Southerner is a creature of fully functioning human
feeling? For that matter, would anyone who has spent an
hour (or a childhood) listening to the content of white
Southern polite conversation make this claim?

Except in the most intimate situations, it seldom gets
beyond politeness. It is stylized, decorative, meaningless
talk, elaborate structure over emptiness, a wondrous slid-
ing further and further from meaning, a virtuoso wander-
ing from irrelevancy to irrelevancy. ("Well, let's see now,
that's old man Will's second cousin who lived next door to
Aunt Cynthia—you remember her, she dyed her hair—
next door to her in that little yellow house, no it was green,
built by you know, Smith, old man Smith the carpenter—
he's dead now . . .")

We hid ourselves within the circumlocutions of these
conversations, out on the porch, rocking, murmuring this
talk in rhythm with the night breezes and frog screechings
—not to avoid thinking so much as out of an inability
mostly to think. But more than this, it was out of a lack of
any real feeling to express.

The affliction of the spirit of the white South has been
Hamlet's. Enterprises of the deepest human meaning have
indeed, without even the benefit of the pale cast of
thought, been sicklied o'er and lost the name of action.
Feeling is short-circuited by cultural conflict and action is
delayed, aimed at the wrong object. It is that most awful
kind of action, perverted—because of an inability to face
the true feelings of a mind, a soul in unresolvable conflict.

Huckleberry Finn knew the Southerner's dilemma in
classical form. He suffered a sudden onslaught of guilt over
the fact that he was helping a Negro, Jim, escape from
slavery. This was the property of a friend he was helping to
free, a friend who had never done Huck any harm. So he

resolved, to ease his conscience, to turn Jim in. But when the time came, he suffered another attack of guilt from the other direction; he remembered Jim's goodness and his friendship, and he couldn't do it. He was damned if he did, damned if he didn't; either way "the wages is the same."

V

It is no wonder that the white Southerner, afflicted by the dilemma that gripped him, has been unable to think straight or feel wholly, or that when he does overcome the paralysis of his spirit, his action is so often impotent, or foolish, or obscene. No wonder that exploiter and exploited whites, year after year, generation after generation, have seemed to act out the terrible myth, unseeing, of the separation of natural allies, of the misdirection of the poor white's hostility—against the Negro instead of the real enemy, the rich white. Guilt breeds upon guilt; the guilty not only flee where no man pursueth; they also keep committing their crime over and over, in quest of punishment.

In the civil rights struggle, many "nice" white Southerners hung motionless on this dilemma, damned by childhood conditioning and by the knowledge of their fellow Southerners' feelings about race. Even the most enlightened white Southerners know a peculiar anguish in affronting the racism of their friends. This was part of the moderate's revulsion from the methods of direct action. For some, speaking out against a man's racism would be comparable to criticizing a person for having cancer; for others, it was just a matter of manners, like not arguing with a man about his religion. The same "nice" white Southerners were also damned by their knowledge (however faint) of the justness of the Negro's cause. In most, probably, the conflicting loyalties amounted to extreme moral uncertainty: they didn't join hecklers and attackers; neither did they speak out for racial justice, let alone join the demonstrations. In a town and even a whole state their failure could unleash murderous violence, allowing the lines of Southern totalitarianism to be drawn tighter. Their failure also probably made the crucial difference between the great original promise of the Negro movement and the sad sort of incomplete revolution that it dwindled down to.

The original strategy—beautiful, not too farfetched psychologically, and entirely Southern—of shaming the whites into acknowledgment of injustice degenerated into the Northern-liberal, tough-minded employment of demonstrations to evoke white violence and force federal legislation. The spirit of loving the whites into integration diminished in the distortions of black power rhetoric to something that sounded like hating the whites and fighting them with inadequate models of their own weapons, separatist political and economic power, such as there was. The hope for full equality of all Negroes was reduced in the late 1960s to a struggle, on the one hand, to achieve and then hold on to token desegregation through federal force, and on the other, for separate but equal—really equal this time. (Thus was the myth perpetuated, enlarged to mutual, rather than one-sided antagonism.)

People who knew better resorted to a variant of the excuse of not wanting to arouse the general public. They did not want, they would say, to lose the influence with their more benighted fellow citizens. The failure of the white church in the racial crises over the years can be largely attributed to this favorite rationalization of preachers. But all sectors of enlightened Southern leadership were guilty of it—editors, politicians, businessmen, lawyers, educators, even, sadly, some writers and artists.

They could usually point to a horrible example of a local leader who had lost his influence, some poor devil driven beyond prudence to stand alone and assert reason. All alone, he was an easy target. Not the least of the ways to do him in was to suggest that he had suddenly gone a little crazy. In the South there has always been precedent for such insinuation; the Negro's cause through history has seemed to attract some disturbed white minds. And even the sanest good man or woman taking the lonely stand against racism might, after such niceties of reprisal as crank phone calls, social ostracism, economic repression, and bombings, succumb to emotional exhaustion. With the backing of only a few other white influentials, however, such heroic people could survive and even prevail.

In towns where this did happen, it was possible, listening to white people who supported Negro advancement, in all the muddle of their reasoning that it was good for business and saved the town's image, to hear also traces of moral reasoning, bits and pieces of what would emerge as one person's hard-thought-out understanding that they all had heard and tried to repeat. Eventually you would find the man who had done this thinking, and he would tell it to you. In one little city it was a thin and crabbed-mouthed, middle-aged merchant who had started from the point of the threat of nuclear war and his conviction that men had to learn to live together, and he had applied this logic to the Negroes and whites of his town. In another, it was an old, Bourbon-type controller of finances who said he had taken in a Japanese student and realized that he was willing to treat this son of his former enemy better than the black people with whom he had grown up and, indeed, fought alongside against the Japanese.

Race (taken as a proposition unencumbered by psychological and cultural distortion) is such a clear-cut, unsubtle, easily resolved moral question. In contrast, even war is a more difficult moral problem. Yet after all the ventilation of race as a moral issue during the years since 1954, despite the hullabaloo about it in Southern streets and politics, and even though most Southern conversations continued to be obsessed with it, it seemed reasonably clear in the late 1960s that most white Southerners had been able to avoid the simple moral question. And even those who had finally faced it intellectually had become moderates, still incapable of accepting the imperatives of basic change and reform that had to follow. This was the chilling, frightening, pathological condition of what was known, in the days before Negroes were acknowledged, as the mind of the South. Whether it was because of all the numbness-inducing dilemmas and myths of culture and conditioning still controlling white people, or whether it was becoming more a matter of a generalized American hysteria and paralysis is one of those questions at the heart of any study of the meaning of the South in American history. Certainly there are no simple answers. The old simplistic explanations—like excusing racism as a manifestation of ignorance—were never adequate and have become downright harmful.

CHAPTER 2

I

THE LEVEL OF IGNORANCE in the South has been one of those bedrock constants which must enter into explanation of any phenomenon, from the Klan to bad politics to the failure to provide decent schools. But the notion that only the most ignorant were racist or that they were even the most extreme racists in the South has been a common error and rationalization. Because they express their racism more crudely is no reason to suppose that the ignorant people have racism more deeply instilled in them; as soon suppose that because their churches are more fervent, they are a more profoundly religious people.

I assert this with full awareness of the preponderance of more than folk opinion to the contrary, summed up in the following statement from a distinguished book on Southern politics:

> Numerous studies have shown that racial prejudice and discrimination tend to be related to low levels of formal education. If southern segregationist sentiments are linked to the low educational levels of the region, then a continued increase in the average schooling of southerners could be expected to lead to a basic modification of attitudes.[1]

The authors then go on to say sadly what a long time this might take, and to point out with the social scientist's fine detachment (not only from the passion of human affairs,

---

[1] Donald R. Matthews and James W. Prothro, *Negroes and the New Southern Politics* (New York, Harcourt, Brace and World, 1966), p. 343.

but really from the meaning of the very numbers to which they labor to reduce human affairs) :

> Education decreases dedication to strict segregation, but extremely high levels of education are apparently necessary to produce actual acceptance of integration. Even among those whose formal education terminated with a college degree, only 14 per cent favor integration. To find substantial support for integration, we must look to those with graduate-school training—and these "eggheads" constitute not quite 3 per cent of the white adults of the South.[2]

Without entering the faith-shaking analysis of methodology behind such sure talk of 14 percent and 3 percent (including all the pitfalls of sampling and interview and interpretative bias), and only acknowledging in passing the magical appeal of numbers used in this way (to the layman, 75 means 75—75 apples, 75 rocks; he is not equipped to handle the mental and mathematical, and maybe mystical, subtleties of 75 percent; how many social scientists really are?), let us merely examine the proposition that substantial acceptance of integration is found only among white Southerners with graduate degrees. Could this possibly mean that only this class of white Southerner has the necessary sophistication and (in sad commentary on what graduate education has come to mean in this country) intellectual dishonesty to know the right answer to questions about integration? What kind of answer would an "opinion survey" have received from the white lady quoted as follows in an article about Atlanta housing? "Sure . . . we got niggers all around. Niggers on this side, niggers on that side, niggers across the street and over yonder, niggers around the corner both ways. They taken over the place." How was it working out? "Jest *fine*! You couldn't ask for nicer neighbors. We don't have no trouble. They all nice people."[3]

---

[2] Matthews and Prothro, p. 343.
[3] Margaret Long, "Neighborhood Transition: The Moods and the Myths," *New South*, Vol. 21, No. 2, Spring, 1966, p. 37.

Not since the days of W. E. B. DuBois, Myrdal, and Howard Odum has social science been applied to main problems of the South. The Matthews and Prothro work was a responsible and informed effort to get its blunt instruments down to the quick of the situation, but what seems obviously needed in this academic discipline is an Einstein to cut through the hypnotic tyranny of numbers and apply thought and understanding, to venture and seek truth. Lillian Smith, magnificently ahead of her time as a Southerner confronting the South, was able as an artist to face and render the real problems of the South. She also probably came as close as anyone has to examining the findings of social science in theoretical and creative perspective. Here is how she described the racism of "nice" people:

> This is Mob No. 2. Not all our business and professional men belong to it, by any means. But many do. It is a quiet well-bred mob. Its members speak in cultivated voices, have courteous manners; some have university degrees, and a few wear Brooks Brothers suits. But they are a mob nevertheless. For they not only protect the rabble, and tolerate its violence, they *think in the same primitive mode,* they share the same irrational anxieties, they are *just as lawless in their own quiet way,* and they are dominated by the same "holy idea" of white supremacy . . .[4]

Of course. Ignorance has been no more the common factor in Southern racism than the possession of power or lack of it. On a practical level, the important point would seem to be that the better educated and thus usually more powerful racist most effectively projects his irrationality.

Indeed, what we see most clearly in any real observation of ignorant Southerners of both races is how cut off they are from any effective expression of whatever is inside them—evil, good, or the elementary hungers of their humanity. But the error of supposing the ignorant to be the real strength of Southern racism enters strongly into the

[4] Lillian Smith, "No Easy Way, Now," *The New Republic*, Vol. 137, No. 26, December 16, 1957, p. 12.

theories about that general public out there ready to be riled up over race, and it is incorporated also, of course, in the myth of the separation of the poorest people.

Racism has been common at all levels of the society and, as in all other things, is expressed most successfully at the top. For that matter, ignorance also may be found at all levels. In the South we are not speaking of even the degrees of difference that prevail in the rest of the country when we speak of relative degrees of education and ignorance. The difference between the holder of an A.B. degree from a Southern university and a high school graduate—or for that matter, a sixth-grade dropout—is not as great as it is in the rest of the nation. And school attendance has never been what it should.

So, even in the 1960s we must assume the presence of a considerable amount of involuntary ignorance, including illiteracy. This has been traditionally a large part of the plight of Negroes, but it has been an affliction of whites also. A continuing strength (and to so many whites of good intention, a positive charm) of the Negro movement and the Negro South has been the stubborn presence of the intelligent unlettered men and women, overcoming lack of book learning with slow-worded, hard, creative thought, displaying a certain advantage of concreteness and realism of mind over the half-formed theory and abstraction and floating contradictions within the minds of the partially and badly educated. This is a remnant of the old frontier tradition, a triumph of common sense over pretentious erudition. One senses some of the vigor of Mark Twain's America, having seen it alive in people of both races in the South. But it is easily romanticized, for Twain's America, whatever its greatness and its failure, is gone. Even the best-trained minds have difficulty coping with the complexity of what has since grown up in America, and this means better training than by far the majority of Southern minds have received.

It is worth noting parenthetically at this point the unwillingness of America (in its welfare laws, its poverty programs, its incredible inability to empathize with the poor) to admit that ignorance and most of the other causes of poverty can be involuntary. The poor are poor because they deserve it is the unconscious concept; if a kid doesn't get a good education, it is his fault, never the school's. The same thinking in rawer form was the heart of popular Southern white resentment of welfare and the poverty program, a sentiment exploited by Goldwater, Wallace, and the right wing generally.

Even in the late 1960s the Klan rallies were still held in the hell-dipped glow of the old rugged cross, raggedly aflame under the soft, lunatic Southern moon. Experts in the frenzied oral tradition of hate goad the crowds on: "We don't want our little white children to go to school with pickaninnies . . . Niggers want our white women. Niggers'll never have our white women."

A little brown-haired girl, eight or nine years old, her ide eyes solemn, holds a Confederate flag over the peaker, and the crowd breathes response to his voice and words. There are young men in T-shirts with faces not impassioned but blankly brutal, at the end of an uneven struggle with learning and the graces of civilization in indifferent, inadequate schools, facing now at best a lifetime of low pay and monotony, at worst joblessness, jail . . . girls in shorts with that most pathetic badge of their place in life, cheap, inept imitations of fashionable makeup and hairdo . . . middle-aged men in shirtsleeves, faces red and fleshy or grey and sunken . . . fat, middle-aged women in playclothes that bare the ravages to their flesh of too much childbirth, too much drudgery, bad diet, boredom.

The crowd, it must be noted, is not all Klan. The Klan members are few and fanatical, having found in racism and an organization of hate what others of similar sickness find in other crackpot cults, from spiritualism to nudity. The crowd is comprised of the curious (including always the varieties of spies, from civil rights enthusiasts to FBI to college students observing contemporary culture), the sympathetic, and simply Southerners who might as easily be drawn to a carnival or an automobile race or a church revival meeting. Probably more old people are there than middle-aged ones; these two generations hold the racist faith close to their strong religious ones, speaking them in the same breath, like the people telling why they supported Lester Maddox. The young on hand, particularly the men, seem to be of that most frightening caliber of American society at its lower levels, moving in mindless and random violence. Racism, like petty crime or motorcycle gang activities, is in one sense just a handy outlet; this sort seems incapable of the faith of our fathers in anything.

The crowd is mostly of the "common" sort, which means people deprived of most of the juiceless joys that make modern America bearable. It is oversimplification to explain them away merely as ignorant.

II

It is merely the difference in style, the difference between the "nice" people and the "common" sort which gives rise to the fallacy that only the most ignorant are racist. "Common" people have, of course, only expressed their racism more vehemently, crude in their expressions of it, and in the Klan has been found the most vehement and crude expression of all. The exact membership of the Klan has never been measurable. The most reliable estimate of its strength in 1966 was somewhere around 50,000 —a quite small proportion of the population. But numbers have little meaning: one would hardly suggest that there is nothing to fear from the Mafia in a crowded city because its membership is less than one percent of the population.

Nor was the subjection of the Klan to the indecency of a House Un-American Activities Committee investigation in

1966 a cause for much comfort. (This spectacle was, incidentally, the inspiration of then Representative Charles Weltner of Georgia, lionized in Washington liberal circles as the new model of Southern congressman, a commentary as much on liberalism as on the South's political heritage.) The effect of the HUAC onslaught against the constitutional rights of the Klan (the Klan, of course, was paradoxically in opposition to the existence of those rights) was to break up whatever cohesion the hundreds of local units across the South had in their several superstructures of regional organization. These superstructures were, by the nature of bureaucracy and the notions of the leadership about "image making," somewhat of a moderating influence. When they were gone, the individual units were left to their own devices, largely a matter of degrees of paranoia and homicidal insanity—a situation truly frightening. One such unit operating in a rather large rural area was described as paramilitary, with summer encampments, weapons, tactical drills, and command posts with nightly patrols communicating from trucks by shortwave radio. The members were watching and waiting nightly for the race war to begin.

The violence of the Klan continued to be a potent menace in the late 1960s, mostly in rural areas and small towns. But it was probably less effective in inhibiting Negro action than it had been in the days before the Southern civil rights movement taught that defiance of the racial taboos did not bring down all-consuming calamity. It still affected whites who were now inching their nervous ways into the new order of race relations.

But most importantly, the Klan had for many years served as a symptom of the serious sickness of Southern society. Here, ignored or despised or ridiculed, were living embodiments of deprivation and emptiness. And here was social psychosis so severe that it constituted a threat to everyone. Lee Harvey Oswald came to his role in assassination out of the pathology of the society; his life history has a dreary familiarity. The social pathology of the Negro poor was considered even less by Southern society, just as it was ignored to the peril of the cities of the North.

The Citizens' Councils, when they flourished during the decade after the 1954 Supreme Court school decision, were the "nice" people's organizational mode of expressing racism and resistance to desegregation. They were far more effective than the Klan—and thus offer further evidence that educated racists were more important than ignorant ones. Claiming to eschew violence, the Councils actually used it as one of a number of weapons or encouraged it in the Klan, using the threat of the Klan as a method of intimidation. But they also used every economic, social, and perverted legal means against Negroes and their white allies. Yet this organization, that included many of the most powerful and prominent white men in the South, could not stop the civil rights movement in its drive to force Congress to complete the job of procedural reform, the overthrow of legal discrimination in the South that the federal courts had begun. They were, in this sense, defeated by the Negro leadership of the South. But their eff its were far more effective than the Klan's in poisoning whatever will there might have been in the masses of whites to accept the reforms fully and in poisoning, too, the minds of many of the bravest and best of the c. rights workers, ending their willingness to work within the American system, ending their will and work toward integration in the South.

III

The South, meanwhile, continued to change. The Klan and Citizens' Councils were on the wane, were less relevant as the society seemed increasingly in a state of flux from the effect of new and contradictory forces at work on it. All the Southern impulses to irrationality were summoned by the state of flux, and, appropriate to the age, often found expression in the absurd. There were scenes, for example, like that at the end-of-the-year "patriotic" program at a fashionable public school in Atlanta where the son and daughter of Martin Luther King, Jr., and the daughter of his chief stalwart, Ralph Abernathy, were enrolled. Their dark faces shining out in the closeness of choral grouping among a sea of little white ones, the children were happily singing what the music teacher had introduced as a favorite song of Abraham Lincoln's: "Dixie." The Reverend Mr. Abernathy, shaking his head and grinning, remarked: "Well if it was good enough for Abraham Lincoln, it ought to be good enough for us." Clearly, we might wander at length in a wryly laughing world of such anecdotage on the Southern anthem alone: the football game crowd in Florida standing as the band plays it, a "liberal" white couple refusing to stand and being berated by the little old lady behind them saying: "After all, when am up North and they play the 'Star Spangled Banner,' I always stand."

A whole book of black humor might be devoted to the psychology of the semantics of race, all the symbolism and surrealism. The "common" sort of white Southerner has employed "nigger" unabashedly; "nice" people in the past said "colored." "Negra" was an affectation by them, an attempt (often difficult, as though the tongue were weighted) to say it right. One might argue, in the way of white Southerners, with relish for deep involvement in superficiality and with great, raw insensitivity, that "Negra" is the natural way the Southern speech patterns would form the word "Negro," as they transform "tomato" into "t'mater," and in remote places, " 'matuh" (as in " 'matuh san'wich"). Negroes use "nigger" among themselves—as a term of approbation, or jokingly. "Nigger, git on out of that car," a harried husband says to his wife during the labor and apprehension of moving into a white

neighborhood, both of them breaking up their tens
with a long laugh at what the anguished, new wh
neighbors might have made of that.

The new legislation and changing racial patterns of
1960s threw the average white Southerner's pronunciati
of the word into wild disarray. In former times, each h
his own word for it and stuck to it—"nigger," "Negra
"colored," "Nee-grow." But with the changes, the sar
white person would use all the terms in the course of a te
or fifteen minute discussion. "Now I've never had an
thing against the colored . . . Th' niggers in this tow
never have given any trouble . . . Why, we've even got
Negro on the city council . . . I don't know what it is th
Negras really want. Do you?" This occurred so often i
interviews and casual conversations that it clearly emerge
as a vivid indication of the ambivalences of individua
white attitudes and the regional white mood.

"Black" and "blacks," not much in usage in the moder
South by whites, were once offensive to Negroes as "darky"
and "colored" were not. In the era of black awareness,
Negro ambiguity was to be noted in the interchangeability
of their use of the terms, "black" and "Negro."

"Negra" is most offensive to middle-class Negroes, not
without their own Southern propensity for the superficial.
They encountered it often t those middle-class gatherings
where falteringly, whites of moderate and even liberal instincts attempt to enter the "interracial" world with little
previous contact with the "better sort" of Negro ("th'
class of niggers we got around here" was a stock-in-trade
explanation for lack of Negro advancement in repressive
areas by more or less moderate leadership acquainted
only with menials of their experience). Negroes enjoy setting them straight. "You know how to say knee," slapping
the knee. "And you know how children grow," with a rapid
upshooting motion of the hands. "Well, just put them together and you have—KneeGrow." Sometimes the lesson
was delivered privately; most enjoyably, it would come as

an interruption to a speech (urging, no doubt, good race relations, or some specific racial reform). A celebrated instance of this, part of the folklore, was when Mrs. Constance Baker Motley, in one of her many appearances in Southern federal courts as counsel for the NAACP Legal Defense and Educational Fund, Inc., (before she became a federal district judge in New York City), delivered the lesson to a United States district judge in Mississippi.

Absurdity has always been at the core of the whole racial situation in the South, and this has not been lost on most Negro and white Southerners. Their ability to laugh at it and at themselves from both sides of the color line has been at once one of the most subtle, elusive (hard not merely to describe but even to suggest), and at the same time most magnificent of their survival mechanisms. The Southerner's laugh—dry, ironic, deeply communicative— stands aside from all his embroilment in evil and human complexity; it asserts humanity and comments on self, the situation, and the world at large, on the tragedy of life. The second-generation white leader of a sleepy, unprepossessing little town lets his laughter resound all through the slurred pronunciation of his words as he praises his hamlet beyond all credibility (his and yours and you both know it) for its peacefulness, self-content, good race relations (never any trouble out of the 49 percent-plus Negro population, as debased as any in the South), sound resistance to the encroachment of new industry upon the fine old one (sawmilling) , and so on. Talking at dusk, outlined against an unbelievable sky of purple clouds behind him to the horizon, colors vivid in the grass and bushes and flowers, he gives a virtuoso performance with his Southern propensity for enjoyment of words, the rhythms and complexities of speech, with little regard for meaning, oral tradition itself rendered absurd. He shouts; he whispers dramatically; he takes his hat off to use as a prop, and leans his large head back. An extraordinarily tall man, with a solemn, respectable, official's face (belied only by the ironic turn of his mouth and the unruliness of his black forelock), he takes three steps backward and runs at you with the point he is making: "Th' niggers have got to quit lookin' backward, feelin' sorry for themselves . . ." (This was preceded by an endless digression into the vicissitudes of the town, the state and the South during and after the Civil War, ostensibly the explanation of why it was impossible in the past for the whites of such a town to help out their Negro fellow citizens as, he implies, they are doing in this happy time.) He hawks, he spits carefully into the grass. He begins to build a poetic image of total absurdity, only his intonations acknowledging that thin line he walks between humor and tragedy with sober argumentation:

> Why we've always been peaceful here. Never any trouble between the races. We've always gotten along fine together. Why I can remember—do you remember during the Depression when they used to drop turkeys out of airplanes, th' merchants did, to drum up business? You never saw that? I have many a time. Drop 'em out, and they'd come flopping down and roost up in th' top of trees. I've seen 'em up in that very tree over yonder on th' courthouse lawn. And great crowds down below waitin' to git 'em, niggers and whites. And they'd go after them turkeys, go streamin' after 'em and not fightin' each other at all—climb up them trees, and tear those turkeys apart, limb from limb, a nigger holdin' to a leg, a white man to a wing. Not fighting. Never any trouble between 'em.

He puts his hat back on his head and lights a cigar, allowing, in the utter stillness of twilight in such a town, the vision of interracial harmony to sink in. Then, finally, he laughs and then he says, looking around at the terrible little town: "Well, I tell you what. If th' niggers take this town, they ain't goin' to have *much*. There's some of us would be happy to get it off our backs."

The encounter with such a figure offers a sense of Amer-

ica as it once must have been, Mark Twain's America, de
Tocqueville's, where all undiscovered and waiting in each
look-alike hamlet was richness and wildly flourishing
diversity of human character not yet subjected to the forces
of personality standardization that were to come to America. In this instance, we had crossed the Mississippi River
only a short distance back. Driving through a landscape of
long, flat fields, the traces of cotton culture still marking
the towns, an agent's office on a main street with a deer-
head staring proudly, a roadside mailbox with the legend
Nil Desperandum (a scholarly farmer or a fanciful family
name?), there was the strong sense of Twain and limitless
possibility of fun and excitement and reward. In such subtle psychological flavoring of the past, we may find understanding of how it could have been that so much evil was
perpetrated in America by people without a sense of evil.
The feeling is of innocence. If, as fashion in historical writing in the 1960s would have it, America's history has been
so full of evil—genocidal tendencies so consistent a dark
thread through it—then it must also be acknowledged that
this was not the drear, stale, urban evil of our time, when
people have generally lost their innocence, have the
knowledge of the good and evil of contemporary historical
forces, without the will or power to shape them. Where
there still can be found innocence, delusions, the lost innocence of America, it is most often, appropriately
enough, in the places where the old evil doing flourished:
in the West of the Indian massacres and the South of the
slave holdings. Nothing is necessarily condoned by such
understanding; it merely enables the mind to comprehend
out of the nothingness of the past, facts that are otherwise
incomprehensible.

The Southerner's laugh. An old Negro man had in it the
high degree of appreciation for his own predicament, for
the folly of mankind, for the vast vagary of chance that is
the cold mechanism of nature and is translated by man
into unpredictable and unreliable machinery. He was

standing by the side of a dirt road with three other Negroes and three white people, all civil rights workers in the
heart of the Black Belt, during the worst of the repression
of such groups. It was darkest night, out in the country,
with woods behind and a field in front. Someone had flat-
tened the car's tire while the group was attending a clandestine and dangerous voter registration meeting, and
local whites had already driven by once, jeering. When the
frightened little group began to fix the tire, the jack
wouldn't work. One of the whites kept fumbling with it,
hands shaking, and the rest of the group waited in terrible,
tense silence—and then the old Negro man laughed. He
laughed at the malfunctioning jack, at himself, at them, at
the white toughs, at all humanity. Everything slid into
perspective; the tension broke; the fragility of life was
shiningly clear; the trouble with the jack was fixed, and
they rode off to safety.

It seems important to understand the Southerner's
laughter, for it is so much of his charm, his genuine char
particularly the white Southerner's. But the temptation
to think that the laugh somehow makes sense of the no
sense. This has, surely, sadly, been part of the mystique, a
the flim-flam and sleight of hand that the white South ha
used mostly by instinct to baffle and intrigue and, perhaps,
to seduce their supposedly morally superior fellow countr
men.

Northern audiences are fascinated by accounts of the
minor specimen of rogue politician still encountered up
and down Southern highways. Leaning back in his chair in
the old courthouse (with a John Birch "Support Your
Local Police" circular on the wall, a tinted photograph of
his sweet-faced children on his desk), he drawls his obsceni-
ties, racial and otherwise, in the comforting shadow of the
Confederate memorial out on the lawn. Some of these fellows are genuinely witty in their cynical fashion.

But they are also murderous. "We had all these-yere
demonstrators in jail, and they complained about the

overcrowding, so ever day we put them out in the yard [in the full glare of ninety-degree-plus sun] so's they could git a lot of fresh air and exercise." The crippled soul of such wit is close to the Southern laugh and close, too, to that attitude which is at once one of the Southerner's unhealthiest and healthiest attributes, an acceptance of evil as part of the human condition. (In the North, there seems to be a conspiracy to deny this, a hypocritical willingness to believe all is well in the face of the most sordid evidence to the contrary.) But the white Southerner's acceptance of evil is linked to a conditioning in him which is at least in part attributable to his history of defeat and disappointment, and which teaches that any amount of availing against evil is futile, indeed, that the more one might tinker with a social structure, the worse it gets.

So you learn to live with ills you have, rather than jump to ones you know not of. Hence the laugh's ability to transcend evil, and such other paradoxes as the well-known phenomenon of the one Negro friend of each segregation- , usually a servant. There were and still are—though on a reatly lessened scale—many instances of genuine love in he servant-master relationship. Expression of this love is often enhanced with the Negro as drinking companion. The picture is unforgettable of a vocal white segregationist and "his" black yard man drinking at dawn together, the two of them sprawled in easy chairs, drawing on long cigars, both drunk as lords. "An' what," the white is asking, "do you think of all this integration, George?" And George, in all solemn earnestness is answering: "Aw Mister Frank, I don't believe in that stuff at all."

IV

It was of course the Negro who was first able—and the process has been going on since slavery—to break out of the fatalism of the social system so set against him; this was possible, of course, precisely because it was set against him.

But the fatalism—so close to the feel of Russian novels describing Czarist times—has lingered; in whites it was most often unconscious or subconscious; in Negroes it still came out in the lamentations of "apathy" regarding the newly won legal rights. "It don't matter what I do. The white man's still the white man, and we can't win."

Too often, this was true. But by the late 1960s the old coercive methods of violence and intimidation were manifest mainly in the dwindling rural areas and small towns. In the cities, things were more nearly on the Northern model—impersonal forces, environmental structurings assuring that the white man would remain the white man and that the Negro had no chance. It was here, in the ghetto-building, in the ugly jungles of petty police venality and brutality, sordid, small-time crime, in the erosive little cruelties of welfarism, filth, decrepitness, ugliness, and in the malaise of near-starvation, that the future of Southern race relations was being determined. Soon, it seemed almost inevitable, the South would catch up with the North —but not in the way we once dreamed. It would catch with the worst, not the best, in race relations.

The Northern city riots boiled up at least in part out of the importation from the South of a people miserably cheated of any capability to cope with the cruel, complex routines of advanced industrial society. So, too, and this includes familiar history (see the film, *Birth of a Nation*), as well as current events (the WALLACE FOR PRESIDENT posters carried north in the cabs of the big transcontinental trucks), has the South's racism been exported. We cannot know to what extent the old original Southern variety has diseased America, or to what extent the proliferation of racism in America is another strain of the virus—which seems worldwide. But we cannot overlook this virulent original source.

The anomaly of the South's being behind the North in the matter of riots was not lost on Southerners. In the summer of 1967, during the height of such outbreaks as

Detroit and Newark, white Southerners peered into your
face and said in a strange kind of tone that was part anx-
ious and part comforted, "Things are worse up there now
than they are down here, aren't they?" The Southerner
seeking change is so conditioned to small hopes that he
might grab onto this and encourage the notion that the
thing might be avoided in the South if we do thus and so.
This has been the traditional approach in human relations
work in the South—to seize on any motivation, to nurture
any sign of wanting to do right. The late Ralph McGill,
publisher of and columnist for the Atlanta *Constitution*,
summed up a gleeful reaction to the riots with this quote
from a white Southerner: "Well, for once, we've got the
niggers and the Yankees fighting each other. Now maybe
they'll leave us alone."

The riots did not occur as soon or as frequently in the
South for obvious reasons, including (1) the lack in the
North of the kind of culture base (churches, extended
families, social affairs, community) which, impoverished
ough the institutions were, long comforted Negro
outherners; (2) the lack in the North of any hope, a final
disillusionment delayed in the South by new laws and visible improvements (where there was so much to improve),
and (3) face it, the tradition of fear in the South, the
lynch-fear conditioning against violence to whites.

While the riots came first in the North, it is interesting
to note that they were foreshadowed in Birmingham, Alabama. Charles Silberman[5] cited the rioting in 1963 in that
dreariest of all the South's cities as the harbinger of what
was to come to the North. For all his recognition of the
inability of nonviolence to hold the forces churning in
great miserable masses of city industrial workers and un-
employed people, Mr. Silberman displayed remarked pre-
science, because the Birmingham riots were not really of
the sort that came later in the North. They were the numb

[5] Charles E. Silberman, *Crisis In Black and White* (New York, Random
House, 1964), pp. 143–44.

reflex of people goaded beyond endurance—by white ter-
rorist bombings and then the onslaught of Colonel Al
Lingo's state troopers randomly beating people. Far more
of a harbinger was the riot that occurred in 1960 in Jacksonville, Florida. It grew out of resistance to sit-ins from
white mobs swinging baseball bats. The riot included an
act unparalleled in the North during the next seven years
—the firing of rifles into white homes. Negroes in Jacksonville were talking two years later of how "we controlled
this city for six hours," the part-pride, part-gleefulness,
part-despair of Watts and all the later ones apparent in
their talk. Remarkably, Jacksonville Negroes repeated the
rioting, in 1963 in connection with public accommodations desegregation and more white recalcitrance, and,
once more, in 1966, in apparent imitation of the season's
Northern riots.

Why Jacksonville behaved so differently from the rest of
the South is not known. Its first riot had an element of
simple retaliatory violence, but there was also—and this
seems to have been the first instance of it in the nation—
the wanton, almost objectiveless property destruction that
was later to distinguish the riots of the 1960s from those of
previous years when racial conflicts pitted man against
man, not man against property.

Could it be that this animus against the impersonal was
more important than the racial content? Here, in a sense,
was man in revolt against man-made environment, against
objects and things, as though a personal enemy could no
longer be discerned. Elements of this were in the young
people's beach riots. Perhaps this was the way of the
future. If so, one could only hope that as in earlier times
when man found his environment intolerable, his impotent lashing out would give way to constructive and purposeful plans to change that environment, to do more than
merely destroy.

James Bevel, one of the most vociferous of the "nonviolent" captains under Dr. Martin Luther King, Jr. (of

Bevel it was said in the early 1960s, "give him an hour to speak and three people in the audience and he'll turn a town upside down"), told a Southern audience in 1965 of his horror at seeing the conditions in Northern ghettos for the first time. "I was with a bunch of radicals," he said. "But what I said shocked them. What I said was, 'Let's get all these black people out of these damn buildings, and let's burn 'em. Then we'll build decent housing back.' "

Aside from Birmingham and Jacksonville, the South's rioting and racial violence was almost entirely white through 1963, and even through 1968, as often white as Negro in origin and not on the scale of the Northern Negro riots. Newspaper clippings through 1963 are a touching reminder of what was offered to the South, then, and to the nation in the nonviolent demonstrations. Story after story told of bands of marchers beset by whites, and of only rare retaliatory violence. Where there was an attempt at self-defense, it consisted of throwing bricks and bottles back, and it didn't spread. But by 1967, in any Southern city the answer to the question of whether there might be a riot was Well, it might be tonight, or it might not, depends on whether anything happens to set it off."

Hector Black, a Northern white, once told me how he had been welcomed in 1964 to the Atlanta Negro slum where he and his family lived and worked:

> You think of who is well and who is sick—you think of the history—what the white man has done and still continues to do to the black man, and here we are a white family n.ɔ ʃ in a black community and received with great warmth, and think of what it's like when the black man goes into the white community and into the white man's school; we even beat up little children. It's clear to me who's sick, which society is sick.

But he said in 1967 that he didn't believe they would let a white family move in then as his had earlier. Attitudes had hardened so.

The strong strain of Negro racism in the rationale and

practices of black power taught Northern and Southern whites many existentialist truths bred into Negroes with the forgotten force of childhood conditioning. To a white Southerner there was an awesome sense of recognition when a good Negro friend, with head shakes and yet fond smiles, began telling of another Negro friend who had come to hate all whites. It was like nothing so much as the way the white Southerner had sometimes tried to explain to Negro friends how he could also be on good terms with whites who were decent people but segregationists. They now felt, in a new kind of rapport, the same kind of anguish about their friends, and for the first time the white understood the kind of distrust that such loyalties to racist friends engender in the person of the other race. Another new understanding came to whites and Negroes of the Southern movement from the spectacle of Negro rioting. This had to do with the old practice in the movement of paying lip service, at least, to the proposition that poor whites should not be blamed for their racist violence, but rather the society. Middle-class whites in the movement particularly, always had difficulty practicing what they preached about this. Their attitude toward the poor whites had been founded in the old conceptions of them as "common," a barbaric horde who must not be riled into racial atrocities, and their distaste for poor whites had been whetted by a thousand unpleasant, if not violent, encounters over race. Moreover, their experience and predilections had built an attitude of benign regard toward equally vast, unknown masses of Negroes, an attitude which bordered on that most despised of Southern sins, niggerloving. (The logic of this special racist epithet was grounded in the all or nothing proposition that if you do not despise all Negroes, you must love all of them. Sadly, some in the movement seemed to employ this logic; it was manifest in reverse in the ability of some Northern liberals, among them congressmen, to abandon the Negro cause quickly, turning against all Negroes, when once they

had loved them all so. But for most blacks and whites who
endured in the Southern movement, the whole point was
the freedom to differentiate—to love whom one pleased,
and for that matter hate whom one pleased, black as well
as white. The tendency to undifferentiated niggerloving
among Southern movement whites was really more a matter of sympathy with all of an oppressed people, and also,
perhaps, an unsentimental and well-warranted admiration
for Negro culture. But only fools among them would be
willing to suffer what the Southern race-mixer had to suffer
on the unreal basis of some sentimental love for all of the
masses of unknown, unseen individuals who happened to
be black. This was why it was less easy for white Southerners in the movement to be browbeaten by black power and
less easy for Negro Southerners to swallow it whole. It,
too, had a logic of undifferentiation.)

At any rate, there was shock of recognition when Negro
riots brought forth the same kinds of assertions that had
been made about white racist violence, that the fault was
ety's, not the rioters'. And this gave new meanings,
re conviction to the assertion when it was applied to
oor whites. Interestingly, the early SNCC workers, who
took terrible punishment from poor whites, seemed from
the start to have this conviction more deeply than others
of the movement. Indeed, they seemed willing to overexcuse
the poor white and the vileness of his actions in their unsuccessful effort to make everybody see that it was the society and the system and the manipulators thereof, the
hobgoblin power structure, which were really at fault.

Here, from a white woman of the movement, is another
example of early understanding of the truth about the
white violence, words written in an article about the murder of Mrs. Viola Liuzzo in Lowndes County, Alabama:

> There were there, also, weary looking women, hand-
> some children and sunburned men, country people, some
> who had gone to town and worked in the steel mills and
> suffered the torments of Hell in the burning mills and

the dirty, smoky town of Bessemer. Such as they are not only exploited but looked down on by the other citizens of Birmingham and Jefferson County. "Poor white trash" is the usual term applied to them. I remembered from way back when the men in the mills worked twelve hours a day and 24 on the swing shift in heat and flame and danger, with no union and no protection or compensation for the injuries they received. They lived when they were off work in dingy company houses, traded with scrip at dingy company stores, and all day the smoke hovered over them, lit by the flames at night. We used to ride out to see a "run" and watch the little figures working with the molten steel and wondered how any human beings could stand the heat.

And out of this life had come many Alabama Ku Kluxers, the men looking slightly askew and their women weary and with that vague, wan look that suggests pellagra sometime in their lives. Some looked as if they had had pellagra of the body, mind, and soul. And I thought once more of the times when the mills closed down and the men were out of work and the credit cut off at the store and while the mules were watered and fed, the people were thrown out of the houses, not fed, not watered, and expected to provide for themselves. I had worked with the Red Cross all during the Depression and I could look back now and see vividly just these same kinds of people coming to the door, so ashamed of having to take charity and trying to excuse themselves for their failure, as if it was their fault. And I remembered the gaunt, fanatic preachers who hollered at them that they had sinned and that their suffering was the price of their sinning, and who, as though they did not have Hell enough on this earth, sent them to an even hotter Hell each Sunday.

Out of these conditions had come these fanatic, joyless, pitiful, and ignorant people who were filled with hate of the "niggers" and of all who helped them out.[6]

Nevertheless, white Southerners who had worked in the Negro cause found tremendous emotional content in the spectacle of Negroes kicking a white to death, or the expe-

[6] Eliza Heard, "Economics and a Murder Trial," *New South*, Vol. 20, No. 10, October, 1965, pp. 4–5.

rience of a good-hearted reporter like Karl Fleming of
Newsweek who was beaten nearly to death in Watts. (In
the South in the early 1960s he had been one of the very
few national reporters who got across to the nation what
was really happening. A white Southerner dedicated to
racial justice, he was able to say on regaining consciousness
after his beating, "I don't blame those kids. I'd be doing
the same thing if I had been brought up in Watts.")

There was the familiar sadness of hearing racism's seduc-
tive insanity (and it is no less insane for having a basis in
real grievance) in the message shouted in a Negro church
to a Negro crowd near to mob mindlessness:

"The honkey ain't got no conscience . . . What have
black people done to white people to make 'em treat us so
bad? Did we burn their churches?" "NO." "Did we make
'em slaves?" "NO." Finally, the young Negro radicals produced a seemingly unconscious parody of white racism
(swaggering, Stokely Carmichael brushes by a news cam-
eraman saying, in the same kind of loud aside the Southern
white has used to hurt and humiliate Negroes through the
years, "I didn't ask for this honkey to take my pictur .
To the Southerner who had seen it all in white racis all
his life, it was another absurdity, a drama of mas on
masks.

Out of all of this, the old, perhaps hypocritical, but at
least enunciated excuses and explanations for the v nt
and racist poor white did indeed take on sudde new
relevancy.

These people, we had cried out, even of the Klan rally
crowd, even of the agents of police and private violence, of
those who beat and shot and burned and bombed, those
who bullied and intimidated Negroes, those who murdered, they are not evil people. They have been indoctri-
nated with evil—but of themselves are not. Take the Klan
rally crowd and with magic out of the theater of the absurd
transplant them to a forest where a child is lost, and you
would have an all-American crowd, acting with steady-

headed courage and intelligence beyond testing or blunt-
ing by bad schools, and with instant self-sacrifice, heroism
and solidarity to make you weep at man's greatness, his
capacity for goodness. In the Vietnam War, it was said, the
men who did the drudgery of the soldiering were for the
very most part white Southerners of the poorest class,
"common" whites, and Negroes. Cruelly intercurling
irony within irony, these old enemies fought well together
against a new enemy, hapless and victimized too in this
ugly, least excusable of wars which was destroying back
home the hope that had been built for a beginning toward
real racial progress.

All along we said it: These are not evil men. Said it of
the respectable whites in their civic clubs and their country clubs and their suburbias, piously performing the
standard rituals of American patriotism, saluting the flag
"with liberty and justice for all," and praying in Jesus'
name while on the town square, within earshot often
enough, Negroes marched and the young punks and blank-
eyed old toughs moved menacingly, and the cops w
curses and clubs attacked not the white aggressors but th
Negro victims, martyrs then to liberty and justice and, for
Jesus' sake, turning the other cheek a millionth time, the
rituals translated into stark reality, all unheard, unseen.

The frightening thing, as at the Klan rally, was that th
evil seemed unseeable. Here, then, was the kind of guil
the Germans of this generation know—the ability not to
perceive evil. Or was it the inability to feel?

In the honkytonks of the white South and in the dives of
the Negro South, the selfsame young men, white, black, sit
alone, faces blank with a strange, objectless hostility.

We said it of the whites, respectable and common, not
altogether believing it in the early 1960s, as ready in pri-
vacy, in the urgency of an emergency—a hate call's vicious
invasion of a peaceful living room or a good friend shot in
the back—to curse them and consider *them* the real evil.

But from childhood, we knew their gentle love of children, knew their laughter, and when anger was gone came back to the truth of it—no, they were not evil. Then more and more frequently, it became necessary to acknowledge that Negroes, in coming into America's mainstream, might learn to lose what it seemed they alone in America were still holding to—an ability to feel. As this happened, the terrible old myths and banal old excuses came terribly and urgently alive, and we returned anew to the only truth we ever really knew, the source of evil and the necessity to change it.

The South's betrayal of its sons, both black and white, is the absurd major fact of modern existence: It betrayed the best in them for the worst possible ends.

V

Yet Southerners are not alone in this peculiar anguish. It has just been easier to see in the South. On the whole and in their potential, white Southerners are no more and no less depraved, or decent, or gallant, than any other human beings. We have known this all along. Negro Southerners in the same particulars are no more or less noble, or bad-smelling, or spiritually gifted than any other human beings. They are all, black and white, after all just people. What has happened to them happens to all men; they are conditioned by their society. That their society has been an evil one is after all not so different from the experience of all men when it is considered that all men live now in a world whose main business remains the building of weapons.

Civilization is the price we pay to—at its most basic functioning—curtail murder. For a civilization to build itself and fashion its style on a foundation of murder (and dehumanization is ultimately murder) is the height of final ironic folly, and evil.

The civilization that the South created has had as a large part of its foundation the dehumanization of a portion of its people.

One looks back in behalf of the benighted white Southerner, red-neck, Bourbon, "common" and "nice," and thinks with some wistfulness of the days before political freedom, with its terrible responsibilities. Along with the stout citizen of a murderous Rome, the good peasant in a tyrannical Russia, the stout shopkeeper in a viciously imperialist Britain, the racist white Southerner would share in the good opinion of history (steady, hard-working, responsible, productive, devoted to family and tradition, right-thinking), if men were still not held accountable for the kind of society in which they live. But if we hold every German who did not fight Buchenwald responsible for it, then we must indict every white Southerner who has not opposed dehumanization; if the question has been raised about the duty of Jews to have resisted the Nazi bestiality, then it must be raised about the duty of Negro Southerners to resist racism. But we are learning that guilt does stop so simply: The nations which might have stopped Nazism are implicated, too. Soon the circle of guilt envelops every man, and that, ultimately, is where blame and responsibility must rest.

VI

The wisdom and greatness of the Southern Negro movement of the first half of the 1960s was based on the fact that it not only assumed the initial responsibility but also offered forgiveness and compassion to those whom it resisted. There is pitifully sad, small evidence that the white South gained from that singular episode in history a capability of accepting such grace even on the simple terms with which it was offered.

The failure of the old white Southern leadership of money and controlled politicians, most spectacular during

the few years when a wiser, more rational Negro Southern
leadership was in command through the streets has continued. Southern money has continued to contribute stin-
gily to answering the most basic, uncontroversial needs of
Southerners, and in their last days of waning power, in the
mid–1960s, the old dinosaur leadership, pea-brained and
still bellowing, and a newer, more cunning, more cynical
leadership were either allowing or abetting the building of
ghettos, the white flight to the suburbs, and a whole new
structure for the continuation of racism on the Northern
de facto model. In the rural areas, Negroes and white civil
rights workers were convinced that a concerted, conspiratorial effort was afoot in the mid–1960s literally to starve
Negroes out, to drive them from the agony of life as sharecropper, day-laborer peasant in the South to the worse
agony of the cities. They were, because of mechanization,
the soil bank, and the minimum wage, no longer needed
on the farm; would be a formidable welfare burden should
their needs ever be met; and were an even more formidable
potential political force as their rights began to be recognized.

A group of medical doctors went into six   cities of
rural Mississippi in the summer of 1967 to document the
clinical evidence (including irreparable damage to bones
and bodies, and even brains) of starvation in children.
Although they were accustomed to the ugliest aspects of
racism and conditioned to sickness and suffering, and
though they expected what they were to find, these men
were nevertheless in a state of emotional shock during and
after the trip. It was a classic case of what has become, all
unacknowledged, one of America's most debilitating schizo-
phrenias: the two worlds of headquarters and the field.
They knew, indeed some had written, of the deplorable
conditions. But they knew this back in headquarters, with
air-conditioning and with other concerns. Then they confronted the total reality of it. SNCC workers had done this
four years ahead of them; SNCC reports in 1963 from

these same and many other counties (and from other states) told the same terrible stories of hunger and cold and crying babies.

Most of the things that have to be understood about the changing South and the South to come can be seen in the tragedy of SNCC. Much of the tragedy involved the schizophrenia of field and headquarters; the SNCC workers were so caught in the reality of the field that they couldn't tolerate or even communicate with the seeming smugness and comfort back in headquarters—that is, with the rest of America, including their political and movement allies. The gap was too wide; what they were seeing —in repression, in rape of democracy, in human misery— was so bad that it couldn't be comprehended by those who had not seen it. Headquarters was concerned with the big picture, and this was little picture stuff. (Never mind that the big picture, if it has any validity, must be merely the composite of all the little ones, faithful to them.) SNCC tried to tell America in 1963 that Negroes were starving in the rural up n. By 1969, America was beginning to comprehend t' SNCC tried to tell the Democratic Party at the 1964 cc vention that the cruel repression of voter registration, the use of totalitarian force against democracy, in much of the South had made it impossible to compromise by splitting up the seats with the regular white party from such a state as Mississippi. The Democratic Party and America, in headquarters fashion, rejected this rationale, saying that in the big picture the whites of Mississippi must not be lost to democracy (and more importantly, Democracy). So instead, SNCC—the last effective combining of young people of both races in a drive deeply within, rather than against, the normal national institutions—was lost to democracy. How much of Negro America was lost with it? Back at headquarters, they set in to worry abstractly over the alienation of the youth, and the growing alienation between the races.

The doctors who went to Mississippi were able to com-

municate better with headquarters; they told their terrible
story before the United States Senate Subcommittee on
Manpower, Employment and Poverty and were subjected
to carping and insults from the two senators from Mississippi, James O. Eastland and John Stennis. One of the
physicians was Dr. Raymond Wheeler of Charlotte, North
Carolina, a serious, modest man who is chairman of the
executive committee of the Southern Regional Council.
Long a dedicated participant in the Southern civil rights
movement, Dr. Wheeler rose to one of those shining hours
when for a moment all the unfairness of the Southern system is overturned: He went out and scribbled off a statement and came back and read it, telling off, as thousands of
Southerners have wanted to, the two senators from Mississippi, making them for at least a moment face truth:

> Throughout these years, my heart has wept for the
> South as I have watched the southern black man and
> white man walk their separate ways distrusting each
> other, separated by false and ridiculous barriers—
> doomed to a way of life tragically less than they deserve
> —when by working together they could achieve a society
> finer and more successful than any which exists in this
> country today.
> And through all of that dreadful pageant of ignorance
> and suspicion and mutual distrust, the most distressing
> figure of all has been the southern political leader who
> has exploited all of our human weaknesses for his own
> personal and selfish gain—refusing to grant us the dig-
> nity and the capability of responding to noble and
> courageous leadership—when all of us had nothing to
> lose but the misery and desolation which surrounds our
> lives . . .
> I invite Senator Eastland and Senator Stennis to come
> with me into the vast farmlands of the Delta and I will
> show you the children of whom we have spoken. I will
> show you their bright eyes and innocent faces, their
> shriveled arms and swollen bellies, their sickness and
> pain and the fear and misery of their parents . . .

Needless to say, the invitation was not accepted.

For all of this, it is difficult to believe that the old leadership, pitilessly sending the farm refugees off to the terrors of the cities, even beginning to build ghettos in the Southern cities, was involved in diabolical conspiracy, acting in any concerted, planned way. Like the old Bourbons and power structures everywhere, they were merely doing what came, had always come, naturally to them. Mainly, they were making money (money rather than ideology had been their main motivation since slavery). The forces behind the migration of the people from the land were more chilling than even human cruelty or revenge. What really was involved where the exodus was worst was the breaking up of the last of the plantation system. It was a full-blown system involving social as well as economic arrangements, the symbiosis of the laborers and the owners, loyalties both ways, and complex community relationships. But the break-up of it, as we shall see, was caused by economic forces that operated despite any human predilections of the owners or the laborers, even as in the larger collapses of obsolete economic systems through history (the transition from feudalism to capitalism comes to mind). Some of the planters may have found sadistic satisfaction in turning black people off the land and perhaps had political motivations. But these were as irrelevant to the ⸢cold⸣ economic forces at work as any humanitarian, ⸢nostalgic⸣ emotions among the planters to let some hands li⸢ve⸣ out their lives on the old places. Certainly, the planters had not needed to plot and conspire. They were being acted upon by the forces, not, of course, in cruel, catastrophic ways, indeed, in ways profitable to them, but acted upon nevertheless. Their plight, common around the world, involved the new bugaboo of technique. Better ways are found to do things, to farm large acreages, to contain the dissident in a society, to wage war, and the human agents of these things are powerless but to adopt the new techniques—or cease to function. In the case of the building of the ghettos in the city, the same patterns seemed to be at work, less clear-cut,

and with possibly more incorporation of racist motivations, but at base, cold and impersonal economic forces at
work (the demand by whites for all-white, cheaply taxed
neighborhoods, attraction of Negroes to central cities by
jobs and welfare) and techniques at hand for implement-
ing them.

It used to seem so simple in the South. Negroes were
right; whites were wrong. That has not changed. But we
begin better to understand the anguish of the nation when
we move beneath the surface of such simplicity in the
South and begin to understand that people, oppressors as
well as the oppressed, have less control over affairs, less
ability to be even all evil (as common sense would tell us
nobody is all good) than it had appeared. In this context
one has to take seriously the New Left's frequent assertion
that the Negro movement's advance was stopped only when
it began to impinge on the larger monied interests. This
certainly seemed true. To challenge housing segregation or
the wage structure is to impinge on the most powerful of
monied interests in America. Even a casual acquaintance-
ship with the real content (as opposed to the ostensible
actions which is all that usually gets into the newspapers)
of American business and *Realpolitik* impresses one re-
peatedly with how quickly and ruthlessly any infringe-
ment on big money is put down.

But knowing this does not suggest a solution; here there
are no more simplistic villains like the rural racist Southern sheriff whose defeat would, it once was thought, solve
everything. Nor is there comfort in the knowledge that
where the white leadership in the South did contribute to
the advance of Negro rights, as in acceptance of the *fait
accompli* of the command of ten-cent-store lunch counters,
it was in the name of good business, not good sense or
morality. To be at the mercy of such a single-minded criterion for basic social change in a civilization is, to say the
least, frightening; the alleged ability to stop progress in this
very advancement of Negro rights is but the most striking

example (not to mention such particulars as pollution of air, land, and water or, for that matter, world peace) of the fact that what is good for business is not necessarily good for society or good morally.

The respectable wing of the Southern movement (that is, the white and Negro interracialists who were working together before direct action, the group Myrdal termed the liberals—though except in race this was not necessarily a correct label) had made an art of seizing on such essentially irrelevant motivations as whether something was good for business to advance and make respectable their cause. The respectables in the South pushed the good business motivation for civil rights hard, using statistics showing how little industry Little Rock could attract in the years after the 1957 school desgregation riots.

This can be seen in retrospect as one of the most severe of mistakes, almost as great as another favorite of theirs, urging law and order as the sole reason for accepting racial justice. Not that these stratagems didn't work; many a biracial committee comprised of blue-ribbon white business leaders, preachers, school officials, and the like sitting across from a handful of Negro middle-class representatives (teachers, preachers, a barber or undertaker or the like) hammered out agreements on public accommodations, schools, even token employment well in advance of the civil rights law for the sole purpose of avoiding demonstrations and their potential violence. In these instances, mayors and chiefs of police who a year or so previously basked in business approval with the most foulmouthed of racist demagoguery and brutal repression were suddenly summoned by these selfsame business leaders and told to get a committee, get an agreement, develop race relations par excellence—and overnight they turned about and did it, even had the effrontery to brag about it, the chambers of commerce holding backpatting press conferences and printing up the sagas of racial progress.

Not always, though, did this happen. In the wretched

old Florida tourist-trap town of St. Augustine, there was
a business leadership, reportedly reducible when it came to
a question of final decision to one old man who either
doubted the bad-for-business theory or had a set of priorities which placed racism and all-around right-wingism
above even moneymaking. There, known Klansmen who
were sheriff's deputies nightly stood by and even abetted a
vicious gang of whites armed with chains and clubs as they
attacked nonviolent demonstrators. Finally, in splendid
indignation over the essential indecency of what was happening, Federal Judge Bryan Simpson put a stop to it with
firm court orders and eloquent tongue-lashings. This, of
course, never touched the real culprits, the business interests.

Judge Simpson, reputedly, was no ardent integrationist;
apparently, he acted out of a high regard for justice. His
court order forbidding attacks on the constitutional demonstrations and ordering the sheriff to protect them happened to have been the only one of its kind ever pro-
pounded and actually carried through[7] despite thousands
of unconstitutional violations of such demonstrations
which occurred up and down the South from 1960 to 1965.
That it came at the request of private civil rights lawyers
(mainly the American Civil Liberties Union) and not the
Justice Department has been noted by critics of the performance of that arm of the Executive Branch during
those crucial years. An even more important point would
seem to be the rarity of Judge Simpson's vision—that not
merely the maintenance of law and order but the protection of constitutional rights is the duty of society. The
failure of the "liberal" South (and, of course, the nation)

---

[7] In Greenwood, Mississippi, such a federal order was sought by
the U. S. Justice Department and prepared during voter registration demonstrations in 1963. But before it could be put in force, an "agreement"
was worked out whereby the court order was put aside on the promise
of local officials not to interfere with voter registration. Fear of white
mob violence was generally attributed to be the reason for abandoning
the procedure.

to see this was to haunt with heavy irony the civil rights cause in the incidence of the Negro riots—when heavy-handed, totalitarian police (and even United States Army) force was used to maintain law and order (with no regard for essential justice, the duty of society). Those disturbed about this sinister new manifestation of national will to apply simple brute force to solve infinitely subtle and complicated problems, likened the police and army actions to an occupation of a foreign nation, and the comparison was apt.

If it was not entirely apparent after the orgies of property destruction in the North that, as in Vietnam, the principle of overkill (or hammering tacks with sledge-hammers) was at work in suppression of the riots, then a look at a lesser affray in the South made things clearer. In the Negro section of Atlanta called Dixie Hills, in June, 1967, after a three-day build-up of what had come to be recognized as the normal provocation of riots, tension with police, a "mass meeting" was held in a small neighborhood church for an airing of grievances.

(These grievances were interesting for what they might show of Southern-style riot potential or the riots of the future. They were not about the worst kind of unspeakable conditions which prevail in most Negro residential areas—shacks on mud alleys—across the South; Dixie Hills seemed to be an area of formerly middle-class apartments of the barracks variety, built after World War II. Better housing for middle-class Negroes in Atlanta had since become accessible, and the more than six hundred hot, cramped little apartments had come to be the dwelling places of working class and welfare recipient Negro citizens, many of them refugees from extensive urban renewal which had replaced the typical mud alley slums with shining luxury apartments, and that cruelest perhaps of all latter-day Southern exhibitions of insensitivity and incapability of response to human suffering, an $18-million sports stadium. Families of twelve and more were existing

in two-bedroom apartments, and hundreds of the brick
boxes stood in long rows with hard red-clay yards bereft of
grass or trees. Among the well-articulated complaints were
faulty garbage collection, lack of playgrounds, faulty
drainage, bad roads, the heat and inhuman qualities of the
apartments themselves, petty bullying by the management
of such apartments, and exploitation by monoply merchants in a little row of stores. They touched finally underlying causes: "The youth don't have nothing to do.
They're just out on the streets. They don't have money or
jobs. They're just on the loose.")

At the church meeting, Stokely Carmichael and others
of SNCC eventually, at the chanting call of a claque, took
the floor from the middle-class, older leaders who were
talking in terms of petitions and even (as late as 1967)
demonstrations. Carmichael harangued the crowd against
the "honkies" but warned them to cool it because the area
was surrounded by police. His suggested strategy: Keep
them waiting. When they leave, do something to make
them come back. A war of nerves.

As in nonviolent days the crowd, numbering no more
than two hundred in the church at any one time, wan-
dered in and out, all ages, women with babes in arms,
children skylarking. It was to the teenagers, already a
claque, that Carmichael spoke, and they, who had been so
much the strength of nonviolence, were the only ones who
responded when another SNCC radical shouted as the
crowd was breaking up: "Remember Watts. Burn Baby
Burn." The teenagers, no more than a hundred and probably nearer fifty, went hollering down to the shopping center and began to throw rocks at its plate-glass windows.

Within minutes, police had sealed off the area and were
swarming through it, arresting the rock-throwers. The
more than a hundred police had enough fire power to
blow up that side of town, patrol cars whizzing about, am-
bulances on hand, paddy wagons, and a special riot-con-
trol armored car (the press called it a tank). Television

lights glared their touch of unreality on the scene; reporters had been watching and waiting all day; radios blared out the news that a "riot" was going full blast. But in fact, the vast majority of apartment occupants were either inside watching television or outside watching the excitement, and during the height of the activity three white reporters were able to walk through four courtyards full of Negroes and not receive a cross look, let alone words, or violence. Looking down at all the police, a young woman said: "Damn. They going to come up here and shoot us like flies." This excessive police force stayed all night and returned the next night, with orders to force everyone back inside the hot apartments. That second night, teenagers threw a fire bomb at a cop, and the police—or police claimed, someone else, presumably a Negro—opened fire, killing a man and severely wounding a boy of nine who were sitting on the front steps of their apartment home. The initial rock-throwing, a very few fire bombs in direct response to the police presence, and an occasional firecracker were the total extent of Negro violence. Police were scrambling around on building tops, losing their footing, cursing, with loaded carbines in hand. They were edgy, some of them downright scared. On a hill opposite was a gasoline pipeline installation with big storage tanks, and a middle-aged Negro who looked as though he knew whereof he spoke, kept saying quietly, "Those double-ought-shells they've got would go right through one of them tanks; I know they would."

VII

To the degree that undiluted pragmatism was allowed to bypass and make irrelevant the beautiful spiritual force of the early civil rights movement, to probably the same degree the old white leadership of the South was able to salvage power, to cut its losses. The American genius has been to hold in some kind of balance the two strains of its soul, pragmatism and spiritual belief (*la politique* and *la mystique*). This was also the great achievement of the early movement, unsurpassed in all of America: Negro Southerners' fully feeling redemptive love for the white man at the very moment that with cold pragmatism they pressed demonstrations designed to bring out the worst of white racism and force federal intervention and reform. For a time, it seemed that all America might, from the example, regain some of its balance. But the march of events worked against it—the Kennedy assassination, the Vietnam War, the countless defeats of individual Negroes seeking simply the basics of American rights in the South (out in the field) even as the victories for these rights were being won (up in headquarters), the Watts riot, the beating of children in Grenada, the defeat of the 1966 civil rights bill which dealt with housing and would have reformed Southern justice, the failures of enforcement of the new legislation, its irrelevance to the ghettos of the North and those a-borning in the South, rats biting babies, Vernon Dahmer of Hattiesburg, Mississippi, murdered by fire bomb six months after passage of the Voting Rights Act because he urged Negroes to register to vote.

The early movement was founded in the creed of Christianity and the maxims of democracy. Perhaps not events but the forces of history and of technological development foredoomed that sweet spirit that rose, anachronistic, perhaps obsolete, out of the innocence of the South. Maybe it was merely irrelevant. The notion has been advanced that black power had its origins and entire basis in the sexual antipathies of black and white men and women. One member of SNCC through its best days looks back and tries to tell how too much was attempted. It was not just the impossible drive by a handful of "freedom fighters" to undo in three years the Southern history of three hundred years. It was also the beginnings of what the hippies still sought a few years later, or the continuation of what the beats had sought a few years earlier—a way somehow

out of the hysteria that human dealings had become
in America and the special hysteria of the mind of the
South. Or perhaps—because SNCC, like the New Left and
all the revolutionary young the world over, never seemed
to have read literature, only a smattering of sociology and
political science—the attempt was to escape the human
condition with no awareness that through the ages this
condition has been essentially a tragic one. "We failed,"
said one who was there, still able to seem puzzled that this
should have happened in the attempt of two impossibili-
ties.

But in the new mythology of the South, success has been
predicted—tentatively, wistfully, but persistently. The
wishful thinking had some basis. Southerners continued to
have the paradoxical ability to believe, to have faith
(white Southerners, Myrdal noted in the 1940s and this
was still true in the 1960s, persisted in believing more
fervently than most Americans in the American creed all
the while their culture and their daily lives denied it; the
Black Belt has remained the Bible Belt; the ability to believe in an age of unbelief was the grandeur and majesty of
the early movement). Illogically and unrealistically, the
South was still convinced that it was going to show the
world a thing or two.

So much foolishness has been written about the South.
James Baldwin said the white man invented the nigger
because he needed him; so, too, the nation may have invented its South. At once damned for daring to show
openly the racism the nation hid in its unconscious and its
ghettos, deplored and cursed for all its backwardness,
stubbornness, stupidity, mosquitoes, heat, speech patterns,
slowness, laziness, and representatives to the national congress, it has also been the repository of every false hope the
nation has known. Not the least of these is the hope that
somehow, out of its long night of political backwardness,
of as arrogant and complete a denial of democracy as any
self-government in the world has known, the South will

somehow emerge as a model of political and governmental acumen. It will of course do well to catch up with the rest of the nation over the next decades, and that, of course, will not amount to much. The same is true of those other fields of endeavor, including business, in which the South has trailed the nation throughout its history. It is cruel to hold out myths to the Southerner, Negro or white, that encourage his propensity to overvalue himself, his region, his civilization. He keeps wanting to show them. But until he solves the simplest problems of public adminstration, until he gets a grasp on the workings of self-government, until he learns the rudimentary instinct of enlightened self-interest to a degree these were mastered over the rest of the nation and most of the globe centuries ago, he is not going to show anybody anything except the horrible example that he now is in all the national statistics. The white Southerner—confirming W. J. Cash's most impo.tant point—has been a romantic. About the only realistic hope of his offering salvation was that he might have deep somewhere in his romantic soul some undisciplined, unstructured, inarticulate ideas of what there is that might be better than the unsavory set of things served up by the rest of American civilization. Or maybe he might only be able to protest the wrongs, and this in a wrong-headed way—as he may have been in part doing when he voted for Wallace. Most of the ideas and ideals the world has lived by and he has been goaded to grasp onto seemed to have outlived their usefulness. Maybe he could come up with the new ones. He has (all the authorities would agree) a certain disposition for leisure, for example.

The new mythology has proclaimed that the white Southerner, having known defeat and having lived with a known evil, more than the rest of America, is disposed to a certain humility and tolerance of human fraility. The point that Negro Southerners have known even more defeat and have lived more intimately, more hurtingly with the evil, is not developed in the mythology, out of that old

Southern custom of ignoring the existence of Negroes. Humility and tolerance have of course been a chief device of overcompensation (and survival) among Negro Southerners; they would do well to get rid of great loads of these virtues (and many have). As for the white Southerners, humility and tolerance are perhaps the last qualities one would ascribe to them after living a lifetime among them, observing them in their off-guard moments, or times of tension, and dealing with them in, say, a political battle or a case in civil court. And yet the mythology is a cornerstone of that grand hope for the South that on the surface and at common-sense evaluation would seem the most absurd of all the idiotic bag of them. This is the hope that the region will emerge as the nation's new model of amicable and sane race relations.

Is it absurd? In 1961 Leslie Dunbar expressed it well and sanely in an article which like the rest of his inestimably sound observation on the South has been little noted.

> . . . I have never met a white Southerner, not even the most determined of segregationists, who did not betray some moral uncertainty; and in that fact he differs and is set apart from the majority of his fellow Americans.
>
> This is possibly a part of the reason why he will, often after the staunchest resistance, adapt so comfortably to new racial practices. Once the fight is decisively lost (the verdict has to be decisive), once the Negro has secured the right to vote, has gained admittance to the public library, has fought his way into a desegregated public school, has been permitted to sit at a lunch counter, the typical white Southerner will shrug his shoulders, resume his stride and go on. He has, after all, shared a land with his black neighbors for a long while; he can manage well enough, even if the patterns change. There is now one fewer fight which history requires of him. He has done his ancestral duty. He is free of part of his load, he can relax a bit more. He has been annealed.[8]

---

[8] Leslie W. Dunbar, "The Annealing of the South," *The Virginia Quarterly Review*, Autumn, 1961, Vol. 37, No. 4, p. 499. The beginning of the article gives the *Webster's New International Dictionary, Second Edition*, definition of anneal: "To subject to high heat, with subsequent

The annealment has not of course been completed; something has gone wrong in the process perhaps. Maybe it's a failure. But the hope is valid, founded in sound psychology, from the truth that whites and Negroes in the South have had a human intercourse of sorts (however crippled and cruel) lacking elsewhere, to the truth that the white Southerner has in his life history and his culture experiences conducive to a great psychological and spiritual crisis of release, the catharsis of renunciation and expiation, just as the Negro Southerner has in his life history and culture similar predisposition to push this crisis upon his white brother. That in effect describes what was attempted in the early movement. It describes also much of the hopeful phenomena of the late 1960s, with the Negro freer, a little more powerful, more mobile, better able to get to a point where he might—either gently which might be unbearable or manfully with gleeful force—rub his white brother's nose in all the evil and cruelty and needless human suffering that the Southern way of life has meant. If the South can ever come to such honest and human settlement of its most ancient antipathies, if the white South can ever bring itself to acknowledge evil within itself, and if the Negro South can stand to make it do so, then a society like the South's might indeed, maybe uniquely in America, be in a shape to reach toward good. Certainly its people, white and black, would be more fit than most on the globe, from having acted out in a public arena (as many are acting out their racial life histories on countless interracial local and state governmental agencies for example) such a universal (and at the moment, historically important) personal conflict.

This is the kind of mythology Lillian Smith must surely have meant when she, in effect, called for a restructuring of the Southern psyche. But it is myth. Few Southerners, white or Negro, have caught their lives up in it. These few,

cooling, for the purpose of softening thoroughly and rendering less brittle . . ." (p. 495).

however, might be in their deviancy like mutants with survival value in the evolutionary process; they might be, in the Biblical sense, a remnant. They have been a small, tight body in the South, a community of race-mixers, known to one another like an underground, often in warm personal contact and cold strategic touch.

They have included not just the civil rights movement "militant activists," but also a large body of white and Negro respectables who never marched or went to jail. Many of these had been working to improve race relations ten and twenty years before the great advances made by the early 1960s movement; if, like the old NAACP, they can be judged to have had the wrong methods, they must at the same time be credited with preparing the way for the great advances. During direct action, the respectables were often go-betweens behind the scenes. Among the whites, often the most valuable thing they possibly could have done was to lend their respectable names to endorse direct action or the militant organizations and leaders in a particular locale. In the heyday of direct action and of the movement, the respectables and the militants worked together amazingly well, with much mutual respect. In the years afterward, with many militants finding themselves relegated to respectable status because of black power (derided as white paternalists, Uncle Toms) and with a proliferation of respectables (particularly whites), things were less cohesive. Nevertheless, it was still possible in the late 1960s to identify a growing body of the race-mixers, with a solid core of old hands still at it, white and Negro, across the South. Long after the movement had been proclaimed dead, they were still at it. With most of the institutional goals achieved, ending legal sanction of discrimination, they concentrated much of their effort on the losing battle to gain compliance with the new laws in the face of continued Southern resistance and irresponsible federal and national indifference and sometimes interference. They kept right on, blacks and whites, holding to integration as a goal even with the rise of black power and more positive local thrusts toward black awareness and separatism. And where there might be ideological disagreement among some about integration, they could keep working together on the terrible problem of Southern poverty among blacks and whites. If one should go into a strange town on some race-mixing matter knowing no one there, he would have names of people to see, white and black, and would be assured of assistance and friendship, a remarkable bond of cooperation and trust. (I went into such a town recently, a tiny one I had never visited. I had my little list: three Negroes and one white man of some prominence, the latter described simply as "decent" and he was. Of the three Negroes, only one answered the phone. I identified myself, my organization, but the Negro woman had not heard of either: her tone was polite, but wary. I mentioned the name of Mrs. Frances Pauley, then director of the Georgia Human Relations Council, a white, apple-cheeked grandmother, as Southern as grits, and the voice at the other end warmed immediately. "Oh yes. We know Mrs. Pauley." I told her I wanted to talk with her and other Negro leaders, reading her the names on my list, and any others she might suggest. "Gi me fifteen minutes," she said, and gave me directions to get to her house. It was full of leaders when I arrived. I found out later that she had been about to leave on a fairly long automobile trip when I called. My request delayed her and her family a good three hours. This could not have been done more graciously; she was genuinely glad "to help the cause." Such words are spoken.

(In the same circumstance in a tiny town in Louisiana, the Negro woman asked where I was calling from. It was on the town square, across from the jail and sheriff's office. "I'll come and get you; you'll never find this place," she said. There were two of us on the trip, both white. It was a matter of delicacy; she surely must have thought I was Negro. But—and one has to sense these things—it didn't seem the proper thing to say, "But I'm white." When she drove up to where we were and saw our color, she stopped; we said quickly we would follow her car; she nodded, and off we went. Before we really began talking, she asked for identification. This was a tough little town; such a request indicated just how tough. The usual thing is for such strangers to accept each other on face value or on mention of a mutually known person. There will sometimes be a little parrying around, asking if you know so-and-so in such-and-such-a-place, all of this delicate and deferential. Unsaid, there is agreement that this is the better part of discretion; at the same time, you have come as a friend and are not to be—in this good Southern way of things—insulted.)

They have been all kinds, these race-mixers, rich and poor, conservative and radical, extrovert and introvert, happy and sad, mean and generous, as capable of folly and cruelty as of the greatness they have shown in the one regard of race. It was this alone that they had in common, a refusal to accept wrong when they know what is right. Unable to be dishonest with themselves and their racial opposites, they have been ennobled in whatever suffering their honesty has cost them. Let it be said, ⸱ race-mixers often fight one another unfairly—cattily ᵢₛ ⸱ term that comes to mind. But they are also generally a rela⸱ed people, and are pleasant to be around. The most important thing is—they are free. This freedom allows them to be—fully and without hidden shame or shameful pretense—at their best moments all that Southerners think of fondly when we say Southern ladies and Southern gentlemen. They are, black and white, living evidence of the hope there is for the South. With history's more or less favorable setting in the late 1960s, the good and strong variants in Southern culture that they embody stood a better chance than ever before of prevailing. If these good things in the culture should survive the necessary death of the evil of racism, then the hope would not necessarily be that the

South would beat the world at race-mixing or anything else, but merely that the South would come to terms with itself and become the kind of good place to live out a life in it ought to be, it almost is, it elusively, like a dream, keeps suggesting it might yet be. . . .

It was one more irony that the South approached the possibility of coming to terms with itself at a time when it was becoming obvious that the rest of the nation was deep into sickness, afflicted in much the manner the South has been, in some ways more deeply, in others less, in everything from race to what was summed up about economic and cultural reality in the term "military-industrial complex." In any examination of what has happened to the South, this raised the central question of whether many of the attainments which Southerners long have been encouraged to overestimate their ability to gain are worth the gaining, and even whether the South's majestic ability to fail through history to attain them might not suggest a secret or unconscious knowledge that they weren't really worth going after—such things as ever-growing cities, efficiency, big industry—that there must be something better. The Southerner's basic mistake has always been that of arming himself with a cotton stalk against repeating rifles when he sets out to prove he can whip ten of somebody else. Maybe he hasn't really wanted to win.

What he has been, what he is becoming, what has happened to his civilization, whether it was indeed moving toward that dream of all it might be or merely toward the rest of the nation's own versions of malaise, was not an easy thing to see in all the flux and contradictory directions of the 1960s. Most non-Southerners have viewed a South beclouded by myth and analysis from the past or seen it superficially in crisis-excited journalism. Their touch with the South's reality has been brief, as in an airport interchange, or looking out a car window bound for some beach or resort, locales not really a part of Southern culture but of beach and resort culture, tourist culture, the same the world over. The South was yet distinctive enough so that, for non-Southerners, seeing it in outline and close detail was like visiting a foreign country. Like people anywhere, the Southerner himself has difficulty seeing the familiar world around him abstractly or objectively. Perhaps the best way to try to see it, really see it, is from familiar vantage, out the car window.

PART TWO

The Changing Face of the South

CHAPTER 3

I

THE ROADS, even the superhighways, but better the old concrete highways, U.S. 1 and 349 and 41 and the like (these better than the rutted trails in sand and red clay or graveled farm roads engineered for 1930s-width cars) lead through it all. They lead through time especially, back to the beginnings, cotton rows green in bright sun color as far as you can see, and forward to the stark rise of a windmill, one arm broken, dangling, by a barn collapsed to ruin and weed-grown waste, through pine forests in efficient, planned rows where no man dwells and where paper mills get federal subsidy and county tax favoritism, then by an old cotton mill of brick and blue-glass windows, and a new one, low-slung, pink and blue brick, and from here to the inhuman twisting and coiling of steel and glass and blinking blue lights that is a chemical plant, and by tracts of land fenced off and marked federal, devoted to nuclear weaponry and space flights and the training of foot soldiers. The roads go on and on, space and time linked along the white cement and black tar, through a tiny town with a railroad cutting through the main street and a row of one-story brick and wooden stores, a cotton warehouse at one end, a general store full of the smell of cloth and seed and the nineteenth century at the other, a tin-roofed shed with iron poles shading their wide sidewalk, and through a "city" of the South with its dune-risings of skyscrapers and its shopping centers (which, big or little, suggest the cere-monial more than do Northern counterparts, sacrificing the utility of multistoried parking garages for the grandeur of open acres of belit and marked-off parking places, looking like a Nazi parade ground) and its federal housing "projects" in ugly, low brick rows and its festering niggertown and poor white slums and its neon-berserk outskirts and over-gardened suburbs, a few all black, the most and best, of course, all white with very little integration, everything interconnected unquestioningly with expressways.

The sense of place is strong in the Southerner's psychology and psyche, his love of the landscape, the smell and feel of the air of home, generalized often in the worst kind of romanticism, but particularized nearly always with sincerity and intensity. A beaming young soldier (who just happens to be Negro) disembarks from a plane at Jackson, Mississippi, surely the world's strongest symbol of all that is evil for him, and says to the stewardess (who nods happily, understanding) : "Oh, it's good to be home. I've got a whole week."

Myth and analysis, as we have tangled them together so far, seeking a certain truth about the South, have their own approach to truth. They do not humbly seek it; they proclaim it. Of all subjects, surely, the South least lends itself to their direct, and detail-lacking generalization. For the richness of the South's reality has always made the myths seem shallow (even those that have sustained its most terrible ways) and has always defied analysis. Wiser students of the region have known this. But then their immersion in the detail and the flavor, the grandness and excess, the merciless contrasts, have more often than not led them further from truth than the oversimplifications of myth and analysis. The best books (like those of Lillian Smith and *The Mind of the South* and James Agee's masterpiece) hold some kind of control over love of place and of people and exhibit a humility, a tentativeness in proclaiming truths of generalization and abstraction.

Of the first-rank regional artists, only a few seem to have

seen and felt deeply the beauty of sun-bleached sheds
aslant on the farms, of sun-faded red and yellow on rusted
tin signs in the sagging little towns, and of the wistful,
lonely lines of railroad tracks leading out of crossroads
hamlets which no one ever leaves, these icons which so
frenzied Wolfe and haunted Faulkner and brought Agee,
ahead of his time, to the threshold of psychedelic descrip-
tive vision.

Inevitably, writers attempt to connect the sense of place,
the feel of weather and climate, of nature and artifact that
combine in the kaleidoscope landscape of color and soft-
ness and splendid disorderliness, with the acts, the psychology, the qualities of mind and manner and activity
that seem typically, uniquely, Southern. This is of course a
common tendency in any literature of any land[1] (though
one wonders at the lack of it in the literature of those
disciplines which seek to explain man and his acts, not
merely psychology, but sociology, political science, even
anthropology). The landscape of the South was changing
like all else in the 1960s, but there remained enough distinctive flavor to warrant speculation about its influence
on personality and psychology. Although air-conditioning
has mitigated the worst (and best) influences of the
Southern summer and standardized construction and the
new-day filling station and motel and shopping center investment capital has penetrated remote byways, a good
deal of picturesque, individualistic man-made scenery remains. This—and such natural wonders as ragged, un-
fenced, unplanned forestry and wantonly neglected, wasted
land—keep the natural setting alive in the minds of
those who study the South, if not in the hearts any more of
all Southerners, and it is the tradition of awareness of the

[1] There are nature passages in Camus' *The Stranger* which might have
been written by a Southerner about his homeland; writings about South
Africa reflect similar feeling, the love of place. Perhaps—and one can
only ponder surface similarities—there is something in the air that
affects the politics in an Algeria, a South Africa, the American South.

influence of the physical world that is important to our purposes. We will not understand fully the South without according the outdoors its place of importance in the Southern scheme of things.

Some of the social consequences of the physical setting were conveyed in a distinctively Southern way by the late George L. Mitchell, former director of the Southern Regional Council. He explained the South of the 1940s and its problems in a "map talk," illustrating his remarks with flourishes of a wooden pointer all over a map of the Southeastern states. The following is taken from a transcript of the talk in the files of the Southern Regional Council:

. . . That gives you four different Souths: the mountains in the middle, the Piedmont next, the plantations next, and the piney woods at the outside. And each is different. Each has a different history, different set of people, different set of problems . . .

Start with the mountains . . . Draw yourself a winding mountain valley. Put a stream down the middle of it— old Hogback Mountain up this side, old Screamer Mountain on this . . . By 1890, other young fellows and other Jessie Bells have [because all available valley land was occupied] gone clean to the top of both mountains. Mind you, they skinned off all the trees. And the people in these bottom farms noticed that every time it rains, the waters seem to come scootin' down the creek bed faster than what it had before. Well, pretty soon there's floods and the floods ruin the crops . . .

Come down from the mountain and take the Piedmont piece. Except for our seaport cities, most of the thriving cities in the Southeastern states today are somewhere inside that Piedmont Country . . . The basic pattern of farming in all this Piedmont Country is the family-owned farm. And wonder of wonders, none of those medium-sized farms today is more than twelve or fifteen miles away from a factory. That's pretty good. That's a balance between industry and agriculture.

Further, the people in that area have two very nice things to have: a firm grasp of political democracy so strong that—in the last fifteen years—it has grown to include some Negro voters in all of those Piedmont cities, and, secondly, a beginning grasp of economic democracy through trade unions . . .

. . . Take the outside piece—the Piney Woods. Except for its rich port cities, except for an occasional patch of land in some speciality crop, in the whole of that outside piece of country there are only four things: sand, swamps, pine trees, and poor folks . . .

That shoots us up to the old plantation belt. That's always the hardest one to unravel . . . Behind each one of the big houses there is . . . either a double row of little black sharecrop shacks and the boss's big mule barn here and they worked the place together, else then a man has his land divided up into little twenty-five to thirty acre tenant farms—little old house and a piece of a barn on each one . . . People ought to be living in these big houses don't live there any more—living in town, belong to the civic club, sell automobiles. But they got some white fellow—probably the wife's brother—though he drinks a good deal—out there, taking charge of the place. People living in the big houses have got money or they can get it if they need it. People living in the little houses are usually poor. People in the big houses—all of them white. People in the little houses—most of them colored. People in the big houses get their sons and daughters to the state university. People in the little houses get their children to about the fourth grade; then they quit. People in the little houses depend upon the people in the big houses for some very important things: land, house, job, what to do, safety, good name, justice . . .

. . . States are important. Let's get in the state lines and see what they mean. Take South Carolina. The mountains just graze the backs of two counties. The Piedmont piece is narrow and short. The plantation piece is wide and long . . . Georgia's the same way. Little piece of mountains, little piece of Piedmont, big piece of Plantation. Nothing changes. . . .

The consequence . . . is that the states in the lower South are all held in every public—and in most private —acts to the attitudes and practices acceptable to that politically predominant part of the state least advanced

in democratic arrangements. For contrast, take North
Carolina: a big piece of mountains, the largest piece of
Piedmont, two shrinking nubbins of Plantation country.
A state that did lead us for sixty-five years. . . .

This 1940s geopolitical description remained in the late
1960s a framework for understanding the import of change
that occurred in the years after Dr. Mitchell used to give
his talk. Sometime between 1950 and 1960, the South
changed from the kind of place where most people lived
out in the country to one where most lived in some kind of
urban setting. (In 1950, 45 percent of the population was
urban; in 1960, 54 percent. The range in 1960 was from
37.7 percent urban in Mississippi to 75 percent urban in
Texas.) The presumption was that most of this urban
population continued to be in the Piedmont. Few new
towns were springing up in the other areas; the old towns
and cities of the Piedmont and coasts were growing.

Dr. Mitchell's flattering evaluation of the political
health of the Piedmont was largely accurate for its time.
The standard was the rest of America; the wretched contrast was the rest of the South. A large part of the political
domination of the Plantation Country that he bemoaned
was then a result of malapportionment and of disenfranchisement of Negroes—both more or less remedied since.

It is typical Southern irony that Negro Southerners were
not allowed—even for a while, for long enough perhaps to
redress the most glaring of their just grievances, to maintain the Plantation Country advantage in Southern politics. But what ensued was a swapping of the overt racism
and general rural reactionaryism of the Plantation Country whites for the hypocrisy, vulgarity, and anachronistic
Babbitry of the Piedmont—which in its essence was the
general tone and taste and moral standards of small-city
America. The Piedmont was, remember, Dr. Mitchell's
place of a Southern "firm grasp of political democracy so
strong that . . . it has grown to include *some* Negro voters
in all of those . . . cities."   .

II

If the South, more than most places, is influenced by its physical setting, it is a diverse physical setting, not a unity of mysterious and mystical forces. Dr. Mitchell's division of all the South into four parts is as handy a description of the diversity as any, and his point that each state incorporates a bit of each part is noteworthy. A drive down those old-fashioned highways in Georgia is illustrative.

One crosses from Tennessee or North Carolina through mountain country with high peaks and raw rocky cliffsides. The winter is fiercely cold here with early snows and ice storms. The towns are sparse and raw-looking; the farms run down the sides of the hills into rocky pastures, or stretch in green valleys under walls of blue-hazed mountains. There are national forests and some merely wild, untamed land whose beauty is comparable to that anywhere, and haunted ghost towns of played out goldmining and other enterprise, but, curiously, the tourist industry has staked no claims that amount to anything.

Farther north, in North Carolina and Tennessee, it has done so in some instances in the worst way. There are Hollywood-mentality pageants of one sort or another, whole towns given over to souvenir shops with "Indians" on display in full headdress and complete degradation or animals in similar plight, ski lodges with artificial snow on the slopes, and ponds where, without owning a license or even equipment, one may pay to pull domesticated mountain trout out of the water. Certainly, no tourism is preferable.

Yet north Georgia is part of Appalachia, nationally noted for its impecuniousness, and more of Appalachia is like north Georgia than the tourist-trap areas. Surely this land might, with the same dignity that rests heavily on the north Georgia town squares with their stone buildings and peculiar double-width streets, and the same sparse good taste and good sense that shows in handicrafts and hand-

hewn tools, share the man-shadowing majesty of its mountains and the flavor of its culture (the Elizabethan twang
and saltiness of speech is still prevalent) with the creatures
of city culture who flee in search of something more than
souvenir shop junk and fabricated quaintness.

Here in Georgia, as newly come across the South, there
are larges lakes (full of houseboats, speedboats, occasional canoes and rowboats, and invariably beer cans and
pollution) created by the federal government's various systems of dams, but only the local folk (and dwellers of the
nearby cities) avail themselves of them. Nothing is done to
develop out of such attractions a decent tourism. The
people would say they don't want it, thinking of the
tourist traps. They tend to be close-mouthed, these mountain people, and tremendously proud. They stubbornly
hold to such hopeless pursuits as moonshining and family
farming, and, far more than the flatland Southerners who
claim the distinction so boisterously in politics, deserve
to be called individualistic—not to mention provincial
and anarchistic. One senses in them the ability to resist
the cheapening and vulgarization of their home country,
if only they might find money for decent tourism, or
even just the concept. "See Rock City," say the signs on
barns and birdhouses all over the Southland, and that has
been about the most of it for the Southern mountains—
blatant exploitation of less than the best that is up there or
no tourism at all. Winding over the well-banked, if narrow
and not altogether well-maintained mountain roads of
north Georgia, one sees some mining, some manufacture
based on exploitation of minerals, and an occasional
quarry. The states to the north permit the crime and
scandal of strip mining and the equally ruthless using up
and throwing aside of the humans once needed to mine
coal underground. Some of the most pitiful poverty in the
South and the most pitiless evidence of the willingness to
dehumanize whites as thoroughly as Negroes, exist in the
ruined land and obsolete humanity of the mining country.

In the familiar pattern one begins to understand that ingrained conservatism of Southerners better, the fatalistic
feeling that it is best not to tinker with things, not to
innovate. As with tourism, north Georgia's failure to develop her mountain-area mineral resources seems preferable to the horror of exploitation that has occurred in the
mountains of Tennessee, Virginia, and Kentucky.

Appearing along the way in north Georgia is a more
familiar kind of exploitation, not confined to the hill
country—textile mills. The manufacture of chenille is
heavy in north Georgia, and numerous little roadside enterprises display tasteless (so grotesque some of them as to
inspire awe) spreads and robes and what-have-you flapping
on lines for the tourist trade. The cotton mill story is, of
course, among the older Southern tragicomedies; Cash
may have overemphasized it with his full, familial knowledge of its intricacies, but it is a wondrous story of romanticized seeking after an industrial cure-all in fine pa-
trician paternalism, with mean-spirited scheming to give
the poor whites something that would prevent their align-
ing themselves with the even poorer Negroes, in merciless
anti-unionism. How has the saga further unraveled?

By the 1960s cotton was no longer king in Southern
agriculture or manufacture, but it kept its hold in manufacture more than in agriculture. United States Department of Commerce figures on sources of personal income
in 1964 give the general picture. In all eleven of the states,
manufacturing had surpassed farming as the major source
of income; in most states manufacturing earnings were
three times greater than those from agriculture. In all
states except North Carolina and South Carolina, contract-
ing and construction also exceeded farming. So did wholesale and retail trade in all but Arkansas; so did services in
all but Mississippi and Arkansas, and so did government
employment (local and state larger than federal) in all
but Mississippi and Arkansas. Even "finance, insurance,
and real estate" exceeded farming as a source of income in

Virginia, Georgia, Florida, and Louisiana. In all but
of the states (Florida, with its tourism dependence
wholesale and retail trade), manufacturing was the larg
source of income. And, sadly, the largest single indu
remained textiles. But it was no longer the only o
Total textile employment in the United States in 1967
924,000. Most of it was the South. But the number
employees in manufacturing in the South that same y
was considerably more—3,942,000. In the four South
states where textiles were heaviest—Georgia, Alaba
South Carolina, and North Carolina—the number of wo
ers in manufacturing was 1,711,000, still higher than
total number in the cotton mills.

As for the cotton mills, *The New York Times*
ported on August 19, 1967, one example of labor re
tions that would seem to sum up the situation since Ca
wrote so dourly about it. In a ruling on anti-union charg
against J. P. Stevens and Company, a combine of most
Southern mills and the world's second largest produc
of textiles, a federal examiner "with a reputation for co
servatism in labor matters" had this to say: "If an e
ployer will offend to the extent of unlawfully d
charging an employee, thereby depriving him of t
means of livelihood—then such an employer would hard
hestitate to commit the other wrongs of denying dece
pay, suitable working conditions, and adequate frin
benefits." The United States Court of Appeals for the Se
ond Circuit found that Stevens had engaged in "a majo
campaign of illegal anti-union activity, spearheaded b
retaliatory discharges." The Textile Workers of Americ
and AFL-CIO considered Stevens a symbol of the still-su
cessful Southern cotton mill resistance to unionism; if i
30,000 workers in fifty-one plants in North and Sout
Carolina could be organized, the rest of the region's mill
would topple like dominoes. But the unions—mountin
impressive campaigns, including the famed "Operatio

Dixie" of the 1940s—had been seeking such footholds for
more than thirty years and had been through the mechanisms and mentalities so well described by Cash, getting
thoroughly beaten every time.

Anti-unionism in other industries continued to separate
the poorest of both races from their natural interests. In
1962, only 1,577,000 of 12,200,000 non-agricultural workers in the eleven states belonged to the AFL-CIO. In 1966,
the figure was 1,923,000. In no state was union membership even 20 percent of the non-agricultural employment;
nationally it was 28.8 percent. Where there were unions,
most notably in the larger manufacturing plants and government-contract installations, one of those trick-mirror
image views of all America through excesses in the South
had been evident since the 1930s. It could be summed up,
in the gleeful statement of a Birmingham segregationist,
"Why, hell, the membership of the union locals and the
local Klan is the same." Only later was the prevalence of
racism and conservatism in the national rank and file of
labor so evident. In the South the erstwhile coalition of
civil rights and labor forces of the early 1960s was never
very important politically before it collapsed in 1965
(partly as a result of this union conservatism and racism
nationally) simply because the unions could not deliver a
vote that approached liberalism on race. Some insight into
the Southern political spectrum may be gained from understanding that the essential conservatism of American
labor in the 1960s was regarded to the detriment of their
own self-interest by most Southern business and political
leaders as ultra-liberal, and was thereby discredited with
the vast majority of white Southern workers despite the
dictums of their self-interest.

In the meantime, liberal forces in the South and the
nation were willing to throw major support to efforts to
desegregate the cotton mills in their non-union state, pushing for the right of the Negro to work at wage rates averag-

ing in 1967 two dollars an hour and to endure such old
cruelties as the stretch-out, piling of more and more work
on fewer and fewer employees.

Of course, in 1967 most Negro workers would have been
better off in the intolerable cotton mills than with the
degrading "domestic" work they were doing: their chief
occupations were still nursemaid, cook, yardman, and
chauffeur. Common labor in construction and on farms
was still important. Indeed, even such jobs were at a pre-
mium; increasingly, men and women, too, had nothing or
not enough to do. For them, the effort to get into the mills
made sense, and there was hope of a better job from there;
other industries recruited from the cotton mills. But in
seeing this as an important project, reformers were either
blind to the real needs of Negroes and the South (and one
suspects there was much such blindness, pragmatism gone
all impractical) or were, more ominously, revealing American liberalism's predicament of the late 1960s. This was in
simple terms that affliction of the spirit which visits political movements of all stripes, an unwillingness to face new
realities, a reflex to rely on old solutions no longer relevant.
It seemed obvious to the most untrained observer that the
international economics of textile manufacturing now
made textiles unfeasible for the American South unless it
increasingly exploited its workers (already and through
history among the most exploited in the land). Real reform would accept this and move on to programs that
would develop more feasible work, or—more to the point
of economic reality—programs like the guaranteed annual
income schemes which sought surrogates for work as the
base of comfortable existence. Possibly even more than the
Northern cities, the South offered evidence that this was
the direction things needed to go.

It is all right for unsophisticated, visionless, homebody
reformers to push for desegregation of the local cotton mill
or its unionization, for that matter, when there is no other
industry around or in sight; it is understandable and

maybe, even with its sick heritage, kind of glorious that the textile industry in the South keeps trying to exist. (Such an assertion reflects the way that the mills are in the blood of the South. "And yet, and yet . . . ," Cash kept seeming to say, as he tried again and again to show that it isn't simple, the subtle, familiar phenomena of the South, isn't reducible to formulae that fit the rest of the country, maybe even the rest of the world. It isn't this, Faulkner kept saying, and not quite that but more nearly this. . . .)

It is necessary to assert an "and yet" about the mills. Are industries and their machines and their managers anywhere else regarded so personally, so proprietorially by their workers and townspeople?

Once I traveled from mill town to mill town, doing a series of newspaper stories on one of the cyclical slumps that afflict the industry, and found that, no matter how bitter the workers were with the general conditions or how desperate from cutbacks in working hours, they invariably possessed a feeling for the work, a love of it; through generations families wove a tradition of it, regarding the mill as some particularly fickle, whimsical, giddy god, about whom they grumbled but seldom withdrew loyalty. Surely the good union organizers know this and have ways to combat it. "How're things running at the mill?" you have only to ask, and it is obvious in their voices that they have great feeling for the damned thing.

At the first mill I stopped in on that same trip, the thin, dour bookkeeper who was designated to show me about the old place soon realized that I was ignorant of the whole threadmaking process. He handed me a poem by some eighteenth-century Englishman that described the process, from machine to machine, all in fine rhyme and old-fashioned language. It hasn't changed a bit, my friend assured me, beaming about the poem, the process, and this particular run-down old mill, ushering me from machine to machine, reading what the poem said about each.

The managers of the mills, probably comprising the core of ultra-conservative influence on the South through the 1960s, were a bad lot. And yet—on my journey among them, they were uniformly courteous (even those too leery of such democratic notions as the newspapers to talk with me). It was not the normal, self-interested and wary kid-glove handling that most businessmen accord reporters; it was courtliness, natural to them. Several had me to their big houses for dinner. I would go into the office—they were uniformly accessible with no advance warning. I would tell them my assignment, mentioning the man in the business who had given me their names as leaders in the industry, and ask if they would give me an interview. Through the recital, to a man, they would stare at my face and, if I looked, hard in my eyes. At the end, to a man, there would be a long moment more of staring, and then an answer, yes or no. They size you up.

Such mill managers—some of the same men I met, surely, and their fathers, for it is a hereditary position often, reaching to the top political power in most of the Southern states—engaged themselves in one of America's most wide-spread and ruthless campaigns to crush an incipient labor movement. This has been largely an untold story of shame,[2] and systematic violence, including killing, and a concentration camp in Georgia and a protracted period of near guerrilla warfare. Never again, down to the late 1960s, was labor to be a mass movement in the textile industry or any other in the South.

Thus, all labor's great gains in the rest of the nation (and the sad degeneration of the union spirit into a smug selfishness) during the 1930s and 1940s were missed in the South. And as long as labor remained supine, liberal re-form efforts like the integration of cotton mills had to be viewed with jaundice, if not alarm.

---

[2] I am indebted to Vera Rony for insights into the untold story from her book in progress which will attempt to tell the story.

What other kinds of industry were there? The answer is not comforting. More money was invested in chemicals than in textiles, but, alas, these were like the petrochemical plants in Texas, Louisiana, and Mississippi, highly automated, not requiring people. Then there were the paper mills, semi-automated, exploiting the land, putting higher priorities on pine trees than on people in many counties, and polluting the air and water. Other manufacture included automobiles and airplanes, machinery and fabricated metals. Much of the smaller industry was of the fly-by-night variety, little garment manufacturing plants and the like. Virtually none of it was of the kind that economists would like to see—industry (such as electronics) which requires relatively inexpensive raw materials and which, by means of very sophisticated manufacturing processes calling for highly trained workers, makes intricate and expensive goods.

Hourly wage rates in 1963 tell the story: in none of the eleven Southern states was there an average as high as the national average; they ranged from $1.68 in textile-dominated North Carolina to $2.39 in chemistry-rich Louisiana, compared with the national average of $2.46.

III

Historically the South lagged behind the rest of the nation in the evolution from agriculture to industrialization and from the economy of scarcity to abundance. Conversely, the rest of the nation was rapidly catching up with the South in the peculiar and frightening fact of excess labor supply: the South's was a legacy of slavery and the collapse of the plantation system; the North's resulted from automation and the rearrangement, if not collapse, of an economic system. In these lags, there was new Southern irony, tragedy.

One of the most astute efforts ever to analyze the economics of the South was the 1967 work, *The Advancing South*. Here is how it described the situation at the time of its publication:

> They [recent economic, social, and political changes] strongly suggest that the South is breaking the bonds of agrarian traditionalism; that it is moving into an era in which science, technology, and urban ways of living play an increasingly important role; that new sets of social values and beliefs are replacing many of those of the past.[3]

and:

> There is a growing emphasis on education. Most southern states are enlarging educational and training facilities and reorientating educational activities to reach more of the population and to meet more adequately the occupational demands of industry.[4]

and:

> By 1960, the proportion of Southern employment in the goods-producing industries had declined to 42 per cent [from about 50 per cent in 1950] and is projected to decline to 38.2 per cent by 1975.
> The very large decline in agricultural employment in the South between 1950 and 1960 was the major factor accounting for the decrease in employment in the goods-producing industries, but there were also modest declines in employment in textiles, mining, sawmills, and planing mills. Further declines in these industries and in tobacco products are expected by 1975.
> In contrast, employment in all other industries in the South is expected to increase—quite significantly in the professional services; wholesale and retail trade; finance, insurance, and real estate; and most manufacturing industries.[5]

and finally:

[3] James G. Maddox *et al., The Advancing South* (New York, The Twentieth Century Fund, 1967), p. 19.
[4] Maddox *et al.,* p. 18.
[5] Maddox *et al.,* pp. 184–185.

If the South fails to take advantage of the opportunity to break the cycle of poverty, while the region is in a period of social and economic transition, it will be following the worst possible course of action. In other words, if the manufacturing and service-producing industries now rising so rapidly in the South are to be based on inefficient, low-wage labor, nothing more than the landscape of the region will be changed. The major development problem will shift from a rural to an urban setting, but southern people and southern institutions will continue to be the poorest of the nation, and the southern intellectual and cultural environment the most backward.[6]

These quotations sum up the thrust of most enlightened analysis of the South's economic plight and possibilities. They have meaning to the extent that one is willing to share assumptions like that in the Maddox book, in its employment projections, that national unemployment will hold at 4 percent of the labor force in 1975. This is to say that one must share the major premise that the national economy has provided enough jobs and will continue to do so, and such minor ones as the assumption that the business ethic will continue as the main guide of national life. But one may doubt the major premise on the basis of unemployment statistics and by understanding the constricting definitions of labor force; and one may look askance at the minor premise on the basis of everything from what seemed an irresistible impulse toward the guaranteed annual income (whose psychological shock waves would shake every element of society) to the refusal of the brightest youngsters to consider business as a career. (So, too, would our traveling through the South at least suggest that there are phenomena there that do not accommodate themselves to conventional economic analysis).

Conventional analyses postulate at least these positive factors at work in the South: expansion of services and finance as well as of manufacture, reflecting a more real-

6 Maddox *et al.*, pp. 205–206.

istic grasp of economics than the old irrational lust for manufacture alone, at any cost; greater federal involvement in the regional economy with liberalizing social influences (upon race relations, among other things) as well as financial benefit; the end of various real and fancied external conditions inhibiting Southern economic development.

Among the fancied (but no less influential) conditions was that set of persecution beliefs that conceived of the South as a colony of the North forced to provide raw materials and kept dependent for manufactures. The real problem was an inability of Southerners to analyze the region's position relative to the national economy. When differential freight rates were finally attacked successfully through the courts in the 1940s, the victory was hailed as the overthrow of the yoke of colonialism. Economists agreed later that the freight rates had negligible effect, really. But insofar as the court victory made thinking in the region a little more realistic, it probably was significant.

Clarence H. Danhof says in *Essays in Southern Economic Development*[7] that analysis became realistic with the realization that the South's main problems were a low per capita ratio of natural and capital resources and a low level of education and training among the people. National, not Southern, developments were responsible for the economic growth in the region after World War II, and even then, a broad base for accelerated growth was not established. He likened the South to the underdeveloped nations and pointed out that problems of such areas are not economic but social and political. "Throughout it has remained true that the economy of the South has evolved as the capabilities of its citizens to respond to their en-

[7] Clarence H. Danhof, "Four Decades of Thought on the South's Economic Problems," in *Essays in Southern Economic Development*, edited by Melvin L. Greenhut and W. Tate Whitman (Chapel Hill, University of North Carolina Press, 1964).

vironment has been enhanced. That experience suggests that persistent adherence to the fundamental task of upgrading human capabilities is the region's best guarantee of continued growth."[8]

This is another way, of course, of saying what the Maddox book said. And the question all of this raises is whether or not it is any longer realistic, in assessing the position of the South relative to that of the nation, to talk and plan educational and cultural enhancement in terms of preparing the people for continued industrial expansion.

It begins to sound like the same old story—the romantic quest for the cotton mills that compelled Cash's sympathetic derision. At the moment the rest of the nation was beginning to shake off or at least resent and resist such integral factors of the going system as the Cold War and the military-industrial complex, the harnessing of education to corporate and governmental needs, and the implications of an economy of abundance were beginning fully to be realized and acted upon in the rest of the nation, here came the South poking along, still psychologically conditioned by its long and intimate experience of an economy of scarcity, pinning its hopes on getting into the goodies of the military-industrial complex, stretching its vision and resources in the effort to educate its sons to take their places, unquestioning, in the best corporation jobs to be found.

Was the South once more too late? Would it be like that sad chapter of history in 1877 when the South had perhaps its greatest political leverage ever in the disputed Hayes-Tilden election? Northern Democrats told its bargainers, anent grand dreams of federal subsidy, that the Great Barbecue was over and retrenchment and reform were the order of the day, and the South found, within a year after having delivered everything to the conservative Republi-

8 Greenhut and Whitman, p. 68.

cans, that the promised railroad and harbor-dredging and other federal help were just not going to materialize because events had moved beyond their needs.

Here, in the late 1960s, the South was once more poised to begin what the rest of the nation seemed ready to end or, at least, to change drastically. Might it not for once avoid the stage from which the rest of the nation was emerging, skip a step, or even—capitalizing on the experience and mistakes of others—plunge ahead innovatively?

The anti-poverty efforts of the Johnson Administration might have been a platform for such innovative thinking, instruction perhaps, if not action. The war on poverty was founded in the notion that poverty could be ended by equipping all the poor people to take advantage of an affluent, industrialized, highly technical economy. That this was impossible for many individuals seemed not to be considered and that it might even be undesirable was not even discussed. And where were the jobs? In the South the fallacy was patently apparent because the problem here was far less the qualification of people than it was the absence of opportunity. (One suspects that in the rest of the nation, should all those poor people suddenly become qualified, the same absence of opportunity would be evident.) Was there any effort from the South, from bureaucrats, recipients or thinkers, to suggest this point? Very little. As Negro college graduates lined up at the community centers for employment assistance, the aim of producing qualified labor was forgotten in the interest of badly needed money pouring immediately into the economy. It might just as well have been pouring in to reorganize billy goat husbandry or build pyramids.

Meanwhile, in every aspect of its culture—in education, employment, job performance, industry, housing patterns, recreation, clothing fashions, religion, construction of roads and public buildings, everything, even, saddest of all, race relations—the dominant white South was striving mightily to attain standards which the rest of the country had already possessed and found wanting—to the extent that revolutionary forces were moving against them, in the colleges and the streets of the ghettos. The black South, the emerging middle class of Negroes especially, were in many ways a generation behind their white counterparts in matters of standards and aspirations. Yet in some important matters, the poorest black people of the South were attempting, desperately, to articulate values far ahead of the whole of American society.

What there was of innovative thinking in the community action centers or voter registration offices or student action committee meetings or black power conclaves or co-op headquarters was not heard much beyond these immediate vicinities. It was inarticulate and ungrammatical thinking, and it had to cope with a reality of national fallacy and Southern haplessness. But it was thinking that became idiomatic across a section of the Southern population, mostly black and almost always poor, and eventually it might be fully heard. It had its formation in the old days of NAACP struggling, burst forth in the direct-action days of the civil rights movement (mainly out of SNCC) with worldwide impact, and gradually spread to masses of people, becoming part of white as well as black folklore.

White farmers in south Georgia might well have wanted to do something about pork prices in the 1930s or 1940s. They might well have used some convention of protest familiar to them from the labor movement, picketing the meat plant, perhaps. But in the 1960s, probably without much thought, certainly without any acknowledgement of where the idea came from, they adopted direct action: a grotesque and characteristically impolitic demonstration, to be sure, killing the hogs rather than selling them cheap, but certainly in the tradition of the sit-ins, the boycotts, the jail-ins. This is the development that we must know in order to understand the contemporary South. The most important point was the emphasis on individual needs and values—the right to stay on the land regardless of its economic worth, the right to economic support regardless of poverty program strategies and mistaken assumptions, even the right to full personality development regardless of role and role expectations. . . .

But all of this happened in the underground, among the underprivileged, the unheard-from. Those who did speak for the South hailed heedlessly the advent of the super-technological revolution without ever bothering to do what this exercise in obsolescence demanded: Prepare the people for it.

What can be said, then, for traditional white Southern business and political leadership? Southern economic history, in one way of reading it, is one long, delightful exposition of the flaws of the American economic system, highlighted by the surface inanities (the usual lack of planning where planning was critically needed) and irrelevant motives (that strange, strong tendency to inject romanticism into the cold and essentially mechanistic processes of the market and production). While the major ineptitudes have continued, the caricature has become less grotesque and the situations more subtle.

For example, industry, no matter how exploitative, remained the golden grail that the states and the cities and the towns sought with uncritical abandon, shamelessly. "Luring" was the straightforward word they used to describe their continued willingness to offer tax favoritism, risk-free land and buildings, government services, and, worst of all, cheap labor to anybody, including fly-by-nighters, with enough capital to take advantage of such favorable circumstances.

Something of a classic example was the announcement in 1967 by Firestone Tire and Rubber Company that it had chosen from among many sites the town of Albany, Georgia, for construction of a $53 million plant for production of car and truck tires, with planned employment of 1,500 persons.[9] Raymond C. Firestone, chairman of the company's board, was quoted by the Associated Press in the Atlanta *Journal-Constitution* of August 27, 1967: "We were also impressed with the attitude of the people in the Albany area. They made us feel as if we're wanted."

That they did. The entire cost of the $53 million plant would be borne by the Dougherty County Payroll Development Authority through an industrial revenue bond issue. The authority would lease the plant to the company; details of land acquisition (343 acres) and tax arrangements were not given, but one may assume they were equally favorable to the company.

Predictably, Albany was congratulated and envied by the rest of the South for its success in luring Firestone; no criticism or questioning was heard, certainly not from the regional press and not, sadly, from any political source nor even the universities.

Not a municipality but the sovereign state of Mississippi passed four new laws in 1967 to issue $130 million worth of state industrial bonds for "the shipyard of the future," to be built in Pascagoula and leased to Ingalls Shipbuilding Corporation of Litton Industries, Inc. Litton was supposed to be guaranteeing retirement of the bonds.

In the late 1960s all of the eleven states had laws allowing tax favoritism for new industries and municipal bonding to provide sites and plants (such bonds, in the final analysis, are the responsibility of taxpayers). Those states whose repression of Negroes had been most notorious were seemingly the most excessive in their "lures" to industry, perhaps in part to put down the impression that racism is

---

[9] In the late 1960s Albany remained the mean-spirited little city which in 1961 and 1962 gave Dr. Martin Luther King, Jr., one of his few Southern defeats by using the same kind of repressive police force against nonviolent demonstrations (and the constitutional rights of those participating in them) that Northern cities later were to use against riots, in the process hanging onto a U.S. Air Force installation and Marine base whose removal from the area was urged by Dr. King and in the end winning the congratulations of the Attorney General for avoiding violence.

bad for business. Not loath to lend themselves to such a purpose, America's big businesses were as oblivious in these instances to moral implications and criticism as they were to those of their involvement in South Africa. Hammermill Paper Company ill-timed its announcement of the selection of Selma, Alabama, as the site for a new plant in 1965 just as that already notorious little center of Alabama racism was erupting into one of the era's worst spectacles of police violence to nonviolent demonstrators (beating marchers protesting disfranchisement and trampling them with horses). The *Wall Street Journal* of April 9, 1965, described the profit motivation dispassionately:

> Hammermill, state, and Selma officials then worked together on plans for the new plant. The state Water Control Board examined and approved Hammermill's plans for waste disposal. Tax benefits, amounting to a 50% deduction in property taxes, were offered and accepted. Financing was arranged through a revenue bond issue by the Industrial Development Board of Selma, an arrangement under which Selma will build the plant and lease it to Hammermill. The state agreed to build Selma a new bridge to accommodate expected increased traffic.

Two years later, the pall and stench of the mill were so heavy that one had to drive ten or twenty miles out of town to escape the low clouds of it, befouling the beauty of early summer morning in the woods and fields. This is not an uncommon experience in the South.

Again, the industry-luring efforts had to be seen in the context that a pittance was better than nothing. Indeed, in one of those rare instances in which modern research techniques were applied to a problem with real meaning in the South, James R. Rinehart, an economist, studied the effect of subsidization of twenty-two industries in ten Southern towns and concluded that in every case the towns received considerably more in overall economic benefits than the six percent return they might expect from conventional uses of their money.[10]

Rinehart made it clear that he was talking about a situation where desperate measures are necessary. What he did not discuss was the helplessness of workers under such circumstances, their and the town's dependence on the "lured" entrepreneur, perpetuating paternalism, making any notion of the dignity or bargaining power of labor laughable. Southerners have fought such aspects of the system for years.

One angry old Southern labor leader told me about a little town where a fiercely anti-union man came in without even a suitcase. He was glib and knowledgeable in the ways of the sweatshop, and, with donated land, plant, and machinery and with willing workers happy to get abysmally low pay, he soon had himself a big house and big name. One year he was faced with the calamity of a threatened increase in his firm's insurance rate because, it turned out, the little town which had given him so much hadn't even a fire department to its name. So with a flourish and considerable savings, he went out and bought the town a fire engine, and they dedicated the fire station to him and built a statue in his honor, falling over themselves in gratitude.

Energy and resources were directed toward living with rather than ending such situations as the prevalent joblessness (and hunger) in much of the South through the enlightened 1960s, and it was intolerable; a moral judgment had to be made of those who knew better and yet engaged in such farces as luring industry (the takers as well as the overgenerous givers).

Moreover, as the stakes grew bigger and the plants more sophisticated (on the comparison level, that is, of a paper

[10] James R. Rinehart, "Rates of Return on Municipal Subsidies to Industry," in *Essays in Southern Economic Development*, edited by Melvin L. Greenhut and W. Tate Whitman (Chapel Hill, The University of North Carolina Press, 1964), pp. 473 ff.

mill with a garment factory), the subsidized industries came to need skilled and semi-skilled labor. In north Georgia during the labor shortage just after World War II, Lockheed Aircraft had to train local people, and bragged about it condescendingly. But most industries imported such workers instead. Previous studies had sometimes shown that a new industry in a town benefited Negroes only in a trickle-down way, providing them such jobs as tending filling stations (after whites had deserted the posts) and providing more money for whites to spend at the filling stations. More recent studies showed that such benefits as there were for local people of either race were of this kind. And an increase in the cost of living resulting from affluence of the imported, skilled workers probably offset the trickle-down gains.

As manufacturing began to prove inadequate as a base for maintaining American living and spending standards in other parts of the country in the late 1960s and as automation made itself felt in Northern joblessness, other parts of the country began luring industry by subsidy, ending the South's monopoly in such endeavor and making it more difficult. Meanwhile, civil rights workers in the South were, with jaundiced but half-hopeful eyes, watching a version of it being tried in a Chicago slum where an industrial park was built on funds collected from, or borrowed in the name of, local slum people. Industries had to agree to hire and train more than 50 percent local people in order to benefit from the subsidized offer. This would seem to be the very least that Southern governments might do, and should civil rights forces decide to enter the field, one of the greatest accomplishments might be to force governments to accept this plan. In Memphis, Negro leaders sought federal funds in 1969 for a black-owned industrial park.

To continue the list of ineptitudes of economic leadership: there was little real planning, even on the state level, even on the level of the little regional planning boards that sprang up after World War II, comprised of a group of counties with more or less common interests in a given state. A talk with a young professional in the office of one of these planning boards in Georgia was revealing.

The organization was financed by county governments and run by a board consisting of two businessmen or business-oriented politicians from each of the participating counties. They saw the planning agency essentially as an industry-luring vehicle; its task was merely to compile data, of interest to persons who might locate an industry in the area, on sewers, water, land, taxes, labor and the like, and to help new prospects decide on a site. The board members, he said a little sadly, just weren't interested in long-range research and planning; they were interested merely in what they could see. During the seven years of its existence it had facilitated the building of industrial parks in various of the counties and attracted tufted-textile plants, the chenille industry. This particular organization did not encourage bond issues for subsidies, but had not been able to prevail against tax favoritism. Its most hopeful gain had been in attracting a chemical plant to service the carpet plants in the area, a satellite industry of some sophistication.

On the regional basis, the need for planning and the failure to achieve it was a familiar tragedy. The University of North Carolina group known as the Regionalists, including Howard Odum and Guy Johnson, had as its central theme this goal of planning. If nothing else, it succeeded in embedding the concept in the consciousness and argumentation of the region; eventually the notion might be acted on. The Regionalists' basic precepts and research remain as valuable tools for the work, should it ever begin.

A little-known recapitulation of the tragedy of failure to plan was enacted during the decade after World War II. An interracial Committee of the South, led by educators, heavy with businessmen, was formed under auspices of the

National Planning Association to try to prevent the South from forsaking its wartime industrial build-up for its old agrarian ways. It soon became evident that no such return was possible, and the committee acted mainly as a record keeper and cheering section for continued postwar industrial expansion. Its foundation support ran out, and it seemed about to die out, but then, through the enthusiasm of one or two leaders, it was revived with a new name, the Committee for Southern Development. Some of the best minds in the South were interested in it, and a brilliant planner, Phillip Hammer, was retained as staff director.

The first meeting of the rejuvenated body was shortly after the 1954 Supreme Court school decision. Members, including businessmen, talked enthusiastically of rallying the South to accept its decree. Considering the power of business, such a campaign might have changed history, but by the next meeting, pressures had been applied to the business members. They walked out on the issue of integration, and the Committee for Southern Development, along with any hope of mitigating massive resistance or of making rational economic and social plans, thereupon died.

IV

We move on down the road in Georgia, out of the mountains, a stream of clear water running along beside us, its lack of pollution reflecting the lack of "progress" in industrial development here. After curving through the roads in the foothills, we enter a tamer landscape of pine hills and flat, green fields.

Dr. Mitchell called the Piedmont a place of urbanization, and industrialization, but it no longer monopolizes the latter. The dubious blessing of the cotton mill, as we have seen, has been bestowed upon the mountains, and similar boons of the advanced industrial age have spread across the flatlands of the coast and even into the old Black

Belt plantation country. In the Piedmont of north Georgia, we pass one big holding of hill land bought up by Lockheed Aircraft Corporation. At that heady time the firm thought that a big nuclear energy contract was coming its way, and it now holds the land in readiness for such a grand eventuality in the military-industrial future. Indeed, the military aspect of the complex predominates in the South, in part reflecting the power of the old Southern Democrats in Congress, still holding on to seniority garnered in one-party days, to gain air fields and army camps for their constituencies.

We pass an Air Force Reserve installation, large enough for jets, and the big Lockheed aircraft plant, which during World War II was the Bell Bomber Plant ("He's got himself a job in the bummer plant," the hill folk would say). In the postwar and Korean War and Vietnam War days, Lockheed waxed fruitful on government contracts. During those same war-shadowed years, nuclear installations have developed in Tennessee (the granddaddy, Oak Ridge), Mississippi, and South Carolina. A famed $2 million "Space Crescent" of installations was also developed from Cape Kennedy (formerly Canaveral, a new-culture outpost set down in the old resort and fishing culture of Florida, pine-floor saloons with rocket ship names) through Huntsville, Alabama (perhaps the South's foremost outpost of Northern-type liberalism on race), through Hancock County, Mississippi, and New Orleans to Houston.

Seeming innocent and even anachronistic alongside such extravagant federal might, the Tennessee Valley Authority is a different kind of venture, life-oriented. Serving primarily Tennessee and Alabama, it has remained a model of rational regional development (foreign visitors on State Department tours include it with race relations as the main things they want to see in the South). TVA provides power, flood and malaria control, and cheap transportation, and some claim that its influence has gone beyond economics, that in improving the economy of the valley, it has enhanced social conditions. TVA country, even in Alabama, is notably superior to most of the South in race relations and social and political attitudes generally. Equal employment policies were firmly established from the beginning with little resistance.

But one has to be wary about ascribing too much to TVA—the Tennessee River runs through country which never had a large Negro population; the axiom applies that race relations are generally good where Negro population is small (and vice versa). The effect of a TVA in the Black Belt might not be so salubrious. (But of course there is no way of telling without trying. People who study the area invariably recommend a vast economic and agricultural reclamation project in the Black Belt, with land reform and public works rebuilding of habitations.) The story of the origins of TVA, however, does not encourage hope for more of even its limited kind of benefit. It is an incredible record of the almost superhuman effort that was required to battle the reflex and special-interest conservatism of America, strong enough even in the experimental atmosphere of the New Deal to compromise the original achievement and over the years continuing to contain and erode it further.[11] Like all else, the good old TVA began to show a sinister side in the late 1960s: the need for coal in its generating plants had made it a customer of the

[11] See Frank Smith's *The Politics of Conservation* (New York, Pantheon Books, 1966) for a comprehensive and acute, though sometimes overly patient, history of American public development of natural resources, including TVA. Here is one of his summations of the TVA struggle: "TVA had to fight hard for its very existence, both during the initial crisis of the board of directors' controversy, and the attempts at a takeover by Harold Ickes. For five years, its whole effort had to be submerged as a vital part of the war effort. The fight for survival had to be resumed in the Eisenhower years. Even today, its future is by no means politically invulnerable, as the views of Senator Barry Goldwater demonstrated during the 1964 election. In view of the scars and bruises of such struggles, it is not surprising that the authority has failed to live up to some of the high hopes of its founders and supporters. Even with these limitations, however, it is still the greatest success story of the New Deal." (p. 237).

stripminers in their continued rape of the Appalachian mountains.[12]

In like manner, the series of river dams developed by the U.S. Army Corps of Engineers concealed an ugly side with a benign provision of flood control, recreational lakes, and improved inland waterways. Such dams have transformed the Chattachoochee, which we cross coming down from the mountains in Georgia, from a sluggish, muddy little river (given in the past to almost annual floods) to a regulated stream as clear as the mountain creek in north Georgia where it originates. Among other things, the new lakes have encouraged the Southern propensity for fishing (working at it with pure joylessness in cold dawns, using it like narcotics, just closing down the business and going off to it for days at a time) and have brought the motorboat culture to full flourish across the Southland.

But the Corps of Engineers has also flooded a lot of productive farmland with little prior consultation with owners (including the vanishing small farmers), contributed to, rather than eased, the stream pollution problem, sacrificed wilderness areas and beautiful streams to interests that in some instances seem no more than big-lake recreation. Many of the projects have been necessary and beneficial; others, like the Cross-Florida Barge Canal, with a projected cost of $145 million, have been of dubious worth except to special interests and land speculators; this one would destroy the scenic Oklawaha River Valley.[13]

V

We pass Atlanta and small satellite cities of the Piedmont. In between them, we drive through decaying county seat towns, with Gothic courthouses and Confederate memori-

[12] See "TVA—The Halo Slips," by John Edgerton, in *The Nation*, Vol. 205, July 3, 1967, pp. 11–15.
[13] See "Corps of Engineers—the Pork-Barrel Soldiers," by Robert Sherrill in *The Nation*, Vol. 202, February 14, 1966, pp. 180–83.

als, and a quietness, stillness, appropriate to death. An old Negro woman in a straw hat moves on some determined journey through hot sun. A farm wagon may be seen, weathered, Negro and mule creaking into oblivion. And between the burgeoning small cities and dying small towns are the wastes of woodland and the ghosts of small farms, houses and outbuildings falling in on themselves, blackened chimneys rising out of weeds. In the Piedmont of Georgia and on down into the softer, semi-tropical coastal plain and Black Belt Alabama, Louisiana, Tennessee, and Texas, the Delta of Mississippi and Arkansas, these evidences of the end of the small farm prevail. And rising like archeological or geological layers of time and history was the new agriculture of huge holdings, mechanization, crop diversification—humpbacked machinery resembling the praying mantis, herds of cattle, in sleek, obscene contrast to the old swaybacked horse and cow of the small, poor farms. These new herds often graze under big plantings of fruit or nut trees, indicating notions of efficiency, full utilization of land that had for so long been abused and wasted.

The lamentations over Southern agriculture—before it began to change in the 1940s and at accelerated pace in the 1950s and 1960s—had centered on the evils of the one-crop system, of the waste of land and animals and human labor, of the sharecrop system with its tradition of cheating those already cheated—the man and his family who did all the work got the lesser share, and the owner did the weighing and figuring so that the lesser share was what he wanted or needed it to be. (A whole tradition of wry, angry, but resigned humor surrounds the sharecropper's plight, dealing with the ways of the man with "the book and the pencil," and with such tenant stratagems as holding back a bale until the man has said that the crop exactly balances what the tenant owes him, and so on.)

The changes that have come to Southern agriculture have, of course, remedied these very problems. That is the

sum of statistics for two and one-half decades. (Increases
above 80 percent in cotton acreage in California, New
Mexico, Arizona, and West Texas since 1938; decreases up
to 40 percent in the old South . . . Increases in the South in
production of corn, peanuts, soybeans, sugar cane, toma-
toes, grapefruit, and rice . . . By the mid–1950s the South
supplied 39 percent of the nation's lumber and 56 percent
of its pulpwood, exceeding all Canadian production of the
latter . . . A decrease of 59 percent between 1940 and 1960
in the number of persons employed in Southern agriculture, from 4.2 million to 1.7 million . . . A decrease in crop
acreage from 111 million in 1940 to 81 million in 1960 . . .
A doubling of the average size of farms . . . A decrease in
the national total of tenant farms [nearly all in the South
and a majority of tenants Negro] from 2,364,923, in 1940
to 537,899 in 1964.)[14]

These were the statistics behind the exodus of black
farmers from the South, reflecting not cupidity and cruelty
and stupidity on the part of white planters, but cold, inex-
orable economic forces—at work on planter and tenant and
field hand alike.

This elimination of the three ancient agrarian curses
upon the South, far from a cause for celebration, had left
an even greater burden of suffering and grief. For as bad as
it had been, the old agrarian system of small farm holdings,
sharecropping, and day labor had been a way of life, a
tradition of generations, and nothing better—indeed,
something worse—was to take its place. Again the statistics
suggest the dimensions, if not the depth, of the tragedy.
First, it should be noted that, as might be expected, those
who suffered most were Negroes, the poorest and most

[14] Primary sources for these figures and those following are the U.S.
Census and U.S. Department of Agriculture publications. Secondary
sources used here include James G. Maddox *et al.*, *The Advancing South:
Manpower Prospects and Problems*; Thomas D. Clark, *The Emerging
South* (New York, Oxford University Press, 1961); Paul Good "Poverty in
the Rural South," *New South*, Vol. 23, No. 1, Winter, 1968, pp. 2–120;
Vivian Henderson, "The Economic Status of Negroes: In the Nation and
the South," Southern Regional Council, Atlanta, 1962.

vulnerable of the rural population. The chief adjustment was to leave home. Thomas D. Clark estimates that between 1939 and 1954, 8,700,000 people left Southern farms. Of these, more than a million were Negro, and another million Negroes left during the next decade. In greater proportion than their white counterparts, they went North. In 1940, Negroes were one-fourth of the South's population; in 1960, they were about one-fifth. The Negro exodus has been estimated at yet another million during the first half of the 1960s, but the rate may have dropped off subsequently. Most of those able to leave had left; however, some stubbornly decided to fight the ills they knew intimately, rather than jump to others in the Northern ghettos that sounded worse. There was no sure way of telling that the tide of immigration had stopped (even though conductors on the Illinois Central Railroad told one newsman that Negro traffic out of Mississippi decreased in 1967).

In the 300-mile triangle of rich earth called the Mississippi Delta (after the shape of the Greek letter, not the delta of the river), the changes in agriculture meant a decline in the number of hand laborers (who chopped and picked cotton, mainly) from 18,890 out of a total farm labor force of 124,318 in 1960 to 4,765 in 1966. By 1966 machines were harvesting 90 percent of the cotton crop. From 1940 to 1968, the number of Negro farmowners in the Delta decreased from 700 (pitifully small to begin with) to 240. [15]

Much has been written about the plight of those who went North. But less has been said (or heard) about those who remained in the South. In 1964, it was estimated that 75 percent of the less than 200,000 Southern Negro farmers, as well as 69 percent of those in rural non-farm situations (whose number increased from two million to

[15] Figures from "The Negro Exodus from the Delta Continues," by Hodding Carter, III, in *The New York Times Magazine*, March 10, 1968, pp. 26, 117–21.

three million between 1940 and 1960), were poverty stricken. This poverty, in counties whose white control was sparing or scornful of welfare or free food distribution, amounted to winters freezing in unheated, dilapidated shacks, lack of clothing so severe that children couldn't go to school, and, for an undocumented but appallingly large number, actual starvation. (We have noted the report of the doctors who found in a random survey in Mississippi terrible evidence of the extent and degree of hunger; other studies have suggested similar situations across the South in 1968 and 1969.)

A Citizens' Board of Inquiry Into Hunger and Malnutrition in the United States, staffed by people from foundations and the Citizens' Crusade Against Poverty and supported largely by foundations, designated in the spring of 1968 a total of 256 counties in the United States as "hunger counties," requiring immediate and emergency attention. The bases for the designation were (1) postneonatal mortality rates of at least 15 per 1,000—double the national average; (2) poor people comprising at least 20 percent of the population—double the national average; (3) level of participation in welfare, food stamp, or commodity programs lower than 25 percent of the poor and needy. Of the 256 counties, 220 were in the eleven states of the South. Mississippi had 37 of the South's 220; Alabama, 17; Arkansas, 4; Florida, 8; Georgia (whose counties are notoriously small and numerous), 47; Louisiana, 9; North Carolina, 27; South Carolina, 16; Tennessee, 11; Texas, 30; Virginia, 14.[16]

The impersonal economic forces that had changed the South, along with the personal animus that grew with the advent of the civil rights movement and particularly with the attaining of the ballot, ended for the most part the paternalistic grace that had allowed many of those who

[16] "Hunger, USA," A Report by the Citizens' Board of Inquiry Into Hunger and Malnutrition (Washington, D. C., New Community Press, 1968), pp. 38, 98–100.

stayed behind in the 1950s and even early 1960s to eke out an existence in the old farm shanties with gardens and occasional work. A slow and not encouraging battle had been waged to extend the benefits of the welfare state to these: many of them were old people too feeble or too afraid or too devoted to the land to move on, and some were children left behind while parents met disappointment in the city. A generation or two before, white smallholders of the East, Midwest, and West had been uprooted by the same economic forces. They and the whites of the South, for the most part, could enter the less laborious, less satisfying life of town and city more easily. It was the fate of the Negro Southerner to show in extremes—in his rioting in the ghettos of the North, in his piteous condition, worsening by the year, in the rural South—what a harsh thing, cruel thing, had been done by the impersonal forces of economics and history to all of a nation which had once been predominantly agricultural.

Negro youth scorned farming, saw the plantation as a symbol of all that had demeaned their race, exploited their parents. It was the middle-aged and older Negro people, particularly, who wanted to cling to the land, the only life they had ever known, cruel as it might have been. Generations of white middle-aged and older Americans before them had had their hearts broken by the severing of the same ties. But the Negro Southerners had another heartbreak. Those earlier generations had the allurement of towns and cities promising grand things and the evidence of the success of their sons and daughters gone there ahead of them. The Negro Southerner had the evidence of the physical torment of the poverty in the cities, and, worse, the psychic damage done their sons and daughters in the destruction of those bundles of beliefs which formed a cohesive culture back home. The result was bewilderment and cynicism, anger and despair.

Beyond the efforts of the faltering and largely uncommitted bureaucracies of the federal government, attempts were underway to let people stay on the land, to resist the horrors of immigration. Chief of these were the various schemes for cooperatives, like SWAFCA (Southwest Alabama Farmers Cooperative Association) and the older, more successful Southern Consumers Cooperative in Louisiana, which with affiliates included various farm production units. A Federation of Southern Cooperatives was formed in 1967, with foundation help, as a clearing house for information, fundraising, education, and the like for the various little struggles to stay on the land. Of course, these did not include the large and prosperous, mainly all-white cooperatives that had been founded during the depression and, sadly, as elsewhere, had become despicably conservative in economic and political stances. Most of the thirty-eight member co-ops of the federation were all-Negro; those which were integrated had only a few whites. In one area of North Carolina, a successful strawberry growing co-op did, reportedly, incorporate a representative mixture of Indians, Negroes, and Ku Klux Klansmen. The thirty-eight included some sewing and quilting and handicraft units. The Poor People's Corporation of Mississippi, itself a statewide federation of largely sewing and handicraft co-ops, was a member of the Southwide federation. The small number of co-ops in the federation was suggestive of the fragility of the movement.

Generally, these combined the organizational skill and emotional fervor and optimism of the civil rights movement with the stubbornness and farming skill and shakier financial skill of the middle-aged and older farmers, landholders and tenants, determined to hang on.

With seven hundred farmers in ten counties, SWAFCA was the largest and probably strongest. Despite fierce local, congressional, and gubernatorial opposition, it had managed to get a half-million dollar grant from the Office of Economic Opportunity in 1967. Nevertheless, it waged a continuous struggle against hostile state and federal officials and white businessmen, faced difficulties with management and organization, and fought problems with crops (such as cucumbers) new to Negro farmers with little help from the United States Department of Agriculture.

Paul Good's article in the Winter, 1968, issue of *New South* (later a book, *The American Serfs*, G. P. Putnam's Sons, 1968) draws a chilling indictment of the active involvement of the Department of Agriculture through the years, under one liberal President after another, in the overt racism of the South, a record of discrimination, abuse, neglect, and—in elections to the crucial Agricultural Stabilization and Conservation Service committees which decide acreage allocations for the soil bank—outright fraud. This has been in addition to fundamental policy of the Department, which is set against the small and the poor farmer. "The Department," Mr. Good wrote, "has tried many schemes to balance production with marketability. Almost without exception, these schemes exact prohibitive penalties on the poor, small farmer and often drive him off the land. For example, a landowner with a 5,000 acre plantation can absorb a ten percent cutback in his acreage allotment and survive grumbling; to a man with only four or five acres in cotton figured to the last penny, it could mean disaster. . . . The Department of Agriculture is geared to the marketing needs of big operators despite all its pious disclaimers."[17]

But the poor farmers persevered, fighting long-established economic trends and federal farm policies. Without considerable subsidy (a not unknown solution to farm problems), these efforts would remain at best small holding actions of the shrewdest and toughest of a dying breed.

In the meantime, what of the hapless and helpless? In the late afternoon sun, the mother, tall with muscular black arms dropping straight down from her sleeveless dress, stands barefooted on her back porch, looking out across a

[17] Good, p. 18.

western Tennessee farmyard with its barn, its chickens
scratching the dirt, and across a field planted in cotton as
far as it runs. Four little girls and a boy, the oldest probably seven, stand behind her, clutching her dress or holding to her, with one of the girls holding in her arms a girl
smaller than the rest. A smaller tot, a boy, sits in the
kitchen behind them, staring, unmoving, as chicks move
before his solemn eyes through the open door onto the
wood floor. The woman's husband is coming across the
field; with him are two older boys. The oldest, probably
fourteen, face sullen, goes off to himself; the other boy
comes with his father into the house. The mother has been
telling how wonderful it has been to have a job for the
summer. It is the first job she has ever had. She is thirty-
five, her husband sixty-five. He doesn't work this land;
they are allowed to stay in the house in return for his looking after things for the owner.

She was born on such a place which her father did farm.
But he died when she was five, and her mother went insane
the next year, and she was reared by her grandmother.
When she was twenty-one, she fell in love with a soldier,
but he had to go overseas and she came home pregnant,
and before the baby was born, her grandmother died. She
went to stay with an uncle on his farm; the birth was
unattended and there were complications, and she was
abed afterward. The uncle had to ask her to leave, for the
white man had said she had to get out in the fields if she
stayed there, not lying abed lazy. Somehow she found her
present husband. (He had been married previously, raised
a family. His wife had gone to visit kin in the North, had
sent word she wasn't coming back, for him to come join
her. Somehow, he just couldn't—couldn't bring himself to
leave the land.) There were now the nine children. All of
them lived in the three rooms of the farmhouse, the four
boys in one room, the five girls in another, the mother and
father in a third. Until recently, they had all eleven lived
in one room on a place nearby. The smallest child, the boy

in the kitchen, had been badly burned there when he fell against a hot stove in that crowded room.

She had come to the attention of various authorities because she had written a complaint to a white man she had heard of—Baxton Bryant, executive director of the Tennessee Council on Human Relations. The family had been approved to get federal food stamps. Her family had no money for stamps, so they had to borrow from a storekeeper who took back in stamps interest greater than the amount he loaned (a not uncommon arrangement). Mr. Bryant, an unbelievable Arkansas preacher turned Texas politician turned rambunctious, effective worker against racism and poverty, big, balding, bellicose, aged fifty, had gotten the stamp situation remedied and had helped the woman find the job she was so proud of in a local Head Start program.

She tells of the job in a soft singsong voice and says her first pay was last week and, then with a grace to it, a great pride, shows what she bought with that first pay check: yellow plastic curtains for their front-room windows, sheets (which they had not had before) for the beds, two in the front room, two in a side room, and a bed and a crib crammed into the third room. There were gauze curtains, too, for the other two rooms. And she told of the other acquisition, something also lacking before, panties for all the girls. The children followed her about, shy and loving her. A full-grown white rabbit, obviously a pet, his presence not needing explanation, flopped from room to room. One of the girls, Mary, proudly showed her report card, numbered marks in the standard subjects, lettered marks in "social development," "personal development," "work habits." With tolerant disapproval, the mother told of catching one of the younger girls chewing tobacco the other day. The culprit grinned, squirmed in embarrassment at all the attention.

The mother was pregnant once more. The job, proud

job, she had would last only for the summer. The father
was trying to find something better, some land he could
really work, but wasn't hopeful. A short while before,
Baxton Bryant had brought an official of the United States
Department of Agriculture, visiting from Washington,
here to show him firsthand some "farm problems" of
which he was innocent, and the father had told feelingly of
how much he wanted to work, to support his children, and
then had to walk away, not wanting to cry in front of
strangers, and had just walked on across the field, and Mr.
Bryant said, "I just said after him, 'So long, so long, Jack,'
and he wouldn't turn around to answer, he just lifted his
hat and kept on walking on off." The rabbit hopped his
slow, easy, gentle hops; now the children laughed; the sun
was bright and happy, the household full of its new things
and its love. But winter would come.

Such households, such human histories are not extreme
for the class of people we are talking about. They might be
along the side of the road that we travel through in middle
Georgia (or any of the Black Belt areas), or might be out
of sight and the reach of our car, isolated and remote, with
fields to cross, paths to walk, streams to hop or wade across
before finding connection on some rutted dirt road with
the world we know, of speed and electricity and doctors
and grocery stores and schools. The mere physical effort
required, say, on an icy, rainy, wind-cold morning for a ten-
year-old boy (who has had no breakfast and has no over-
coat and is lucky if he has shoes) to get from the drafty and
likely crowded and as likely filthy shack that is his home to
the road where the school bus comes is exertion of a kind
no child (and few adults) of our world has known, and
explains the absentee and dropout rates of the schools of
the rural South. Schools . . . ? Even in the empathy we
might get from a few hours' visit with the families of the
rural poor, *we* can know the irrelevancy, the luxurious-
ness, of such a notion as school.

VI

We move along now in middle Georgia, with its beauty of soft-colored vegetation and rolling land, with its places where the woods, thick near to jungle-like, come with their fresh spirit of fecund life, their cool breath of deepest shade and damp, luxuriant growth, out onto the highway and into the car, and along here, in a valley of the unlikely little chain of glacier mountains called Pine Mountain, we pass the remains, mainly the ruins of one of those hopeful 1930s efforts of the federal government to alleviate, to remedy the terrible farm problems that long ago.

This goes back into another chapter of unheeded recent history, a little known, futile move toward land reform. A 108-page book, *Farm Tenancy, Report of the President's Committee,* published in 1937 by the United States Government Printing Office, gave the dimensions of the problem as it then existed, bad but remediable, two of every five farmers tenant farmers, increasing at the rate of 40,000 a year; thousands of farm owners as insecure as tenants with equity in their property as little as one-fifth; farm laborers, including migrants, comprising more than one-fourth of the total gainfully employed in agriculture. In its land reform program, the book recommends the formation of the Farm Security Administration, proposes that a Farm Security Corporation buy and resell land with safeguards against reconsolidation, and suggests cooperative arrangements for purchasing and machinery and marketing. It sounds like the fondest of the wistful and angry dreams of the older Negro farmers with the co-op confederation of the 1960s, a remedy that might have worked, that might yet.

The program was attempted in the Pine Mountain Valley area, and in other little islands around the South, notably in Holmes County, Mississippi, where the mark of improved conditions still lay on the land thirty years later, an ironic suggestion of what might have been. The failure of the program (its humanitarianism done in by the same forces that eroded the TVA) shows as well—here, as everywhere else, farm homes are deserted and falling down, weeds covering over the lane to the barn and the path to the well, the mark of generations of living people almost gone, a way of life weed-covered. The big operators have moved in.

And what are they like? Villains? Westwardly, in Alabama, Louisiana, Mississippi, Texas, Arkansas, they seemed arrogant in big hats and boots, the ruthlessness and wildness of the frontier vestigially alive in them. Certainly they were an exploitative, reactionary, and (in driving out Negroes) vindictive force. They still were capable of putting their holdings up as poker stakes—some of the plantations were named for the time of night they changed hands: Midnight Plantation and the Rising Sun.

But these were the spectacular traits; in profile, the South's large farm operators, even the plantation owners, likely differed little from large farm operators the nation over (or world over, or through time, the alternately greedy and grabbing or whining and begging universal farmer, of Mencken's "Let the farmer, so far as I am concerned, be damned forever. To hell with him and bad luck to him"). In the 1960s most of them were descendants of landowners, ag school graduates, possessing the same veneer of learning the state universities had provided their fellows in business and the professions—no worse, no better than these others, perhaps with a better, certainly a freer means of existence. Their fathers wore overalls and straw hats and had skin like leather and drew upon the various but equally grim wisdoms of fundamentalist religion, Populism, and the sad thing populism became—hating niggers and cities instead of the banks—and their own intimate knowledge of the hard ways of life, whether from the weather and soil or mule orneriness of farming, or cupidity and cruelty of their fellow man. But they, the sons, wore sport shirts and expensive twilled cotton britches stuffed in boots, had the sleek, healthy flesh of the middle class of their generation, and took trips afar, and had the television and the slick magazines, maybe *Playboy*, to augment their state college education.

If they were the villains in the latest tragedy of Southern agriculture, they were no longer uniquely Southern ones; they partook of that strange villainy and guilt consuming the American mainstream middle class—which was guilty of being exactly what America had patterned them to be. If there were people all around them who had not had their chances, if direct suffering resulted for other people from their success, were they personally accountable, to blame? Or was the blame the nation's, in its economic and farm policies, in its neglect of the victims of the economic forces at work on such institutions as Southern agriculture? Was the real villain the very value system that produced these new-model Southern planters in the same sleek and unseeing condition as the rest of the American middle class, just as it produced the racist poor whites of the South and the violence-prone black people of the Northern ghettos?

Even with their advantages, they had a hard time, the post-cotton farmers of the South, settling on a new dream of a seller's market. They have tried truck farming and soybeans, cattle, poultry, hogs, pine trees, such exotica, even, as tung trees, always with spectacular success for the pioneers in each new crop; then immediately many more would jump in until finally they would glut the market and send prices spiraling nationally. (Southerners told of such wildly speculative leaps as the tung tree venture with appreciation of their humor.)

In Georgia during the 1940s, the Atlanta *Constitution* had a farm editor who wrote frequently and enthusiastically of the excellence of kudzu as a controller of erosion and restorer of soil. Over the state, farmers were persuaded to put it on their ruined and wasted lands, and, sure enough, it held the dirt and improved it. But the vine also has a rapacious growth rate and iron tenacity, spreading across arable land, pastures, and farm buildings themselves with dismaying rapidity, and soon it seemed that all of Georgia would be entwined by its limber green tendrils and hidden under its wide leaves. Other states had similar experiences with it; it still abounds. In later years came a bitter experience in Alabama and Mississippi with a legume called crotalaria which turned out to have toxic seeds with a surreptitious cumulative effect; farm animals might eat thirty-nine of them with no visible effect and then keel over dead on ingestion of the fortieth.

As through history, though, Southern agriculture was most often deep into tragedy, rather than hovering on its borderline to humor. The poultry industry, as it was called, developed a form of factor farming whereby packing plants waxed rich on the plight of poor devils who had been set up with the long, low brooder houses (now as characteristic of Southern landscapes as the squat, high-chimneyed tobacco barns or cotton gins of yesteryear) and chickens in such abundance that prices fell to an established low, and the one-time luxury of the chicken dinner became nationally cheaper than hamburgers. When enthusiasm for hog raising (with a vogue of "feeder farms") sent pork prices down in 1968, Georgia farmers engaged in that macabre protest, killing and burying the hogs rather than selling them at the low prices. These ritual slaughters, with savagery attendant on some of the shootings of the beasts, offended many citizens, and most of the protest centered not sentimentally on the hogs, but on the waste of good food when there were so many people in the proximity of the slaughters who were near to starvation.

These procedures were, in their way, protesting the same blind forces that had driven Negroes from the land. A little-known Southern historical precedent shows the continuity of failure and federal irresponsibility in such efforts at farm protest. Vera Rony has described the neo-Populist, biracial Southern Tenant Farmers' Union, formed with high hopefulness in 1934, built by 1936 to

31,000 members, but destroyed before World War II, mainly by ruthless strike-breaking methods of the planters.[18] The usual alley-fighting power struggles within the labor movement abetted the destruction process, but more important was the fatal willingness of the labor movement, the federal government, and liberalism generally to abandon the South to its own miseries at the first sign of resistance by the powerful.

The civil rights movement was never able even to begin to weld black and white poor farmers together again. The tough, civil rights-touched organizing spirit which had started with Cesar Chavez in the vineyards of California made itself felt in a continuing organization and strike effort in the Rio Grande Valley of Texas. But it met repression similar to that in the 1930s, state police a factor in both, and was anyhow more a national and Western and Mexican-relations matter than a Southern one. There was some hope that it might spread to other rural poor, perhaps to the migrant laborers, another national disgrace centering to a great extent in the South. Of the three main waves of these people who move from the bottom to the top of the country following crops as they ripen, two originate in the South. (The third is in the Pacific Coast area.) The migrants harvest the fruit and vegetables that other Americans eat in abundance, while the migrants go hungry—and exhibit more plainly than the other rural poor of the South the national responsibility for their plight, moving as they do over the nation. Robert Coles has described how they can have inadequate diets even during picking season because of a natural enough (and eloquent) antipathy for the crops they labor over, and he has summed up other miseries and debilities they know:

> They live apart from the rest of us in a number of ways. By definition they are on the move, regularly or irregularly living each year in several states and in the process

[18] Vera Rony, "Sorrow Song In Black and White," *New South*, Vol. 22, No. 3, Summer, 1967; pp. 3–38.

managing usually to lose the many advantages of a permanent residence in any of them. For example, migrants usually do not vote. They are rarely eligible for any local unemployment assistance. They may hardly see the towns whose nearby fields they harvest. Their rights to adequate schooling for their children, to police protection, to sanitary inspection and regulation of their homes, to enforcement of fire regulations for those same homes, are in many cases prejudiced.[19]

At least a quarter of a million such people were in the Southern migrant bands. Many were refugees from the collapse of the plantation system and tenant farming, fleeing that situation and trying desperately and with determination and admirable self-reliance to avoid the city slums. Who was to blame for so brutally betraying *their* braveness —the farmers who exploited their love of the land, or the contractors who herded them from place to place at high profit, or the operators of the camps, usually unfit for human habitation, where they stayed?[20] Or was it all the Americans who partake of the abundance the migrants harvest?

Surely, real guilt was involved in the scandal of federal subsidization of the planters, the paying of public monies to take large landholdings out of cultivation, so vital a part of the transition to agribusiness. In 1967, one of the five recipients of more than $1 million in such subsidy was Southern (a Florida firm), and three of the fifteen receiving between $500,000 and $1 million were Southern (in Arkansas, Mississippi, and Florida). A disproportionately large number of those receiving more than $50,000 was Southern. And a safe guess would be that of all these sub-

[19] Robert Coles, "The Migrant Farmer: A Psychiatric Study," Southern Regional Council, 1965.

[20] The American Farm Bureau Federation was among those culpable in the matter of the camps. Citing this and other activities of the federation, Representative Joseph Y. Resnick was quoted in *The New York Times* (Sept. 3, 1967) as saying it "is not an organization representing the interests of the American farmer, but is, instead, a vast combine of business interests operating under the protective umbrella of its tax exemption."

sidized Southern agrarians, upwards of 95 percent were
hard-line conservatives, opposed to the "socialism" of welfare and food subsidies for the poor, admirers of such an
anti-socialist as Senator James O. Eastland of Mississippi,
the Eastland Plantation, Inc. of suffering Sunflower
County having received one of the larger 1967 subsidies,
$157,930.[21] But even in this most flagrant adding of insult
to injury of the Southern rural poor, villainy proliferates.
For despite the iron grip of Southerners on relevant congressional committees, it was still a national Congress—
capable in other matters of overriding the Southerners,
and more than once warned of the implications of its willingness to subsidize the rich but not the poor. Senator
Williams tried to put a ceiling on the amount any single
individual or corporation could receive in the subsidies,
and was defeated.

Those intimate with the South and its hunger often suggested an obvious solution to the problem—to plant food
on those subsidized fields lying fallow and distribute it free
to the poor. Would the Congress, with its ties to grocery
lobbyists and the like, even consider it? Food stamps were
its answer. A devastating study of the impersonal system of
askew values at work in national economics and politics
simply recorded the considerations and compulsions involved in a hearing before the Agriculture Subcommittee
of the Senate Appropriations Committee. It cited the more
than $3 billion paid to the full total of 92,720 recipients of
soil-bank subsidies in 1967 and compared that to the $1.9
billion war on poverty budget for fiscal 1969. Then it
told of fervent lobbyist appeals and great committee concern for such subsidy matters as fire ant eradication
($6.4 million in fiscal 1968); research on problems of

[21] Data on the subsidies are from a Senate statement by Senator John
J. Williams, Republican of Delaware, May 23, 1968. Among his comments:
"At a time when the Administration is shedding so many crocodile tears
over the plight of the hungry in America, it is a farce to see them at the
same time paying millions to corporate-type farming operations not to
produce crops."

poultry processing plants, including poor hatchability of some eggs, chicken house odor control, etc.; increase of a $225,000 program of research into employee inefficiency in wholesale and retail food service to $500,000; a proposal to spend $50,700 for the "development of physiological and psychological measures of well-being of dogs and cats," and so on. The projects, most of them, were harmless enough, even worthwhile. But measured against the refusal to feed starving children, help hapless adults, their evil showed plain. Of more than $150 million in United States Department of Agriculture research spending in 1968, the article pointed out, only $4.2 million went for study of human nutrition and consumer and food economics.[22]

But then why single out agriculture? A representative of the National Limestone Institute who appeared before the Subcommittee chided members for quibbling over a couple of hundred million dollars for water and soil conservation when the government was subsidizing industries by more than $5 billion annually. He cited payments of $500 million each to Lockheed Aircraft and General Dynamics, $393,842,000 to American Telephone and Telegraph, and $356,079,000 to General Electric.

Villainy, villainy. It is hard to sort the villains out, to separate them from the routine complexities and banalities of advanced industrial organization. If understanding of Southern rural poverty was to be anything other than superficial and scapegoating, it had to be seen in the perspective of national economics and politics, of a long and apparently intensifying national policy of valuing things over people. As for the Southern individual villains, even they, the hated planter just as much as the cotton mill owners, dissolved stereotypes in the individual confrontation. I remember the peach farmer who had, somehow, gotten himself involved in a State Department exchange

[22] Warren Pritchard, "The Poor People's Campaign and Other Lobbies," *New South*, Vol. 23, No. 4, Fall, 1968, pp. 21–27.

trip to Russia and came back impressed, telling of the
social welfare benefits to all people there, honestly overcoming a lifetime's conditioning, and telling scornfully of
some of the backward notions and technology still prevailing in farming there. He remembered watching his father
struggle through the Depression to hold on to his land and
then lose it. Since college, he himself had struggled to buy
it back, a piece at a time, using elaborate and compli-
catedly technical methods to squeeze more money from
each parcel when he got it, his holdings at the time far
beyond what his father would have wanted, but less, still,
than was needed for success. His ten-year-old boy, he
hoped, would continue after him; it was a good life, he
said, and profitable if you knew how. What came through
strongest in his talk was not just his love of the land
(shared with those older Negroes of the cooperatives) but
his sense of having something important to do, something
worth all his studying and thinking and working, something worthy of his manhood. Here, too, his similarity to
the Negro farmers was striking. For it was the value of
their manhood, of dignity, that they asserted most strongly,
values beyond economics and efficiency. These were not
even considered in the feeble and futile gesture toward
rectifying farm tenancy in 1937, but thirty years later they
were of the essence of such newer problems as urban rioting, upon which Presidential committee cerebration was
lavished, and newer, lengthier reports produced (with still
futile and feeble recommendations).

The stereotypes dissolve. That white farmer who had
been to Russia would call the Negroes of the cooperatives
"nigger" without a thought about it, in a friendly, conde-
scending way that somehow, maybe almost shamefacedly,
recognized far more of their humanity and the values they
so much shared with him than the lengthiest of Presidential committee reports down through the years of liberalism. He had taken his slides of Russia to the civic clubs and
churches all around the county, he said, and had developed

a pretty good little lecture to go with them, part of his duty, he felt, in recompense for the privilege of going over there and learning so much about the world which before he had only dimly sensed. And one meeting was held at the nigger school so all of them could hear about Russia, too, and derned (not all of sterotype is dissolvable, dern was his word) if that meeting wasn't the best one of them all. They had the high school band to play, and then when he got to talking, the niggers got to answering, responding back, with "amen" and "yes, that's right," and "that got me to going, seemed like the talk just went better, and all in all it was the best talk I gave of them all."

VII

The land flattens out as we drive southward, and the earth which was black or dark red in the mountain area and became salmon-colored in the Piedmont becomes black or gray and richer. The vegetation is more luxuriant, tree limbs bending with weight of leaves, downward plumes of green. Palmettos and beautiful chinaberry trees, deli-cate-leafed and round-topped, flourish here. In hottest sum-mer, the towns and small cities gleam in the sun. This is the Black Belt. This is still county-seat country.

Georgia has 159 county seats all laid out close enough together so that each could be reached in a few hours by mule and wagon from any point in the county. This is an excess of a traditional Southern pattern from the horse-and-wagon past. Despite the demands of common sense and administrative logic through nearly half a century, con-solidation remained impossible. No small-town county seat would give up its power, its overbearing, overprivilged public wards and their friends and kinfolk and town businesses benefiting from the largesse of various state pro-grams administered through the courthouse. Their power and patronage had greatly decreased. But it was about all they had; they clung to it. Georgia, as other Southern states, was trying to live with the impossibility of changing the anachronism of too many counties by developing multi-county administrative units in such matters as welfare and juvenile detention and education. But the people who stood most to profit, who desperately needed better schools, fought even this, hearkening to some of the faint strains of Jeffersonian democracy running through their political heritage (even as did Negroes in their groping after some concrete reality of a controllable, human unit for administrative purposes in civil rights organizations and poverty programs). In a manner that would surely bring howlingly, ironic joy to a Paul Goodman, they resisted even the consolidation of town and county schools.

The Negro population of the Black Belt is large, but no one, not even the United States Bureau of the Census, knows how large. This was the bemused discovery of Don Jelinek, one of those young white civil rights workers from the North who stayed on in the South in grim love of the fight to somehow make it make sense. He discovered that even in 1960 the Census Bureau had contented itself in Alabama with the estimates and guesses of white census takers (partaking of a decennial boon descended from the federals upon the courthouse). The method of the more conscientious of these, Mr. Jelenik in half incredulity learned, was to go to the white-owned crossroads store and inquire of its proprietor, "How many head of niggers live down this road?" Similar methods were in use across the South, the Bureau feared, and made conscientious efforts to improve the situation by the 1970 census, and with good cause. For what scholarly work, what governmental report, what law based on population was untainted? The ironic symbolism was exquisite: the perfect national acquiescence, willy-nilly, to Southern dehumanization, reduced to numbers.

This is the Black Belt of legend and gory lore, of Faulknerian groping to achieve the universal human epic poem, of Cash's insights into the savage and irrational at the base of a civilization's psyche, of Negro terror and love of place, filling blacks in the North with nostalgia. Here lies the mystical meaning of the Negro's vast, cataclysmic influence on America's destiny and character.

The past holds more strongly down here, in the very landscape and shape of the towns, and in the minds of people. There lives yet the practice and legacy of the mixing of the blood: true integration, perverted in the fantastic ability at compartmentalization, in the frightening ability of men to let run free the worst, most animal instincts of the parental process, which allowed them at the first to sell into unknown horror the little children sired of black women, and in later times to allow them to live out their lives as untouchables. Many Negroes and whites can trace their kinship across the color line, and accommodate the complexities and insanities of status and class involved.

Here, in such a diminishing form as the brute sheriff or the peonage turpentine farm, lives yet the South's old overt racism, the genuine article. Proliferation of racism in subtler form across the nation and generally a toning down of it in the rest of the South makes the Black Belt version seem unbelievable—like the story of the dweller in one little hamlet saying that sure enough racial agitation was occurring there: "They've gotten to where they want to walk on the sidewalks."

Except for scattered instances, lynching ended in the 1940s, largely as a result of the embarrassment it caused, and as part of a taming down of life over all the nation. Efforts of the Association of Southern Women for the Prevention of Lynching were also instrumental. The wonderment of all the change that has come, not necessarily in any meaningful improvement of the lot of the average Negro (or white), but in the whole temper and tone of America, is strong in sitting and listening for all of a day in 1967 to one of the organizers of the Association tell its saga and success.

Mrs. Jesse Daniel Ames, in her eighties at the time, told

it in such a way as to make real again the fact that so many score lynchings occurred each year in the Southern states, to make understandable how the threat of them haunted the minds of white liberals and the lives of Negroes. The more fanciful version of her story, repeated in Southern liberal circles, is that the women, dressed in their Sunday best, flowered hats, and white gloves, stood on the steps of the jailhouse, shaming the mob: "You must harm us first. You are not doing this in the name of white womanhood. We don't want it." This was the message, but the method was less spectacular in most instances. It consisted of an elaborate information network, including secret outposts in the Associated Press, which would inform members when a dangerous situation seemed to be developing. They would, with the expertise Southern liberals have developed, pressure sheriffs, police forces, town and state officials, businessmen, preachers, all those who could have stopped lynchings all along, to do the necessary things to stop this one. The organization opposed federal antilynching laws, probably in part because it smacked to them of Reconstruction, but more importantly because as Southerners they wanted to work things out for themselves, solve their own problems.

The less spectacular, more hidden cruelties have continued in the Black Belt: the atrocities that occur in jails (in all jails, but here with Negroes often the victims and intimidation intended, more purposefully), economic intimidations and methodical petty swindling of Negroes, perversions of political and court processes. In recent times, these have been directed most often against local civil rights leaders and the hated white outside agitators, "people messed up in that civil rights," or more simply, "Communists," pronounced "Commonists."

The memory of past repression could be almost as strong an influence as a current campaign of it. In a town with a particularly bad history, attitudes of fear and caution were handed down through generations of Negroes, and even more than ordinary harshness existed in the white racism. "People gets things like that in them; it is hard for them to get rid of it," said a black leader in Dorchester County, South Carolina. There as in many other places, the memory lived of a Negro-killing sheriff. Before being rewarded with higher office, he had, in the line of duty, killed more than twelve Negroes. In the late 1960s, the county's whites were markedly unfriendly to such Negro rights as welfare and voting, when most other counties of the state had learned to be on-the-surface friendly and industry-attracting peaceful in race relations.

Human relations experts and even civil rights workers talked glibly of "apathy" and the unfounded fears in such a community. And for most Americans who have never known the utter helplessness and terror of totalitarian control and completely unrestrained official violence, it is almost impossible to empathize with black people in such a community, to know the force and holding power of their fear. (One could only hope—against some frightening evidence to the contrary—that other segments of America, the rebellious young, for example, might continue innocent of such knowledge.) Always—in such communities especially, but in the South generally—it was remarkable to see the courage which individual Negroes were able to muster in order to present themselves at such occasions as hearings before the United States Commission on Civil Rights. They testified the terrible truths of local grievances with the hope that at last something would be done, with true sacrificial regard for the general good. The Commission's persisting into the late 1960s to hold the hearings and publish the findings with seldom even general results, let alone alleviation of local conditions, had become obscene. The grievances had all been told, the remedies had all been obvious for years, the risks to the witnesses were still great, and the erosive effect of disappointment grew more devastating by the year. Here again, liberalism, with the best of intentions but with dependence on obsolete methods, seemed to be doing far more harm than good.

We can begin to understand that other cruelty, the driving of Negroes out because their presence had become an economic and political liability, in all its depths down here —in the sun, in the heat-shimmering, mirage-touched landscape of the Black Belt, in the motionless, soundless towns. This place, this land was home, and these white people, with whom in a lifetime through generations these Negroes were intimately bound (as servants, victims, equipped in exquisite degree with all the retaliatory mechanisms, shaming, mocking, outwitting in a thousand subtle ways), these white people were part of home, too. In the curious and twisted ways that human love finds expression, these Negroes loved these white people. Carson McCullers, more than any Southern writer, told the strange truth of such twisted expressions of human love out of a knowledge of the most intimate of Southern racial human dealings, told it best not in *Member of the Wedding*, but in *Ballad of the Sad Cafe*. ("We don't hate our colored," insisted the whites, and most assuredly, in the strange ways of the human heart, they did not.)

The cruelest thing was this driving of the Negroes out, to end forever the perverted but human bond and disappoint forever that hope some of the Negroes had always held—as unfounded and majestic as the will of people without food or warmth not only to keep alive but send the children to school—that wistful faith that some day the whites would be all right.

We see other signs of a mechanistic and hysterical hand upon the land. The pine forests of the pulpwood plants flourish down here, held with small taxation, as the number of people dwindles year by year. Congressmen from these areas, despite reapportionment, represent pine trees and those who grow them, not the ordinary people.

Then there are the big hunting preserve plantation holdings of absentee owners. In Baker County, Georgia, known until recent years of black voting and poverty program strivings simply as Bad Baker, there were two such plantations, vast holdings—one 35,000 acres and the other 24,000 acres—mostly woodland for hunting. It has been for years an open secret, a scandal that one of these was owned by an Atlanta man of considerable influence, his money generously given to various Atlanta charities. The other was owned by a Northern family whose name is synonymous with philanthropy, including efforts to achieve better human conditions.

Such plantations stand there, a symbol of the greater problem—America's style in a world in which half the people are hungry: heedless, insensitive, impersonal exploitation, a seeming inability, akin to compulsion, to do otherwise. Here, in the midst of starvation, parallel with royal forests and the like of antiquity is obvious; the fact that it is the pleasure of the kill to which they are dedicated (tame wildlife, birds, turkeys, deer, are kept at these places to be released for the pleasure of greenhorns to slaughter) is suggestive of America's worst history and recent foreign policy postures.

The few Negroes who work at these places would tell you that the absentee owners were just about the best white folks there ever were. Wages were higher (if below the law's minimum and statistician's definition of poverty), and living conditions better. In fear of losing such sinecure, these privileged few rarely became involved in civil rights.

It seems worth seeking the full culpability here, the exactitudes of the evil, for it is far more representative than the raw racism of the Black Belt of what is wrong with America in the world. In the worst situations, it was not just the exploitation of the Negroes, using available, cheap, and pliable labor. It was as much an exploitation of the ruling whites, taking advantage of their tax structure, their property values, their human values. But more than either of these, it was a pitiless, thoughtless exploitation that was not even greedy; essentially it was the frivolous using of a whole society. These owners were taking the land out of production, giving nothing to the general welfare; they were oblivious to the wretched schools, to the lack of hospitals and the lack of flood control, oblivious to all the deprivation and misery of the people of both races around them, oblivious to starvation. We may begin to understand how Americans were able to ravage Vietnam, to napalm babies, to brandish nuclear holocaust, to play calmly with the life and death of a planet, if we can begin to understand some of the hunting preserve plantations of the Black Belt. Alongside them, the indigenous swaggering plantation lords are of a more innocent tradition of evil; at least they have greed as a motivation.

For the Negro, such plantations were probably no more or less damaging psychologically than all the other manifestations of white power; they were a part of an unfair system into which he was born, and which, gropingly, afraid of himself, he was coming to understand and hate. For the white of the Black Belt, who was equally enmeshed in the system, such places were proof positive of his various creeds and prejudices, most notably his rightful contempt for the hypocrisy of the white North and, even more, his secret knowledge that for all white men it was the same, this ability, this readiness to use the Negro and consider him inferior.

Coming upon such phenomena, the Negro intellectual was beyond anger: his blood ran icy with an aversion for all whites. All of America, he proclaimed, is racist. Let us examine this proposition from the vantage point of the Black Belt.

One of the generally accepted axioms in the monumental political science work on the South by V. O. Key, Jr. (*Southern Politics in State and Nation*, New York, Alfred A. Knopf, 1949) was that the white mind of the

Black Belt held sway over the South, extending its racism into all the practices of the society and all the sanctuaries of power, particularly political. A corollary was that in the rest of the South, where Negro population was proportionately less and race relations generally better, the crime of political exclusion, all the denial of civil liberties, might have been avoided, or mitigated, had it not been for the sinister influence of the Black Belt. An inference suggested by the racist upsurge of the 1960s and inherent in any contemplation of Black Belt racism would be that the Black Belt had extended its sway to the nation, to the highest sanctuaries of power, with global impact. But, thinking of the worst of these hunting preserve plantations and ways in which the non-Black Belt South acquiesced to political manipulation for their own direct disadvantage, one may at least doubt the original axiom. It is one more version of the central question of this book: In its worst attributes, how different is the South from America? How much is it an influence, how much a reflection?

VIII

There is another part of the question: How impervious might the best of the South be to that in the rest of America which degrades quality and deadens creativity? No more appalling examples of that degrading and deadening effect might be found than the tourist attractions that flourish in parts of the South, surpassing vulgarity along the main routes of Florida.

On the other hand, some work of the federal parks department had a dignity and respect for the tourists and the site. Occasionally, similar respect was institutionalized by local business or a municipality, like the Okefenokee Swamp Park operated by the city of Waycross, Georgia.

The Okefenokee itself offers an appropriate metaphor for anyone touring the South or trying to fathom its mysteries. An Indian word meaning "Land of the Trembling

Earth," the name stands for the islands of floating vegetation that comprise much of the swamp; these islands are called by swamp people "houses," and some are large enough to support trees with roots trailing in the water below. To step from a boat onto one of the "houses" is a dismaying experience; the land does literally shake and bob underfoot. If you don't know how to walk this land, your feet quickly sink into the muck and then the cold water below. The swamp people walk it with quick jerking steps, barely letting a foot touch down before lifting it, moving in a hopping lope. So it is, with contemplation of the South. If one jumps to what seems an obvious conclusion, likely as not the solid-seeming fact that ought to be supporting it will give way underneath. Better it is to hop from one point of fact or judgment to another with the tentativeness of the swamp people, distrusting the obvious but aware, always, that somewhere back through the jungle trails and across trembling earth, solid truth will be found. One of the real islands in the Okefenokee Swamp once supported a good-sized logging town, with a main street and even a picture show.

There are indeed many Souths, and generalizations about the South have to be taken with consideration for all the differences, for the trembling earth foundation. Indeed, generalizations about this or that part of the South must also be qualified; not all of the Deep South is isolated, sleepy, and not everything on the main tourist lines is neon and chrome; the five counties at the border of Tennessee and Mississippi are of Mississippi, not the generally moderate civilization of Tennessee.

The point is better belabored than missed. We may take each state and turn it over and examine it in generalization. Virginia partakes of the Washington metropolitan complex, of the Black Belt, of genuine roots and pretensions out of the colonial period; its race relations seem to have as much in common with southern Illinois (their

particular meanness) as with those of a state like South
Carolina, where administrative trickery was ever to be preferred to violence. More than any other Southern state,
Virginia, the cradle of American democracy, was willing to
disfranchise whites if it took that to disfranchise Negroes.

North Carolina, I have suggested, was atypical in its
progressiveness, but by the late 1960s there were areas of
other states surpassing it, for its social development has
been generally static since the 1940s. Tennessee, with its
small Negro population, its TVA, its ability to produce a
Kefauver, tended also, alas, to be satisfied with a reputation out of the past. Nashville emerged with something of
the ugliness of Northern-city Negro debasement, as bad as
there was in the South, and, in 1968, through the recalcitrance and callousness of a city administration and society,
Memphis became another of those Southern places of
infamy when a mad dog killed the symbol of the best of
the South, Dr. Martin Luther King, Jr.

South Carolina hearkened to the myth of a Southern
nobility longer than most of the states; it liked to look
upon itself as gentlemanly. Yet it had not avoided violence
completely; indeed, its rural areas were nearly as bloody as
Georgia's, but its newspapers were uniformly bad, and the
public seldom learned about the atrocities. Cotton mills
flourished here as viciously as in North Carolina; white
society in Charleston was probably as provincial, as inter-
necinely cruel and snobbish as any in America. Yet in the
1960s, South Carolina's gentlemanly instincts and its
yearnings for industry led it to surpass states that were
formerly noted as progressive; in such efforts as its program of integrated technical training schools for high
school dropouts and adults driven from the farm, it was
ahead of the region.

Arkansas was ever a place to itself, touched by the border states, by the West, by mountain culture, and by Mississippi. It had contrasts of beauty of landscape and un-

adulterated ugliness both of nature and towns surpassing any in the South. Arkansas spawned Orval Faubus, the first of a new breed of demagogue whose devotion to racism was patently opportunistic; it was successfully cited for several years by liberals in the rest of the South as the horrible example of a state in which racist notoriety deflected industry and harmed business.

Texas was more of the West than of the South, with its peculiar problems attendant on a large Mexican-American population, but its eastern reaches were thoroughly Southern, reflecting in place and family names and racial mores the movement west from the rest of the South. Louisiana was a mixture even more flavorful than the other states, in the grandeur and beauty of its coastal country, bayous and the touch of French culture on towns and speech, in the Black Belt harshness and lushness of its Protestant North, the studied individuality of New Orleans, the cruel (like unto Texas) exploitation of the oil lands, and the flourishing of its political specimens—the Long lineage, and such Falstaffian a villain as Leander Perez. Governor John J. McKeithen probably represented the progressive and better-instinct moderation of the rest of the South more skillfully than most and exemplified the new art of Southern statesmanship. This consisted in contriving to appear progressive to the rest of the nation and convincing native Negroes of much the same while holding them and most other unfortunates of the old system precisely where they had been all along, and communicating this to the native whites.

Mississippi was for so long (and in Negro folklore, "Mississippi Goddamn" remained so) the worst, the place of cruelest, most brutal racism, the home of the poorest, most degraded Negro life, and the bottom of the list in all the social indices for all the society, white as well as black. The lust for industry, the emergence of business interests over agrarian ones, perhaps the shame of the concentrated exposure by the Southern as well as Northern press of the excesses of private and official brutality to Negroes and their white friends (the murder of civil rights workers in Neshoba County), and perhaps the influence of the civil rights movement itself in the 1964 Freedom Summer, all of these—or some of all of them, and who knows what else—brought an effort toward reform. By the late 1960s this had achieved some success on the surface of race relations and in the statistics of such matters as education.

But Alabama, close through the years in reputation and performance to Mississippi, showed little tendency to reform. This must have been due, in large part, to the hold of the totalitarian mind and method of Governor George C. Wallace. Here, as in no other state in the late 1960s, large numbers of young whites, high school age and over, still spouted unquestioningly the old catechisms of racism and Southern aristocracy.

Before 1964 Mississippi had been more totalitarian, but in the late 1960s Alabama was the last bastion of Southern totalitarianism, and it was not incapable of spreading its influence across the South—or the nation.

Florida, the unknowledgeable liked to say, was not Southern at all. Miami was indeed an extension of some of the sorrier aspects of New Y   nd the coasts were lined with that nameless, regionless (indeed unearthly) vulgarity of motel culture gone crazy. But the centerland—and most of all the northern scrub country—was Black Belt Southern: the Klan flourished there into the late 1960s, and it was as likely a place as any for the nation's first rural or small-town racial guerrilla warfare to break out.

In all of this diversity in the past, institutionalized racism and a backward agriculture, with resultant material and spiritual poverty, were common factors which gave the region unity and distinctiveness from the rest of the nation. All of that has changed or was changing, as we have seen. Racism was no longer institutionalized; agriculture was no longer dominant and was undergoing radical modernization. And most of the people were living in the emerging cities and burgeoning towns. In these, far more than out in the country, the crucial developments were underway that would determine whether the South would emerge with any but superficial regional differences. Race remained the most important struggle, but in many other ways, the cities and towns of the South were undergoing tremendous stress from the pressures of regional traditions and national influences. Perhaps the most illuminating insights about the South and the nation to be found in these cities and towns were that not all the national and regional pressures were counter to each other, and where they were, not all the regional ones were negative.

PART THREE

The Cities and Towns

CHAPTER 4

―――――――――

I

BY THE END of the 1960s the South still had no real cities.
That is to say none on the scale of those in the North or in
the advanced countries of Europe and Asia, none with
their degrees of density and immenseness, inconvenience,
dehumanization, or development of the fine arts. Atlanta
and Houston were the largest. Census estimates in July,
1966, put Atlanta's metropolitan area population at 1,258,
000 and Houston's at 1,740,000. Atlanta's central city had
almost half a million, and Houston's more than 900,000.

Atlanta was merely an overgrown version of most of the
other cities: Nashville, Montgomery, Jackson, Little Rock,
Raleigh, Richmond, Columbia. Only an occasional Southern city possessed especially flavorful qualities—Birmingham, Gothic in the ugliness of its industry and spirit,
Charleston or Miami, coastal and each contrary in its own
way, New Orleans, with its own idiosyncratic blend of Old
World cynicism, Northern abruptness, and excessive
Southern inefficiency. (Nothing, it was common to observe
in Southern civil rights circles, ever really gets accomplished in New Orleans.)

If Atlanta was an overgrown (or more aptly, multiplied
and outspread) county seat and trade center town, Houston was both of these and a port town as well, with the
braggadocio and vulgarity imparted by the frontier tradition and oil wealth. These two cities, keep in mind, were
the pace and tone setters, the more sophisticated, the

models of urbanization imitated by the other cities, large
and small.

It was possible in Atlanta in the late 1960s to sit, of a
late spring evening, in a residential section no more than
ten minutes from the downtown and to breathe the air of a
small-town America (not suburbia) of the American past,
suffused with the coolness and blossom-fragrances of trees
and bushes, roses, honeysuckle, and the wet smell of grass
and weeds. The present intrudes, recedes—nature seems
dominant, but it is an altered nature, the patterns and
artifacts of the city somehow fitted into nature. The full,
heavy vegetation muffles sound—the motor and jangled
television noises of a city neighborhood, cries of children;
the wail of sirens seems far away, not of the present. Only
the bird sounds are clear and present, jays piercing
through everything, outrageous and glad. A jet airliner
streaks high over window-lit skyscrapers and primary-
colored glow of neon in the downtown, and it all seems a
thing of decoration, not of immediate, functional, frantic
reality. The mood is contemplative, appreciative, abstract.
Later, in the absolute stillness of deep night, an owl wails
his weird laughter, and later still, in wet grayness of before
day, a mockingbird pushes the limits of his sanity with
lyrical delight, in praise of dawn.

This is the best of Atlanta and the myriad cities of the
South. In order to find the worst or to gauge these cities,
we may travel a few of the more obvious byways and boule-
vards of Atlanta's blend of good, bad, and bland. By sampling what the best of Southern cities has been like, we
may better understand the rest of them, including the
worst.

II

At its economic base, Atlanta was better off than most of
the other Southern cities, for it was not a manufacturing
center. By luck, it had escaped selling its birthright for

that dubious and increasingly obsolete pottage. Atlanta was, instead, a regional center of finance, transportation, trade, and, increasingly, services, including recreational and cultural; it was close to the economists' models of what the Southern city of the future ought to be. The manufacture that it did have was diversified, and much of it sophisticated; even in this, Atlanta was more fortunate than many of its sister Southern cities.

The hulks and culture of a few cotton mills still appeared in scattered sections of the city (with the lean, blankly hostile faces and stooped shoulders of the workers unmistakable), but Atlanta grew up around railroad tracks. It was, as it proclaimed, the gateway to the South. Downtown Atlanta was constructed curiously over the railroad tracks: many of its main streets and building lots were perched on stilts in elaborate viaducts—in order to hide the tracks as much as to avoid downtown grade crossings (which still imposed their maddening influence on downtown traffic even in such large Southern cities as Columbia and Mobile).

Atlanta's airport (a grand new terminal built in 1961 with as little foresight as architectural distinction and outgrown by 1965) boasted that at peak periods it had the largest number of landings and departures of any in the world. But most of the passengers were just making connections. This tradition of travel, of people coming and going, had from the beginning influenced Atlanta's soul, making it more urbane and more tolerant of differences as well as more greedy—this suggesting the origins (in isolation) of the provinciality of so much of the rest of the South, the hostility to strangers (people or ideas) and the slower, more human pace.

When Southern business expanded after World War II, Atlanta's gateway existence gave it a greater number of branch offices than most Southern cities had. Thus, the image-seeking, respectability-bent national business and corporation mentality moving into (and making their adjustments with) Southern culture could be seen in extreme in Atlanta. Thus came, too, the influence of American mobility more than the South had known before, including a tendency among adults on the move to be incapable of very deep commitment to any local phenomenon. (In racial matters, this helped explain the holier-than-thou Yankee who never bothered to penetrate the subtleties or understand the agony of whites as he thought he understood it of blacks, and the Yankee-turned-racist who superficially accepted the shibboleths as part of his adjusting. Another kind of Yankee, who came to embrace and embody the best of the South, acquired the Southerner's own kind of exasperated love of the place, the people. He was valuable, since he usually had a superior education and could keep a detached perspective, and he usually stayed on.)

Branch office temporariness involved also a wary unwillingness, among people who stayed put as well as among the transients (and even among children), to make friends too deeply, out of the trauma of so many leave-takings. These were, of course, national phenomena—their impact on the South was probably more pronounced because they had been so little felt there before.

The South might be said to have lost many of its most ambitious, brightest people since World War II, keeping mainly the mediocre in both the small towns and the cities. (This has more to do with qualitative than quantitative factors.) In terms of amount of education, the South was exporting people with little schooling (many with less than eight grades of it) and importing ones with college degrees or at least some college. On the other hand, the South had larger numbers of functionally illiterate people than the rest of the country, and these tended to be left behind by the emigration.[1] And among those better edu-

[1] For quantitative data, see "Human Inequalities and Southern Underdevelopment," by Mary Jean Bowman, in *The Southern Economic Journal*, Vol. 32, No. 73, July, 1965, pp. 73 ff.

cated immigrants, what would their quality be? Consider the educators who, unless fired with missionary zeal, would choose to come South to teach.

The proliferation of branch offices illustrated one other sad fact—the rarity of business of any size or national influence with origins and headquarters in the South. Coca-Cola, with both in Atlanta, was an exception that proved the rule, as were the tobacco manufacturers of North Carolina. A true measure of the massive cultural influence of big business lies not so much in a comparison of these more benevolent industries with such reactionary and rapacious ones as the oil baronies of Louisiana and Texas or the textile firms. Rather, the better industries might be compared with what business ought to be.

On the whole, business had been inaccessible to Southern Negroes, but Atlanta had an exception to this rule, too. The largest amount of Negro capital and corporate wealth in the nation was centered here in a row of insurance and banking and small business firms along Auburn Avenue, developed painstakingly and concomitantly with the city's Negro educational complex. Southwide, Atlanta in earlier years was looked to as a mecca of Negro business; Auburn Avenue was known as "Sweet Auburn," blessed with much sugar.

Other accumulations of black capital, mostly in insurance and banking, developed here and there in the other large cities and some smaller ones. But Negro banking was notorious for hindering black people from purchasing homes in white neighborhoods in most Southern locales; similarly, Negro insurance firms trafficked largely in the low-interest burial policies so important and costly to the poorest of Negro Southerners. In practice neither of these industries differed notably from its white counterpart. In the late 1960s it was a fashionable political gimmick to consider the munificences of white capitalism and a burgeoning of black capitalism as the solutions to problems of race and poverty. This was merely the least promising of any number of ironic efforts in which the South strained to achieve what had already gone sour and sorry in the rest of the nation.

As for equality of opportunity in the mainstream of white businesses, Atlanta differed little from the other cities of the South. Characteristically, older firms effected token desegregation, if any at all, and newer ones made various efforts to comply with federal contract regulations and the civil rights law. Most of the older firms would more or less rightfully say that they could not lay off satisfactory white employees merely to hire black ones. But the attitudes of Southern-based industry, homegrown or national corporation, and the need for firm enforcement of equal job opportunity—as well as of all other facets of civil rights law—were well illustrated in Atlanta's experience with the Kennedy Administration efforts to gain voluntary fair employment from government contractors. (This was the ill-fated Plans for Progress program wherein then Vice President Johnson sought to show that such voluntary action from business was preferable to firm regulation and law.)

A Southern Regional Council report in 1963 noted that of the first fifty-two firms in the country to sign the Plans for Progress pledges, twenty-four were located in Atlanta; it then attempted to assess their performance. These twenty-four companies had about 26,000 employees at the time, including Lockheed with 14,500, a General Motors assembly plant with 6,490, and a Ford plant with 2,000. Only seven of the twenty-four produced any evidence of compliance with their pledges, and only three—Lockheed and a Western Electric and a Goodyear plant—demonstrated what the report termed a "vigorous desire to create job opportunities." The other seventeen indicated everything from "ignorance to indifference." Of the vigorous three, Lockheed, the largest by far, seemed to have been influenced more by NAACP complaints than the voluntary pledge.[2]

If evasion was to become more difficult in the South, rationalization came more easily. We can't find qualified Negroes, employers said. This could mean almost anything, but usually it involved the variety of unconscious prejudice that led people to demand more of the black worker than of the white and made them willing to extend far less training and patience to blacks. Or it might involve the even more cruelly debilitating practice of never demanding anything of black workers, never enforcing any standards, saying in effect to them and their white co-workers that they had been hired merely to satisfy government regulations and couldn't be expected to be competent. If the quest for "qualified" Negroes ever became honest, there would be opportunity to know the real dimensions of the problems of education for Negro Southerners and—as we shall see—the not unrelated problem of nutrition.

III

Something of the real meaning of Atlanta's status as pacemaker for the other Southern cities could be seen in its performance in this vital matter of education of Negro children. In fact, Atlanta probably did set the pace for the other cities (though not, as we shall see, for the towns and rural places where the civil rights law was often better enforced), but the pace was tragically slow. In 1968 a citi-

---

[2] "Plans for Progress: Atlanta Survey," Southern Regional Council, January, 1963. The report points out ruefully that the Plans for Progress scheme followed recommendations of the Southern Regional Council made in 1961, except in one vital particular. The 1961 recommendations had called for required, not voluntary, compliance, citing federal executive power then available to achieve this. The reason Atlanta had so many of the original signers was that an Atlantan, Robert Troutman, Jr., was an enthusiast official of the program.

zens' group compiled statistics that shocked even those who had been generally aware that the pace was indeed slow. The figures showed that in 1966–67 a total of 92.3 percent of black elementary students in the Atlanta system attended all-black schools. Of the remainder, 3.1 percent were in schools with token integration (less than five percent black), leaving only 4.6 percent in situations in any way describable as integrated. Of black high school students, 77.5 percent were in all-black schools, 14.9 percent in schools with token integration, and 7.6 percent in integrated schools. Ninety-seven percent of the elementary schools had three teachers or less of the opposite race from that of the majority of students, and 85 percent of the high schools had four or less.

Students in the black schools attended larger elementary schools, larger first grade classes than in the rest of the system. They had fewer textbooks per student, were in buildings of less value per student, equipped with less valuable furniture and equipment per student, and with less site area per student than in the rest of the system. And black students, who needed speech therapy programs more than whites did, were less likely to have them.

This latter was less a matter of willful neglect than of ignorance of the need. One of the unexpected results of desegregation had been the discovery that, contrary to fond belief (the white refrain: "We know our Negras"), the two races could not even communicate with each other. This failure was partly a result of white prejudice, a willful unwillingness on the part of, say, a white mother to concede that the Negro teacher of her child could speak good English. But much of it was genuine—a matter of differing dialects more than of improper usage, the latter a common fault of both races. There might be some philosophical cause to question whether it was right that the dialect of the dominant whites be imposed on the blacks should they be blessed with speech therapy programs. But the same question might be raised about college-level efforts to impose upon drawling whites the flavorless intonations of the Midwest. On the practical level, the question in both instances was moot. The practical need was communication with a dominant majority in order to get along. Never mind that the black speech patterns were prettier than those of the whites or that white Southern spoken English was more graceful than Midwestern. The whole matter of speech was a Southern mark of distinction worthy of the attention of specialists, including semanticists. The Southerner who drawled, no matter what his erudition or, if white, social enlightenment, had two strikes against him in conversation with strangers in the North. It was not really stereotyping, one sometimes felt, but more like the communication barrier between different cultures with different languages. This was much of the problem between the two races in the South in their startled discovery that they couldn't understand what the other was saying.

The results of Atlanta's discriminatory neglect of educational needs of the black children were summed up succinctly in the citizens' report. Fourth-grade pupils in the black schools were more than one year behind pupils in the other schools of the system in median reading scores. By the eighth grade, they were four years behind.

Such statistics always bear the danger of being misread, of implying that by contrast white students were faring well, if in terms of nothing more hopeful than national standards. The Atlanta citizens' group found that in 1966–67, the city was spending $472 per child. By Southern standards, this was high, ranking with such cities of similar per capita income as Houston and New Orleans, running slightly above Columbia and Dallas (both less than $450), and considerably above Memphis ($370). But it was below Miami, and such comparable metropolitan systems as Cleveland, Milwaukee, St. Louis, Baltimore, San Diego, and Los Angeles, all spending between $500 and $600 per pupil, and far below Washington, D. C., and Philadelphia, which were spending above $700 per pupil.[3]

In a 1967–68 ranking of the states on expenditures per pupil, no Southern state was as high as the national average of $619. Louisiana spent the most, $618 per pupil, ranking twenty-first among the states. (But it had large numbers of children in parochial schools.) The others were Florida and Virginia, each spending $554, thirtieth; Georgia, $498, thirty-eighth; Texas, $492, thirty-ninth; North Carolina, $461, forty-fourth; Tennessee, $450, forty-sixth; Arkansas, $441, forty-seventh; South Carolina, $418, forty-eighth; Alabama, $403, forty-ninth; Mississippi, $346, fiftieth. A comparison with 1951 figures showed, despite all the economic improvement since then, little change in the rankings. Of course, the Southern states were spending more in 1964 than in 1951, and all along probably higher percentages of state revenues, and they had more children proportionate to adults in the population. But the rest of the country had increased its expenditures at a faster rate. So even considering the kind of separate but unequal imbalance between education of whites and blacks revealed in the Atlanta statistics, it becomes obvious how badly handicapped Southern children of both races were in the essentials of getting along in America and in solving Southern problems.

The most heartbreaking set of statistics had to do with dropouts. In the 1960 Census listing of school years completed, the medians for the Southern states were: Florida, 10.9; Texas, 10.4; Virginia, 9.9; Alabama, 9.1; Georgia, 9.0; North Carolina, 8.9; Mississippi 8.9; Louisiana, 8.8; South Carolina, 8.7. These compared with the national median of 10.6. Even when it is considered once again that there was great imbalance between white and black per-

[3] All the data on Atlanta schools from "Student Achievement in Atlanta Public Schools," published by Better Schools-Atlanta. The group sought without much immediate success to remedy the situations they described.

formance, like Mississippi's medians of 11.0 for white, and 6.0 for Negroes, with each state at the national median for whites and below it for Negroes,[4] the main import of the figures was to underscore the faith of the people in education (as opposed to the cynical indifference of their political and other leaders). The parents, white and black, got their children to the schools. But the schools failed them.

There were many stories like that very sad one in Harry Caudill's *Night Comes to the Cumberlands*[5] of the mountain white man who sacrificed so terribly to send his son through high school, something never attained in the family before. But the son was unable to find a job locally and went off to California and discovered there that his proud diploma meant nothing; the schools of his state rated so low that he had to take tests to get even a job in a factory. Then, in the final shame and tragedy of Southern education, he found that his schooling hadn't prepared him enough to enable him to pass the tests.

At their best, the public schools in a modern city system like Atlanta's were capable of being warm and cheerful places full of a maternalistic love for the children. They were also the bland and essentially anti-intellectual places that American public schools have come to be, with object lessons to instill standard values, materialism not preached but objectified in the emphasis on buildings and equipment, erudition not openly despised but put in its place by the emphasis on sports. Even the grade schools might have a football team, with coaches and grueling practice sessions and little girl cheerleaders.

High school fraternities and sororities continued to exist

[4] Besides Mississippi's, these medians for white and Negro were respectively: Florida, 11.6, 7.0; Virginia, 10.1, 7.2; North Carolina, 9.8, 7.0; South Carolina, 10.3, 5.9; Georgia, 10.3, 6.1; Tennessee, 9.0, 7.5; Alabama, 10.2, 6.5; Arkansas, 9.5, 6.5; Louisiana, 10.5, 6.0; Texas, 10.8, 8.1.

[5] Harry M. Caudill, *Night Comes to the Cumberlands* (Boston, Atlantic Little-Brown, 1962), pp. 335–36.

in many of the cities with society page attention to their activities, an adolescent institutionalization of the snobbery and anti-democratic tendencies of the adult society. Atlanta had outlawed them in the early 1950s, but there were other involvements of the young, down to the toddlers, in all the complex stratifications (clubs and circles and hierarchies of elitism) of high society that the South continued to take more seriously than the rest of the country did. Similarly, the college fraternity system continued to flourish in the South long after it was abandoned elsewhere to the most backwardly bourgeois kids.

If there had been a regrettable tendency in Southern public education to indulge the young in all manner of frivolity, mostly harmless but not part of the aim of education, and if this continued full tilt into the late 1960s in most of the small cities and towns, there was in Atlanta the example of an overreaction in the large cities even more degrading of the young. When Atlanta abolished the high school fraternities and sororities, it instituted little to replace them as channels for adolescent time and energy, and there were strong evidences of an authoritarian kind of approach, seeking containment rather than development of the young. The educators were becoming policemen, and the police, in their own terrible ways, educated the young.

Another regrettable tendency in the larger cities was a process of school decentralization when much evidence suggested that the nation could not long continue the social and educational wastes of the neighborhood school, New York's complicated Ocean Hill controversy not withstanding. Until 1946, Atlanta, for example, had only four white high schools, accommodating youngsters from every part of the city, with every background, and developing a sense of community between widely disparate elements that lived on in adult affairs. There was similar centralization of Negro high schools. Where such centralized schools continued to exist in the South and where desegregation was advanced beyond tokenism, there was something approaching real community integration, overcoming not only racial barriers but the drear stratifications of subdivision and suburbia as well. But such things were happening mostly in the small cities and towns and these, as we shall see, were only transitional. In this and much else, Atlanta was indeed, sadly, the pace setter. One could sense in Atlanta's previous segregated centralization what real integration of the two cultures in such a large city might be, what richness might be derived. Those inclined to liberalism in race could approach it by diligent exploration into the opposite culture, but among whites and even among Negroes in the late 1960s, the more successful the exploration of the opposite culture, the more likely a cutting off of contact and intimacy within one's own.

Accentuating differentiation, separation, and alienation even more than the classline locations of the public schools were the private schools, catering mainly to children of parents of social ambition or pretension, but also actually the only sources often of quality education, that joyless and forced brand considered necessary for attaining to the better universities outside the region which were considered touchstones of unlimited opportunity. (Harvard ever had its special mystique in the South, imposing on its graduates-come-home mystical and magical qualities beyond the American norm of such superstition, imparting to them individuality beyond even the Southern norm. I met once in a rural area a middle-aged gentleman farmer who affected a ring in his nose and got by with it—a Harvard man.) Middle-class parents were strained in a dilemma of their ambitions for their children, knowing that the big far-off universities offered them the best chance of bettering their fellows economically, but knowing, also, fearing all the alien indoctrination of those places, not the drastic change in social and moral standards reflected in drugs and open sex so much as the standards of modern liberal thought, race, of course, predominant in this. Another sort of dilemma posed itself to parents with liberal leanings in the question of the local private secondary schools. For in addition to being exorbitantly expensive, they were by their nature undemocratic and tended to be anti-liberal. Of the ones in Atlanta, one, sponsored by the Episcopal Church, held out against desegregation long after the public schools capitulated. A sensitive teacher at another of Atlanta's private schools called the students culturally deprived. She told of reading to one of her classes a piece of fiction that described a farm cabin, not a shack but a rustic country home, and of her astonishment to hear expressions of disbelief that anyone lived like that any more. Those parents who took their chances with the scholastic inadequacies of the public schools and lost for their children, some of them, the coveted far-off college opportunities, at least by the late 1960s had the consolation that these, too, were dubious in some of the same ways as the local private schools.

Even more pitiful were the private schools which, since 1954, provided hastily formed retreats from the democracy of the Supreme Court school decision, often without standards or accreditation, and sometimes even lacking sane faculties, neglecting the educational needs of the children for the sake of the parents' prejudices. In 1967–68, there were two hundred of these, with enrollments totaling 40,000, a relatively small but tragically excessive waste amid the dangerous general wastefulness of Southern education.[6]

The approaches of the three largest school systems of

[6] Jim Leeson, "Private Schools For Whites Face Some Hurdles," *Southern Education Report*, November, 1967. All but about a dozen of the schools were in Mississippi, Alabama, Louisiana, South Carolina, and Virginia; none was in Florida or Texas. They were still on the increase in 1968–69, charters sought for twenty-two that year in North Carolina alone. "If the desegregation rate keeps increasing," said an official in a small Louisiana city to a newspaper reporter, "we're going to have to build us a private school. The rate doubled last year." Asked how many Negro children this meant were going to previously all-white schools, he said: "Two."

metropolitan Atlanta nicely sum up the varying ways of Southern city resistance to the law. During a decade the cities were the main targets of the court suits that sought Southern compliance with the 1954 decision. It was only after the 1964 Civil Rights Act that school desegregation spread generally into the towns and rural areas. The cities were sophisticated in their resistance; there was less violence in them and also less desegregation. As late as 1967 –68, Atlanta still had little or no better desegregation than most of the rest of Georgia, and this was the situation generally, a mark of the slow starts in the cities and of their continued ability to thwart court orders and, as in Fulton and DeKalb Counties, HEW guidelines too. In the Atlanta city school system this had been a matter of cunning and trickery; in the Fulton County system, self-righteousness and aggrieved pressuring of federal officials, and in the DeKalb County system, arrogant and crude defiance. Much of the failure of courts and the federal educational bureaucracy to desegregate Southern schools might be summed up in the abilities of Southern school officials in the varieties of dishonesty demonstrated in the three Atlanta approaches, and in the recent pressures they were able to exert against the federal bureaucrats, not the least of which were powerful Southern congressmen as willing to intercede in squabbles over guidelines as they were to try to further weaken the 1964 act itself.

School officials, the men entrusted with teaching the young and with setting educational policy for towns, cities, and states, engaged in more than a decade of defiance and disobedience to fundamental law. The implications of this have not been fully examined, perhaps because they are so revealing, not only about the South but also about education and America as well. It was not, of course, that these school officials across the South considered themselves engaged in dishonesty. In their own lights, they were acting conscionably. They could rationalize their dishonesty in the ways of the professional, with his practical knowledge of the reality of the problems, ranging from racist-conditioned misapprehensions about the educability or sanitary standards of black children to the authoritarian reflex, strong in American education professionalism, of servility to any and all authority, whether that of the PTA or the local government or the state one. The federal government might also have exploited this reflex had its enforcement been more firm (and its evaluation of Southern school professionals more realistic), and the law it sought to enforce less flabby.

And yet in many Southern cities at least one courageous school official sought to counteract the object lesson in sophisticated dishonesty on display before the children. In Atlanta, it had been Mrs. Sarah Mitchell who rose up in one of those moments of wrath that come upon moderate white Southerners to tell their people, like Old Testament prophets, they are full of folly and ruinous. Using her own children's experiences in Atlanta schools and her work with the League of Women Voters, she wrote an article in the Sunday magazine of the Atlanta papers attacking such indecencies as the emphasis upon football over learning, the stinginess, the stupidities. Parental response was strong enough to get her elected to the school board where she precariously fought (like the Southern "nice" lady she was, tactfully, self-depreciatingly, but fiercely) with typical members of such a board, mostly businessmen, mostly opposed in spirit to the meaning of real education. When finally she retired and hopefully suggested to the board several excellent candidates to replace her, they rewarded her efforts by rejecting her choices and electing the vice president of an airline.

Negro public school educators had a sad record in the 1960s, largely because of white control of education. Until the civil rights changes of the decade and with lingering effect after that, they were, in the harshest terms, among the most controlled of all Negro Southerners. The reasons were obvious. Teaching jobs were among the very few above the menial level that were open to educated Negro Southerners up to the late 1960s. They were precious jobs; one did not risk losing such sinecures by offending any of the hierarchy controlling them. This became painfully, often poignantly clear during the civil rights campaigns when these people, among the best educated and most well-off of the Negro community, were unable to join the movement—and some even opposed it. Many suffered a great deal of guilt about it, and there were brave exceptions. A number lost their precious jobs, some of them becoming "professionals" in the civil rights organizations. One such man who was fired in Sumter, South Carolina, in the early 1960s was still working there on voter registration in 1968. But the majority of Negro public school educators, not to mention faculties and administrators at Negro state colleges and even at some private colleges, could not act during the historic days of the South's revolution against racism.

These were the intellectual elite of the Negro South, —not only because most of the best educated had nowhere else to go but teaching, but also because education could more nearly be equated with intellectual ability since ability and ambition, more than money, still determined for many which Negro Southerners got to college. So the movement was in large part deprived of the Negro intellectual elite in the South. Such considerations have seldom been taken into account in assessing weaknesses in the Southern movement, its anti-intellectual strain and susceptibility to irrational impulses, its need of a stabilizing and thoughtful influence to match its incomparable courage and fierce honesty. And when one considers the influence of the Southern movement—particularly of the early SNCC where knowledge and criticism of the condition of the educators was greatest—on the New Left and the campus movement of the late 1960s, there is once more startlement at how much Southern racism in so many hidden ways has influenced the history and direction of America and, indeed, the world.

White teachers, who were not the intellectual elite Negroes were but more of one than in the rest of America and more middle-class, showed similar subjugation. It seems safe to say that a majority of white teachers were against school desegregation when it occurred. But they accepted whatever degrees of it the officials conceded —another paradoxically frightening instance of vitally important functionaries supinely accepting innovation entirely against their personal principles. That in this instance their principles happened to be wrong is no comfort in contemplation of what might happen when there came an order against those principles, most that they held, which were right. No outstanding leadership favoring integration rose out of the ranks of the educators, either. This was true even in the colleges where probably a majority of younger faculty members supported integrated education. Petitions were circulated here and there, and on rare occasions there appeared such courageous men as James Silver, who went beyond befriending beleaguered Negro students to acting against gross injustices of administrators and viciousness of white students. But most educators acquiesced or even supported racism, denying the deepest meanings of the disciplines they were teaching.

Despite a few evidences that stronger enforcement might someday evolve, another development in Atlanta presaged the future of Southern big-city school desegregation. Atlanta's system began desegregating under court order on a grade-a-year plan in 1961, with all grades covered by 1966. Yet each year more and more Negro youngsters were attending segregated schools. Indeed in 1966, when all grades were supposed to be desegregated, there were more black youngsters in segregated schools than in the year of the Supreme Court school decision. This was, of course, because the Negro population of the inner city

was increasing, and the white, decreasing, so that Negro
population was nearing 50 percent in 1969, the year of the
mayoralty election, and Negro pupils made up 62 percent
of the school enrollment. The familiar white exodus to the
suburbs was often sped up by school desegregation as
whites fled any area whose school population neared 50
percent black. School officials, of course, exerted no leadership to persuade parents to experiment in the democracy
of such a situation; indeed, they occasionally abetted the
exodus with advance warnings about black enrollments.
Once more, Atlanta led the way—in the irresponsibility of
white citizenship and other dishonesties of *de facto* segregation. It was, of course, impervious to the 1964 civil rights
law, that statute deliberately designed by an irresponsible
Congress to do deference to big Northern metropolises
which had already collected black majorities in the inner-
cities.

In Atlanta, as in most of the large cities, the cruelties
encountered by Negro youngsters in desegregated schools
were minor contrasted to the terror known in the towns
and rural areas. Robert Coles, with exquisite respect for
the humanity of all people, has written not only about the
Negro children's suffering, but also about the experience
of white children in desegregation.[7] Again, here was
the spectacle of the "adjusted," duteous, young Southerner
who, accepting his parentage and culture, was affronted in
the presence of desegregating Negroes and tended to ugly
actions. He was subject to all the stress of opposing impulses; the natural and cultural one to friendliness to the
black youngsters opposed by the taboo against such friendships, the natural and cultural sense of justice and fair play
opposed by the cultural conditioning against desegregation, as well as by fear of attracting the consensus of cruelty
to himself should he take up for the Negroes. White
youngsters who emerged from this with a new attitude
toward Negroes and segregation—and even those with a

[7] Robert Coles, *Children of Crisis* (Boston, Atlantic Little-Brown, 1967).

new sense of moral uncertainty—were launched on that terrifying, yet ennobling experience of needing to re-examine all the "truths" that childhood conditioning had instilled in them. It was a painful experience, but necessary for the survival of the South, and, increasingly, of the nation.

The pain Negroes knew even in city situations could be devastating. I talked with one of the first nine Negro students to desegregate Atlanta high schools on the day before she was to enter that middle-class white world. She was hopeful, optimistic. When I talked with her again at the end of the year, she emphasized the good things, showing proudly the pitifully few inscriptions by white class-mates in her year book, glossing over such unpleasant incidents as the times food was thrown at her as she sat alone in the school cafeteria, or the administrative effort to keep her from attending an honors banquet. But when I asked her if she still planned to go to the (integrated) Ivy League college she had told me about, she shook her head sharply—no. She would go to (all-black) Spelman College.

Things were more gentle in many of the big-city grade schools. But the teachers' kindnesses had to be understood in their Southern context of condescension and racist conditioning: in that tone of moralizing allowed them in all things (from personal hygiene to religious instruction) a teacher would tell a class of thirty white, middle-class eight-year-olds that in a few moments a colored child would join the class, and we all must be nice to him, no matter how we feel, now musn't we, children? Moreover, many Negro Southern parents of such lonely, little black strangers would understand and be grateful for the warning. White parents would understand it, too, and could assimilate the entire desegregation experience in this way, in the "nice" people's tradition—trying always to avoid personal touch with racism's cruelty, avoiding ever saying "nigger" to a Negro. Thus, at a PTA meeting, a John Birch-style

WASP mama takes in tow the coal-black mama of her child's classmate and introduces her to the other mamas, many of them segregationists, and all, on both sides of the color line, display elaborate manners. To get the feeling of the white's role in it, one should appreciate the sense of charity and pity and yet pride in manners that was involved in the ability of a plain and entirely undistinguished middle-class matron to sit at PTA beside a black man who just happened to be world renowned—the only citizen of the South ever to win the Nobel Peace Prize and by far the greatest man it would ever be her privilege to meet. To know the black's role in such situations, one must understand all the scorn that sophisticated, middle-class blacks have stored up for lesser people than themselves of either race, and most particularly for the gauche or overdressed white female. Despite all its change and big-city modernity, the South of the late 1960s was not a simple place.

In the spring of 1967 one could attend, in such a big Southern city as Atlanta, an all-city musical program with mixed groups of children in bands, orchestras, dancing groups, and choruses, and the mix of black faces and white faces was random, near to balance. In the audience, black sets of proud parents and the stair-step range of brothers and sisters sat alongside white sets of the same, not self-consciously nor even it seemed with any awareness of one another, or that such a thing could not have occurred six years earlier. Such programs represent middle-class striving; it was a middle-class crowd, Southern at that; the double-edged sword of politeness served both races well. Getting in their cars afterward, the big and battered cars, station wagons of families with growing children, they were so many units of sameness, and this must have been apparent to them without their even thinking about it or remarking it.

Beyond the heartbreaking small hopes and large betrayals in the Southern school desegregation situation, such trends as *de facto* segregation, decentralization, and increasingly harsh authoritarian attitudes toward children in the large Southern cities—and maybe in the smaller places too—offered a sense of the great crisis in education that had come upon all of America. In the South, where public schools had been late coming and where action had ever been stressed over erudition, this crisis was best characterized not by the fact that the children hated the schools (for they always had), but by the new way they had of showing it. Possessed of new national values, of a new cynicism, a new idealism, this new generation no longer regarded the schools as an ordeal somehow to be got through, vital to future success. Most eloquently, they disdained the school's own pressures to conform, to succeed. Schoolchildren in the South, from a variety of reports, no longer cheated in order to make passing grades.

IV

Atlanta was a center of higher education for whites and Negroes. This is to say that it had an exceptionally large number of the mediocre, mainly undergraduate institutions that served the South into the late 1960s. The development of Southern higher education is suggested by the few advanced degrees among those awarded in 1962 by all public and private institutions: 86,518 B.A.'s, 13,403 M.A.'s, 1,352 Ph.D.'s. None of the Southern schools, one is tempted to say (though the criteria conflict), was of the first rank. Individual departments or schools of a college had considerable strength or tradition, but no one institution could be compared with the Ivy League or West Coast giants or even with the better institutions of the Midwest.

The predominantly white institutions of Atlanta included most of the kinds of such institutions to be found in the South. Emory University and Agnes Scott College were among the best of the large number of Southern liberal arts and (at Emory) professional schools supported in part by church funds and controlled by the narrowness and public morality of the white Protestant denominations. (In 1967 Agnes Scott still refused to hire Jewish faculty members, but in 1968 it acquiesced after local newspaper publicity and pressure from the American Jewish Committee. Out in the rawer areas, whether to allow students to have dances could still be a policy issue breaking asunder a denominational college's board of trustees.) Oglethorpe College was one of those thinly endowed, struggling little schools which seemed to move in cycles from exciting innovation to hidebound conservatism. Georgia Tech was a state-supported, factory-like engineering school geared almost entirely to the middle-echelon needs of industry, and to the football enthusiasms of small-town old grads. Georgia State College was a state-supported, standard, commuter's liberal arts institution, turning out teachers, corporation and small business employees, and such urban exotica as abstractionist painters and paramedical technicians. An Atlanta suburb had one of the state's junior colleges, part of an effort to contain the numbers of the less prepared (or endowed) of the postwar baby boom. There were similar programs of one kind or another in the other states.

All that is lacking in this profile is the state university, in most of the states located in some small central town, generally the *de rigueur* place to send all but the most obstinately bright of the children of the prominent. Here, football, social life, contacts and a sense of the special tradition of each state are the important things. Political careers are begun at them. The law schools are of more than ordinary importance—training grounds for generations of Southern statesmen and utilities attorneys. Some people smiled wryly at the news of a special foundation program to strengthen the University of Mississippi Law School in the late 1960s: for years its graduates had been using all varieties of legalistic means to thwart public policy and hamstring the Congress itself.

Another kind of law school, possibly more prevalent and more influential in the South than elsewhere, was the unaccredited little factories with no frills or pretense to anything but mechanical preparation for the bar exam, long the jackleg origins of much of the legislative wisdom of the South and even of elements of the judiciary. Similarly unaccredited "business schools" abounded, but these had evolved, taking on frills—pragmatic ones to be sure, but somehow more admirable than the more pretentious offerings of culture on the standard campuses. In addition to bookkeeping, shorthand, typing, and the mysteries of the new office machinery, the young women (and a few young men) in attendance learned a smattering of art (how to recognize the painters and periods and, more to the point, how to talk of paintings), music, literature, and how to act at cocktail parties, or even how to manage the boss's dinner party. The students seem to come mostly from the small towns and farms. They learn to dress in high fashion, to fix their hair and faces tastefully in extreme styles. Each is a formidable "career woman" package when she finishes, with only a flat or nasal accent, the glint of an eye or honest spread of freckles on a nose betraying origins, and this for the most part—particularly if the employer is Southern and wants to feel comfortable around his modishly packaged help—enhances. Here, in the setting of better times, is the old yeomanry of the South, the female of the species: tough, resilient, hard-eyed, enduring, and— sad for the male left behind or gone to the Army or struggling in junior college or trade school—upwardly mobile. Maybe it is merely Scarlett O'Hara.

At the state universities the sport of football was developed just as elaborately as it was nationally, to the neglect of learning. But it was even more raw in the South, as year after year the Southeastern and Southwestern Conference teams ranked highest in all the statistics of yardage and points made, appearing in every listing of All-Americans, while the schools themselves rated among the lowest in all

the indices of endowment and attainment. And yet . . .
Somehow in the worst excesses of the football ceremonials,
there remained an innocence, an exuberant enjoyment of
the whole thing, if not on the playing field, then still in
the stands, an amateur and enthusiast spirit long since
gone from the sports spectacles of California, from the
grim grandstands of the Midwest. They played hard,
mean, romantically tricky football in the South, out of a
hard, mean, tricky school of coaching, still predominantly
Southern in this respect, if not in the recruitment-scandal
line-ups. And in the half-time shows was all the excitement
and innocent corniness of a Fourth of July parade—all that
band music, baton twirling, pretty-girl marching units, all
those kids skilled in undemanding, banal performances,
projected a democratic, town-gathering quality, in contrast
to the highly selective, professional skills of the teams. The
faces in the stands, probably predominantly middle-aged,
reflected the best of the innocence, the anachronistic life-
style of the white South, proudly enjoying this banal exercise of a bygone age's recreation and ritual. The evil in
their innocence, neglect of the real needs of education, is
an expression not of individual irresponsibility but of the
natural values of their society. Somehow it seemed less sinister than the newer evils in the country perverting higher
education to national goals somehow gone crazy, with corporate mindlessness, with war.

Something closer to the national failure could be seen in
the history of desegregation of Southern higher education.
By the late 1960s most of the colleges, after state government or private board crises, were what was called desegregated. Insights into Southern education—so terrible that
they were generally brushed over—were on display during
student riots attendant on desegregation of the University
of Mississippi in 1962 and the University of Georgia in
1961 and the futile attempt to desegregate the University
of Alabama in 1956. But disgrace far deeper than the riots
lay in the performance of administrations and governing

boards of the South's state colleges and universities when they had their days in court.

In his excellent book about the University of Georgia desegregation,[8] Calvin Trillin reviewed the terrible and tragic and typical record not merely of evasion in testimony but of lying under oath by these highest officials of the university and the state system of public colleges. In these federal suits, there was no question about the law; segregation was unconstitutional. So the only defense of states resisting desegregation was to deny a policy of segregation was ever employed to keep Negroes from enrolling at the particular institution. The highest education officials, like those in Georgia, had to get up and swear to lies supporting such an absurd position. This degradation of everything that education must mean occurred down the line in the public school suits. Under such conditions (and they were not ended in the late 1960s), real education cannot be achieved.

Nor can the system of law survive. Trillin quoted Mrs. Constance Baker Motley, attorney in many of the Southern federal cases:

> . . . It's not funny, really. The system is based on people getting on the stand and telling the truth. But people who talk about their respect for tradition and integrity and the Constitution get involved in one lie after another. They're willing to break down the system to keep a Negro out. In Mississippi, university officials got up on the stand and said they had never even discussed the Meredith case. They do the same kind of thing in voting cases . . . This is one of the most serious byproducts of segregation. The people get a disregard for the law. They see supposedly important people get up day after day on the stand and lie.[9]

Have national education figures behaved much differently when other values, other goals have come into con-

---

[8] Calvin Trillin, *An Education in Georgia* (New York, Viking Press, 1963).

[9] Trillin, p. 42.

flict with educational values? The university riots may not have exposed Northern educators quite so nakedly, but many have been shown just as caught up in systems inimical to true education, with the true interest of students, just as incapable of acting for those interests and those alone, as the Southerners were of telling the truth. Perhaps the plight of the Southerner in all his cultural conflicts can best be seen in the helplessness of men elsewhere to act on true principle. The most revered and best-intentioned of modern national statesmen have not been immune. In 1963, all that education might mean for some time to come at the University of Alabama (and in much of the rest of the South) was blighted when the Kennedy Administration allowed then Governor George Wallace to stage his stand in the door of the University of Alabama (incidentally vouchsafing for Wallace the future of his political career of reckless racism). The term had not come into vogue at the time, but it was a political scenario, planned in advance, Wallace allowed the drama of pretending to bow to federal arms before the two Negro students were allowed to enter the campus. (A similar scenario had been planned for Ole Miss but it got out of hand, from all accounts mainly because of a certain denseness, an inability to follow the script on the part of then Governor Ross Barnett.)

Where do we come to an understanding of history, of the reality and meaning underlying the surface appearance we so readily praise or condemn? I remember sitting with other reporters in a Tuscaloosa motel room on the evening of that infamous day of the schoolhouse door stand, in the company of key aides in the Justice Department, which had engineered the thing. We gathered around a television to hear President Kennedy deliver his famous speech demanding across-the-board civil rights legislation after a week of nonviolent demonstrations in more than seven hundred Southern towns and cities. The reporters there included the most knowledgeable of the South and the race issue of the time, a hard audience for such a speech, and as it neared its end, they were agreeing with the Justice Department men that it had been good—apt and honest and to the main points. Then one of the men said, in a tone that indicated the thought came out of many experiences, something to the effect that, yes, the old boy took a long time to do something like this, but once he did, he did it right. No one there, probably least of all we reporters, realized how deeply betrayed and defeated were the noble aims of the speech and the ideals of true education in the events of that day in Tuscaloosa at the University of Alabama.

V

Negro higher education was degraded to lesser degrees by white administrative and political dishonesty. We have noted the control over public school educators and state college faculties and administrators. But there were outstanding examples of courageous leadership from Negro educators even in the state colleges, and more of it from the private colleges. The greatest contribution, particularly of the private colleges, was summed up in the statement of the president of one of them in a small city who explained why he and his faculty had wholeheartedly supported their students in the sit-ins of 1960 and 1961: "We had been teaching the very principles, every single one of them, on which these students acted, as long as this university has existed. How could we fail to back them up?" (After the sit-ins, college students faded out of the Southern civil rights movement as a major force. There were various causes, but not the least of them was the kind of thinking expressed by the late Dr. Rufus Clement, canny, conservative president of Atlanta University, when, after backing the sit-ins, he said that education could not survive if the campus were to continue to be the staging ground for a social revolution. Thus, in the early 1960s, he summed up the conservative position of college administrators that was at the nub of the campus revolts of the late 1960s, a striking example of how the South, like some pilot project, had already experienced in the microcosm of race what the rest of the nation was only beginning to experience.)

The early history of school desegregation litigation centered on higher education and such subterfuges as the old regional compact (one of the few instances of state governmental cooperation in anything) to shunt Negro graduate students to whatever separate-but-equal facilities were available, wherever they might be. Things were only a little improved by the late 1960s; there was still much inequality between predominantly white and black state institutions, and again this reflected only greater and lesser degrees of inadequacy. The thirty-nine surviving private Negro institutions of higher learning were in little better shape. Those in Atlanta were considered among the best, the four undergraduate colleges and graduate school confederation known as the Atlanta University complex, with its adjunctive Interdenominational Theological Seminary. Supported by black Protestant churches or foundations or Southern and Northern business and combinations of these, they had their own problems with conservative boards.[10] Like their counterparts across the South, they had their own hard-to-reshape traditions—turning out teachers and preachers and a few other professionals to fit into the limited and segregated niches in the old Southern society. And because of their struggles with ill-prepared students, they tended to let standards and ambitions remain low even after changes in law provided middle-class opportunities unprecedented in the South in business and the professions. There was debate whether these private

[10] See Robert Terrell, "Black Awareness versus Negro Traditions: Atlanta University Center," *New South*, Vol. 24. No. 1, Winter, 1969, pp. 29–40. He pointed out that the same wealthy white Northerners were on the boards of all five of the Atlanta University schools and in control of their main committees. (The undergraduate colleges are Clark, Morehouse, Spelman, and Morris Brown.)

Negro colleges should be built into first-rank institutions or simply allowed to perish along with the Negro state colleges. But black power doubt about the validity of integration and rightful insistence that true integration would mean improving, not closing black schools—along with the compelling need for any kind of plant for the burgeoning number of Southern college students—tended to make the debate moot. Most, meanwhile, were groping toward some pattern accommodating the concept of black pride, with programs geared to Negro American history and culture and Afro-Asian studies. In addition, civil liberties was being developed as a specialty in Negro law schools, and small numbers of white students with this interest were enrolling in them. Certainly, the urge to replace the black schools with ones run by whites was only an arrogant expression of white-superiority attitudes; like all other Southern schools, they needed to be strengthened.

The smaller, out-of-the-way Negro colleges had a sleepy beauty and a fading but impressive grandeur, of big, well-constructed (usually bespeaking New England good sense), well-designed buildings. Noting their contrast in the 1960s with surrounding squalor of city slums or rural dilapidation, one could sense their past meaning—what such buildings represented to a poor, unsophisticated Negro youngster entering them for the first time. Most of them were built in one of America's better moments of real faith in its ideals, in the days immediately after the slaves were freed, and they had their legends of children and grown men walking across whole states, barefooted, to get to them. Calling themselves colleges, they had to begin with the three R's. With their New England Puritan style and their Southern Negro students accepting and, as always, subtly adapting this white style, they persevered and stubbornly built themselves, if not into the New England models of the best tradition of American education, then certainly into far better institutions than their resources and psychological setting in the segregationist South ("ed-

ucate a nigger and you ruin a good field hand") ever war-
ranted, certainly truer to education's real meaning than
the white colleges. They overemphasized social life and
football, were snobbish and self-centered—they did not
serve the surrounding communities any more than Columbia University did, but Columbia had far less excuse.
But they did keep alive more of a humane love of letters
than most white Southern higher education, and in the
late 1960s they came off well in comparison to the mainline institutions in the rest of the nation.

The development of black power-oriented groups on the
Negro campuses across the South in the school year 1967–
68 was a probably important, mostly heartening new departure—marking the Negro students' return to social
responsibilities for the first time on any regionwide scale
since the sit-ins. These groups were variously called Black
Awareness Committees, Black Awareness Coordinating
Committees, and Black Awareness Youth Groups. There
seemed no regional or national organization behind them;
they sprang up separately, spontaneously. More importantly, in this first period none of the groups seemed to
desire to unite in any way, to form confederations or, as
happened with SNCC, to evolve regional action organizations. They were in the New Left tradition of indigenous
groups working away at local problems, deliberately avoiding broad views, on the supposition that without local
solutions, general efforts are meaningless. (Some day,
surely, as in the old SNCC, both kinds of efforts would be
joined again.) Though the general framework was the
same (study groups concentrating on Negro history, Negro
culture, with some actionist effort in specific crises or in
such matters as voter registration and organization), there
were individual, indigenous differences.

They struggled as much against the elaborate regulations governing conduct and decorum (compulsory
chapel, stringent curfews, even dress requirements) as for
educational reform. The regulations were often a hang-

over from the Victorian notions of the founders but also part of the old Negro strategic tradition of overcompensation, disproving white canards by being zealously more decorous than the whites. (I remember the grudging admiration of the most racist of whites at the Georgia State Capitol for the always superior conduct of the black schoolchildren who came, hand-in-hand, to tour the wonders of that public edifice.) Renunciation of such a strategy—and it was a part of the old SNCC disdain for conventional dress and hairstyles—was of the essence of the justice the new student movement sought. The worst dangers of the movement were of the kind threatening that larger student movement in the world of which theirs was a part —a tendency to dogmatism and uncompensated destructiveness, various expressions of the very lack of real education that they rightfully protested. In some instances the Southern students were going so far as to demand no contact with white culture, banning, for example, symphony concerts. But out of their demands were coming needed reforms and, in the struggles to develop black-oriented curricula, the potential of something innovative and fresh in American education.

As always, whatever dangers existed in the student movement were tame by contrast with the terrifying capacities of reactionary overreaction to such movements of dissidence and protest. The situation in Orangeburg, South Carolina, in 1968 illustrated both the feel of the new black Southern student movement and the terrible response. A small black awareness group of students from South Carolina State College and the private Claflin College began demonstrations in early 1968 at a segregated bowling alley (one of those many segregationist hold-outs the South allowed to continue to taunt, to demoralize Negro citizens), and saw students respond to state police brutality (needless clubbings, abuse of women as well as men students) with near riotous clamor, including rock-throwing for two nights, on the second of which state police fired shotguns

pointblank into a defenseless crowd of the students, hitting
them in the back, on the soles of feet, killing three young
men and injuring thirty young men and women. Besides
being a neat reflection of all the Southern movement's sad
history, from peaceful demonstration to police brutality to
near-riot to lethal police suppression, the episode was the
South's most serious showing to that date of what had become a national tendency to police-state repression out of
fear of riots. From all accounts, the police, over-armed and
in a state of undisciplined panic, opened fire after a student threw a stick at one of their number and he cried,
"I'm hit." They thought he had been shot. Amid all the
national pathos of hysterical mourning after the deaths of
Dr. Martin Luther King, Jr., and Robert F. Kennedy in
the ensuing months, all the denouncing and renunciation
of violence, the state of South Carolina continued to insist,
n the voice of its supposedly moderate governor, Robert F.
McNair, that the shootings had been justified. The press,
including wire services, did a worse than usual job of reporting the shooting itself, leaving the impression that a
riot had occurred and police were shooting in self-defense.
Later, Jack Nelson of the Los Angeles *Times* and other
responsible reporters put the story into perspective. But
after what little furor of concern this created, the nation
forgot Orangeburg. Nearly a year later, when students
demonstrated before state police headquarters, one of their
signs eloquently summarized the situation: "Just Us For
Justice. Doesn't Anybody Else Give a Damn?" The matter
had been presented to a federal grand jury in October,
1968, in Columbia. Indictments were sought against nine
state highway patrolmen under an 1870 statute prohibit-
ing officers from violating a person's civil rights while performing their duty. The grand jury, with two Negro members among twenty-three, refused to indict. Nelson quoted
students who were shot and appeared before the grand
jury as saying the jurors were more interested in trying to
establish that students provoked the attack than in estab-

lishing what actually happened. "They wanted to know how many signs we had and what the signs said," one of the students said. "That's the kind of questions they asked. They just beat around the bush, that's all. I don't trust any white man any more. They're afraid to get us in court, that's what I think."[11] The college newspaper said editorially the hearing was "little more than a legal formality . . . a serious jolt to our faith in American justice." Subsequently the Justice Department filed a criminal information charging the nine with violation of civil rights of the students. The patrolmen were acquitted. Earlier, the Orangeburg students had been able to gain some paltry monetary concessions out of the sorry episode from the state legislature for their school, the only Negro state-supported institution of higher learning in South Carolina. The increase in bitterness among Negroes southwide from the Orangeburg disgrace was great.[12]

The wonder was, as ever, the amount of quietly desperate, grim, and grieving responsibility that Negroes showed, even in Orangeburg. In the days immediately after the shooting, I watched Negro students at their headquarters, the home of Dr. Charles H. Thomas, Jr., a South Carolina State faculty member. The whole thrust of their concern was to compel, somehow, lawful, within-the-system redress. When three youths from Cincinnati showed up at the headquarters seeking bond money for one of their number who had gratuitously clubbed a white reporter from the Washington *Post*, the reaction was quick. Another faculty member there snapped out: "We can't help them. We don't go along with criminals." The others there, students as well as adults, agreed. In the terrible and tense aftermath of the murder of Dr. Martin Luther King, Jr., rioting or near-rioting was at the same minimum it had been all along in the South. At Atlanta University,

11 The Los Angeles *Times*, December 8, 1968.
12 See "Events at Orangeburg," by Pat Watters and Weldon Rougeau, Southern Regional Council, February 25, 1968.

students, including a black awareness group, met and discussed going into the streets. Those urging responsibility, including faculty members (English professor Finley Campbell, the most persuasive), prevailed; a lawful protest march was organized. Similar struggles, between unreasoning, entirely understandable outrage beyond outrage and the old, self-preservative, cold strategy, must have occurred across the South. With students once more rising in protest, it remained a question of how long such persuasion—with so few visible results—could prevail.

But there were many evidences in the South that the situation was still salvable and that there was no need for it to deteriorate into the violent kind of breakdown of all civility that threatened much of America and from which— no matter what the apparent social gains—people who must share an increasingly crowded land may never recover. In Orangeburg, they had begun their demonstrations against the segregated bowling alleys not with anti-honkey tirades but by singing the old freedom songs, ". . . black and white together, we shall overcome." Faculty members and administrations of the two colleges were not separated from the initial effort in a gap of generations and goals, but supported the students.

A 1967 opinion survey of a representative sample of Negro high school students in Atlanta developed a remarkably moderate, even conservative profile, suggesting the reservoir of faith existent even among the young with which the white South and white America might have negotiated, should they have been able to muster good faith of their own. A near majority thought their schools and colleges, the city's race relations, and even the police were good. Seventy-six percent disagreed with separatism and 51 percent advocated nonviolence in protests. Perhaps the most touching index of faith and innocence was their rating of qualities important to getting ahead in life. The quality considered "very important" by the largest number of students (89 percent) was "pleasant personality," and the one deemed important by the fewest (5 percent) was "being slick." Eighty-six percent rated ability as "very important," and only 12 percent so rated "being a white person."[13]

I talked with an extraordinarily personable young man in Spartanburg, South Carolina, during that fateful spring of 1968. He had organized a Black Youth Awareness Coordinating Committee among high school students and dropouts, neighborhood toughs. A high school senior, he had earlier organized a class boycott that won such concessions as teaching of Negro history in the (illegal) all-Negro high school, improvement of the library, and the like. He had led a demonstration that resulted in desegregation of the YMCA and was talking of organizing one large parade of Negroes protesting all the many injustices; it would take his lifetime, he said, to try to pick them off single-shot. Intelligence and humor were in his eyes behind his faddish, round, steel-rimmed glasses; an infectious grin accompanied his telling me, a white stranger, how profoundly he distrusted whites. I had met him in a Negro drugstore where the proprietor was one of those mild, middle-class, middle-aged men of the Negro South who gave time and energy to such activities as voter registration in the same spirit in which their white counterparts worked in charity drives. He had spoken of the youth, Wayne (J. Wayne Watson, it was, when Wayne introduced himself), with affection and pride. *That* Wayne. While I was there, in the midst of an interview, a high school teacher came in and sat down with us, listened, and began interjecting comments, then rebuttals to some of Wayne's standard black power comments, and suddenly the two were deep in, not argument or debate, but discussion, examining, analyzing the points of black power.

---

[13] "Black Youth in a Southern Metropolis," by Dr. James E. Conyers and William J. Farmar, with assistance of Dr. Martin Levin, Southern Regional Council, 1967.

There was a mutual respect, a transcending of the generation gap to warm the heart of Socrates, and there was
a sense of the community that the Negro South's
middle-class life has built. Another adult there ordered
and ate—with no sense of the self-conscious, faddish soul
food cult in the North—an order of pig's knuckles. At one
point, when Wayne said with a grin that, sure, he could see
himself engaged in killing his enemies, the teacher said,
"Aw, Wayne—you ought to understand. You've got the
good life here. You have a place. People like you. You have
our life here. You go doing to yourself what you'll have to
do to get what the white man's got, and you'll find out he
doesn't have anything like what you've already got, doesn't
have anything worth what you'll do to yourself." His argu-
ments throughout were humanist, and full of the Negro
Southerner's sane (not cowardly) wisdom of self-preserva-
tion. Wayne was, in part, enjoying shocking this wisdom
and the teacher's humanist instincts with outrageously
revolutionary sentiment (Oh, yes, I'm aware that the rich
must be destroyed before the poor can get what they
should have: I just want my share) but was also, one felt,
expressing a buried anger, desperation for these grown
men around him. Certainly, they were not offended or
frightened by his views. The teacher was disappointed that
day that Wayne could not have supper with him later in
the week when he would be entertaining an honor student
whom he felt needed to hear Wayne's kind of talk.
"Wayne says he does all that he does for Buckwheat," the
teacher confided to me later, pointing to a little neighborhood Negro boy of the age of the old Our Gang comedy
star. "That's what he calls all those little ones like that."
Wayne had showed himself conversant with the most extreme of the black militant ideas and strategies, had talked
of his lack of hope and faith in democratic procedure, the
normal channels of the American social order. He had also
talked of his loss of religious faith, revealing with more

than usual disingenuousness how much of faith remained in so much of all the Negro avowals of disenchantment, alienation. The teacher had said in answer to some of this, "Aw, yes, yes. I talked to Skeeter down at the pool hall, one of those pool hall boys, and he got to telling me about how there ain't no God, that he knows there ain't no God, because if there was, He wouldn't allow those little babies to starve to death in Mississippi, and I said oh-oh, oh-oh, Wayne's been down here telling Skeeter all this. Skeeter ain't got sense enough to figure that out for himself." Wayne grinned modestly, devilishly. Finally, I asked Wayne how it was that, with all the doubt, distrust, and dismay he felt, he came to be leading his Black Youth Awareness Committee in that most believing of American system activities, voter registration. His face became quite serious. "I guess you could say," said Wayne Watson, J. Wayne Watson, "I am still divided within myself."

Southern white students, meanwhile, were no more a part of the campus movement of the late 1960s than they had been of the great civil rights struggle when it was occurring all around them. For the most part, they, like the colleges they attended, were straining for the blessings and benefits of that which students elsewhere protested, servitude to the military-industrial complex. The ability of that leviathan to have held so much of American education in thralldom becomes more understandable when one considers the denominational colleges of the South. Take a Methodist one. For years, it would have been a creature of the whims, if not purposes, of the Methodist Church, never noted in its Southern branch for rationality. It would have been embroiled always in politics of Southern Methodism, acutely sensitive to the powers of proximate bishops, and further in servitude to the larger individual benefactors of the faith. Administrators and faculty were fully conditioned to control and long accustomed to carrying out mandates irrelevant, if not actually harmful, to education. The colder and more rational controls imposed by the corporate and military mind probably came as a relief.

Most students seemed unaware that there were new masters. Students for a Democratic Society and a Southern version, Southern Students' Organizing Committee (SSOC) had in the heyday of SDS power elsewhere only the most precarious of footholds in the larger institutions. Such small groups as those at the University of Florida and the University of Texas added a few white bodies to the early civil rights demonstrations and later to protests of the Vietnam War. Notable protests did break out in the spring of 1968 at the University of Georgia and at Duke University, perhaps indicating an awakening. The first was put down ruthlessly with the same kind of harsh punishment of leaders and dishonest legalisms that the civil rights movement had experienced, a parallel hopefully not lost on the young whites. The one at Duke was conducted with great decorum, marshals measuring off sit-in spaces and the University president allowing co-eds desiring to sit-in all night before his home to sign out from their dormitories as his house guests. Repression, curtailment of student rights, set in later, and then harsher student protests. Some concessions were gained in both instances; the Duke protest seemed significant for its interest in Negro labor on the campus and its protest of racism.

There were the similarly small beginnings in such manifestations of the New Left as the anti-war coffee houses and enclaves near Southern military bases and the hippie colonies that sprang up in most Southern cities. The latter tended to be milder than those in the rest of the country, less involved with drugs beyond marijuana and more inclined to fun than ideology. They were, however, in their cult idiosyncrasies of dress, if anything more offensive to ordinary folk than elsewhere and were generally roundly persecuted by police. Perhaps the measure of the movement in its Southern manifestations was to be found in the remark in nasal rural accents of a pretty teenaged little

Atlanta hippie girl: "Why we have the bes' time you ever heard of down there, talkin' 'n' dancin' 'n' sittin' 'roun' medy-tatin'."

The national folly and personal tragedy of jailing conscientious objectors had its white as well as black martyrs, probably in representative numbers (which were among the most difficult to ascertain in a nation where all facts that were embarrassing began to be elusive). A brave and hopeful sight out of the past of the South was posed in an anti-war demonstration in 1968 when a young towheaded Southerner, absent without leave from a base which had canceled leaves because of the demonstration, and seventy-three-year-old retired General Hugh Hester, of Hester, North Carolina, together, in the thickest of Southern accents, denounced the Vietnam War. The young man's speech was full of the classical Confederate soldier's disdain for military formality, and the old general's was mostly a critique of the breaks in military and legal precedent going on in the war. But both expressed with great feeling their abhorrence of the waste of human life in that ill-begot war, and this was a notable departure from their shared Southern heritage.

The South did have a proud tradition of dissension and rebelliousness, and not all of its causes had, like the evil of racism, deserved to fail. If, as it seemed in the late 1960s, the nation were only beginning to encounter the kind of soul struggle through dissent and righteous discontent which the South had confronted for more than a decade over race, there were better models that might be followed than the acute statement of conservatism we noted by the late Dr. Clement of Atlanta University.

Through the turbulent 1960s Dr. Lucius Pitts served as president of struggling, unaccredited little Miles College in Birmingham. An entirely middle-class, courtly black gentleman, portly, with balding head fringed in gray, with a gray mustache, eyeglasses, he struggled with fund-raising, campus development, library building, seeking accreditation for his college. His students were involved more than the ordinary in the 1963 police dog and fire hose days of direct action in Birmingham. As black power, in its more appealing forms, later made itself felt on his campus, with its arousal of Negro students to dissatisfaction with conditions of American education, a demonstration of a different kind got underway at Miles, not against the old white segregationist enemy, but against the black bourgeois administration of the college—against the old civil rights warrior, Dr. Pitts, himself. Students marched, seized buildings, and finally gathered outside his office, demanding that he come out and hear them.

The superiority of Dr. Pitts over the kind of manager humanity which has prevailed at the most prestigious mainline universities became apparent later when he recounted the episode. Proud of his students, he knew what it meant for them to be able to rise up against inadequacies in their own institutions, to challenge such a father figure as himself. It meant more, in a way, than rising up against the old white enemy. Further evidence of Dr. Pitts' superiority was his handling of the most dangerous aspect of the situation. Someone, he learned, had in panic called the hated white police of the suburban municipality in which Miles is located. He grabbed the phone, got hold of the chief of police, and told the chief that whatever he did, if he didn't want serious trouble, to keep his men off Miles' campus. He told the chief to phone him if there were any more calls from the campus. "Don't you dare send one of your men here unless you hear me ask for it."

Then he turned to the students, clamoring for him to come out among them. "You tell them," he instructed an aide, "that I'll do no such thing. If they want to deal with me, let them send in their leaders, and we will negotiate in my office." Here was the most impressive mark of all of Dr. Pitts' superiority. He was sure enough of himself, of his own proper role, and knowledgeable enough about his students and about the dynamics of power (he was not merely incapable of lowering his dignity—he was aware of the disadvantage of wrangling with a mob). Thus, he kept his advantage and maintained the dignity and power of his office. He had (with two heart attacks to pay for it) endured the tensions of his role of negotiator and go-between during Birmingham's worst civil rights turmoil, and had lived through the anxiety of white threats to blow up his school and kill him. He was capable of coolly sitting and waiting out the students, who finally did send in their leaders, and then, in the way of aristocrats and kings, Dr. Pitts and his students worked out solutions to the democratic demands of the uprising. Dr. Pitts clearly regarded it all as educational, as part of the education of his students. Obviously, he respected them enough to provide them with a formidable adversary. It was a far cry from Berkeley or Columbia.

VI

The snobbery of the white South, instilled from the start in the young, was founded in the old pretensions to an aristocracy that never existed. In a few of the cities, like Charleston, and many of the small towns this snobbery was attached to notions of family, but it was always—with Atlanta long the most frank and blatant about it—vulnerable in its highest reaches to money, no matter how new or dubiously acquired.

And yet . . . in the absurdity of snobbery whose institutions were so numerous as to include anyone who wanted in, and in the pitifulness of a snobbery based on no particular distinction within an ill-educated, provincial, mass-taste society, there was a kind of energy and even constructiveness. There was a kind of democratic quality; persons of the lowest origin might, with earnestness and diligent conformity, enter into the leadership. One suspected that such people might be doing real harm otherwise engaged, in politics for example. Indeed, much of the success of John

Birchism in the South must have derived from its encouragement of that same dumb patience required to endure club meetings and junior league activity in its own evil designs over the minutia of PTA and other diverse democratic meetings.

The Negro South had its own versions and outlets of snobbery; probably nowhere in Christendom were such institutions as the college fraternity and sorority, the men's lodges, the ladies' clubs, and church work more enthusiastically developed than in the Southern Negro middle class. The Negro's participation in white snobbery since the days of the house slave is, of course, legend, and this survived in its waiter and butler forms, in exquisite forms of the put-down, through all of the upheaval and overturning of racial mores in the 1960s. James McBride Dabbs has suggested that most Southern white snobbery was inspired in its origins and encouraged by the Negro slaves, bringing from Africa a propensity for style and ceremony, and, out of self-interest, involving the white barbarians who owned them in such practices as would enable them, the slaves, to avoid the onerousness of labor. I attended once an annual banquet of the Brotherhood of Pullman Car Porters in Atlanta. In style, in tone, in the demand for perfection, and in sheer splendor, I have never seen anything to equal it.

Out of the South's generally impecunious past and the Negro South's continuing state of impoverishment, class distinctions remained in the 1960s for both races, but more so for Negroes, a matter more of standards and values than of money. The Negro middle class, moneyed or not, seemed in its moral rectitude and devotion to the Protestant Ethic often a generation behind the white South, which has lost most of both. The white middle class often seemed mired down in fascination with material things and ill health, maybe with a more obsessive quality to it than in the rest of the nation. They attended funerals with almost joyous relish. I made these notes on the content of one harrowing conversation of comfortable, middle-aged, middle-class Southerners: "Of new furniture and the family motorboat, of a child operated on for some rare kidney infection, of the pedigree of the dog, of diverse deaths of distant kin, of operations generally, of doctors good and evil, of who among old friends has recently been afflicted with cancer of the prostate, of the country club, of a suicide, of a divorce involving frequent institutionalization of one of the partners for alcoholism, of the construction of a new church building, of the frantic social calendar of the teenage children, of epidemic and rumor of unwholesome condition of the water supply, of other operations, of the elderly kin in nursing homes . . ."

Such concern is not an anomaly to Southern hysterical hypocrisy, the studied ability to ignore the unpleasant and the real, to act as though these don't stare an individual, a family, a society in the face. For it is mostly other people's troubles, other family's ills with which these middle-class jeremiads are concerned, as merely morbid developments of the general Southern propensity for gossip. Maybe one of the main devices Southerners have used to pretend nothing is wrong when nearly everything is has been gossip's ability to abstract the awesome and awful facts of human existence, to project them onto others. In one of his dialogues John Henry Faulk follows the thread of old Southern lady gossip through all of its nuances, from sexual innuendo ("Now mind you, I don't say they's nothing wrong with her settin' out there with that boy—but he goes down to the University of Texas and ever'body knows that's jest a cesspool of atheism and nastiness . . .") to every kind of grotesquery imaginable, from a little boy falling from a tree onto an old gentleman, addling him for life, to a young lady strewn up and down a railroad track when hit by a locomotive, to the terrible accusation that a certain old lady's little old spitz dog has running fits despite all her fierce denials. Of course, gossip is a universal vice and delight of humanity. The suggestion here is merely that it might have a more highly developed function in the South

than elsewhere of catharsis and release for people otherwise blocked from talking about unpleasantnesses.

Fashionableness in dress has not been a notable part of the snobbishness of Southern womanhood (white and black). They seem to come late and infrequently to the extremes of style. Sometimes it seems that it is a matter of sameness, that no matter what their style magazines say about hemlines and necklines, Southern women just wear the same dress, year in and year out, decade after decade. Among those who attain to high style, often there seems something offbeat, a little less or more than should be, as though they were at the mercy of retail store buyers with some fatal flaw of taste or competence, or perhaps contempt for customers, like those main street merchants of the small towns who know that the people who come to them rather than to the bargain racks of the big cities are hopelessly captive and can be sent out arrayed in expensive outfits of three seasons past. Mostly, it was a matter of money. It takes much to change wardrobes each year, as Dallas career women were conditioned by Nieman-Marcus to do. Negro coeds about the South, meantime, with Afros and boots and their own adaptations of mod styles, seemed the most creative feminine fashion element.

Offsetting the more typical disability in dress, if such it were, was the distinctiveness of person still recognizable among Southern women of both races—sure of themselves, of poise, place, and charm, with—chin outthrust—endless, terrible strength. Most of the old Victorian cult of white Southern womanhood was happily gone in the generally healthier, more open climate of the 1960s. But women and sexual attitudes among both sexes and races were probably more repressed, less free than in the rest of the country. How much the cult of pure white Southern womanhood, of sexual panic, remained the basis of racial antagonism in the Southern unconscious, was problematical. Negroes still often repeated the old truism that only the Southern white man and Negro woman were free sexually. But in the

1960s a thoughtful Negro man in a small Southern city could add after speaking the truism: "The Negro doesn't feel the white man as he once did. I don't know if the white man has changed. Maybe he has; maybe he doesn't feel as great as he used to."

One may also be permitted to doubt that the Negro woman in the truism was so greatly blessed, or that she has been guilty of the sinister inferences in the use of the term "matriarchal" to describe her role in Northern and Southern Negro life. Surely, social science has never reduced people to numbers in such a gratuitously cruel way as when it blamed matriarchal family structure for the social pathologies of ghetto and poor Southern Negroes. This struck at the self-respect of both sexes and had a cultural arrogance about it, too; it implied smugly that the norm of white middle-class family structure was preferable and blindly ignored the possibility that something better might evolve. God knows, the patriarchal pattern has not served us well. It is like those American pediatricians who found children in Israel's communal nurseries more secure than the norm of American, family-raised children, and doubted the validity of their tests rather than that of the American cultural norms.

How can the great and beautiful strengths of Negro culture, of all its institutions, including family structure, be ignored? It has become unfashionable to mention, but surely no greater human achievement exists than the Negro Southerner's ability (and it was primarily the Negro's achievement) to humanize somehow the inhuman Southern racial situation, in slavery and through segregation—making it endurable for both races. Those Negro families who served white families for generations in the South and who finally, with sadness, broke away from the old, twisted love between the two races, left to seek better opportunities, better status as human beings were saying—probably consciously more often than not—that they were weary with that one-sided demand on them; they were finished not merely with taking the smallest economic share and suffering all the white contumely, but also bearing the responsibility of holding it all together, making it work. Maybe the explanation of all the pathology in the poor is even simpler than the stark fact that poverty produces pathology, which social science has sought in every conceivable way to avoid. (Blaming it on white racism was as ingeniously designed to catch the discontent off-balance as blaming it on matriarchy was cruel.) Maybe what poor, ghetto Negroes (and whites, too, for that matter) have been saying is that they are weary, too, of trying to fit themselves into all the conformities necessary to get along in a society the basic sanity of which many wise men doubt and where the patterns of conformity cause most average men terrible stress. Maybe, rather than being left out and left behind, the poor were in the vanguard.

One thinks of those Southern whites mainly of the lower middle class with their morbid preoccupation with acquiring and ailing and dying. For such people, most of them middle-aged refugees from rural and small-town life, the simple mechanical complexities of the big-city South are terribly strenuous; getting to the few places they go, complying with tax and other laws that touch them, getting medical attention as they feel they need it, seeking out some kind of activity that has the feel of recreation—those things that ought to be automatic and autonomic drain away most of their physical and intellectual energy as well as their time. (The poor of both races floundered more haplessly on these routines—one reason they were poor.) So many Southern city dwellers are a gray and grim people, as wretched as their conversation suggests, and have not even the unconscious courage to say no more, for they are rightly terrified of the poverty that looms one payday away. Precisely because they are in that terrifying condition the rest of the country dreads, ghetto Negroes especially and the poor generally have been compelled to act.

The South, at any rate, moving toward urbanization and ever more like the rest of America, could no longer explain the conditions of its soul with truisms about the white man and the Negro woman. It was probably not yet finished, however, with race as a major symbolic expression of its worst sexual misgivings and maladjustments. The old perversions of emotion die slowly. I remember the first time I saw an interracial couple in the South, a very black college youth escorting a very blonde young lady, and not gingerly (in the way of the then relatively scarce encounters between the races in the late 1950s), but like any young man dating an extraordinarily pretty young woman, fussing over her wrap, holding her hand, flirting, hugging her. Watching, I felt the startling surge of my Southern conditioning against this and stifled it quickly, but was surely not alone among whites present in this betrayal of all my white liberal beliefs. The young man and his date were attending one of the earlier integrated theaters in Atlanta. No one in the "nice" audience set about to lynch him; indeed, like me, they contrived to act as though they saw this sort of thing every day.

Among the "common" people, of course, both might in those days and into the late 1960s have been in real danger. Without thought, a white civil rights worker went from a late-night meeting with a young white woman and Negro man into an all-night restaurant in 1967 in Montgomery, Alabama, and the two men were attacked and stabbed by whites. On the other hand, during the Freedom Summer of 1964 citizens of Jackson, Mississippi, became conditioned to seeing interracial couples, hand in hand. Their lurid speculations about what went on among such couples were, of course, in the familiar pattern of projection, confirming all the theories of sexual fear as the basis of Southern racism. But the Southern white man had, indeed, changed. More and more frequently, among those white Southerners in daily contact with their Negro fellow Southerners—whether by choice or in accord with the formal requirements of desegregation law—there occurred that hopeful kind of forgetfulness that betrayed the young white man in Montgomery—obliviousness to race and the old artificial cultural pressures.

VII

The condition of the big-city press in the South could generally be judged in terms of Atlanta's two newspapers. Long reputed to be the best and most liberal in the South, they were, indeed, superior to the vast run of dailies in the region, certainly to be preferred to the gross fat slug that the New Orleans *Times-Picayune* degenerated into under the Newhouse chain, heavy with ads and almost devoid of hard news, or the vicious little rodents, rabid and racist beyond rationality, that the Jackson, Mississippi, *Daily News* and *Clarion-Ledger* had been for many years under home ownership of the Hederman family. But Atlanta papers were bad.[14] From make-up to reporting to editorial writing, they had seldom neared greatness and were at times downright incompetent, and seemed, year by year, to get worse.

Like nearly all the Southern papers but maybe even more baldly than most, they refused to pay decent wages to their news staffs. And again characteristically of the South, the management was unwilling to tolerate and exploit standards of excellence in staffers willing to forego decent pay for the pleasure of competent newspapering. Bad professional practices in the Southern press, probably more than in the rest of the nation, drove good men away and demoralized those who stayed, and this was particularly

[14] See "Atlanta in Suspense: Crisis of the *Constitution*," by Arlie Schardt, *The Nation*, December 23, 1968, Vol. 207, No. 22, pp. 679–84, for particulars on failings of both papers. "Despite its unwillingness to become a regional leader, to cover the news adequately, to pay decent wages, or to respect its staff, ANI continues to thrive in its monopoly market. But . . . while Atlanta's population has recently been increasing at the rate of more than 150,000 every five years, daily circulation of both papers has actually decreased," the article summed up (pp. 682–83).

true in Atlanta because the reputation of the papers attracted many of the best of beginners from throughout the South.

It was not really strange that a good many of the nation's top newsmen came out of the South whose newspapers have been so sorry. The proliferation of Southerners in the top echelons of national journalism in the 1960s, though, was something to give one pause; they were all about the upper reaches of the news magazines, the network news agencies, the newspapers with national impact (*The New York Times* most notably, but the Washington *Post* as well) and slick magazines, including the *Saturday Evening Post* before its demise and *Harper's*. It was no wonder that such men left the bad Southern papers as soon as they could; it was more of a puzzle why so many Southerners of high intelligence and ability went into journalism in the first place. A guess would be that until, say, the postwar years, the height of intellectual attainment outside the schools that was visible to a Southern lad of ambition was the editorship of the local newspaper. The Southern penchant for action would make newspapering preferable to being a professor, and the young Southerner's education did little to encourage a view of the world that would suggest loftier ambition—not even in literature, let alone such esoteric pursuits as science or public relations or psychoanalysis. By the 1960s city Southerners were getting beyond such narrowness, but even the largest cities still attached an aura to the journalist that more sophisticated places reserved for the more distinguished and dignified callings. What other large city in the world had, like Atlanta, named its general hospital (Grady Memorial) after a journalist?

The reputation of the two Atlanta papers for "liberalism" was largely undeserved though, once more, by comparison with the dismal no-think right-wingism of most Southern editorial pages, they were indeed far to the left.

This meant in the South being moderate on race or at least not blatantly racist, supporting the national Democrats in their domestic as well as foreign policy after, first, straining against any innovation in social legislation, and urging such reforms at home that did not threaten the tax benefits of the larger business interests. Most Southern city papers, moreover, were jingoist; like the *Constitution,* most threw the usual patriotic support behind the Vietnam War with seeming unawareness that it might be different from previous wars. The Miami *News,* under the late Bill Baggs, was a notable exception. Much of the reputation both Atlanta papers enjoyed nationally was due to the brave and intelligent writings of the late Ralph McGill. The bulk of his braveness was unseen, fighting, like so many good Southern journalists, behind the scenes for decent standards in all phases of operation of the papers. Sadly, his influence behind the scenes waned with the years. And like most of the best of the Southern press and like liberalism generally, he seemed to cling in the late 1960s to an old general strategy that had become obsolete. Since the 1930s this had consisted of a courageous support of the national Democratic Party in its liberal wing against the racism and reactionaryism which controlled the Democratic Party in the South. When national party liberalism in the mid- and late 1960s seemed to have lost its cohesion and effectiveness and, indeed, in foreign and domestic policy seemed often little different from the Southern wing, Mr. McGill and the Southern liberal press generally continued right on with the formula. They seemed unaware or unwilling to admit that there was no longer a cohesive national majority against racism to protect them in their Southern minority stand against it or that the Democratic international and domestic policies were no longer completely supportive of Southern liberal goals on race and economics.

No Southern paper attempted to cover the whole region. Most of the big-city ones did a better job of covering their states and adjacent states than did the Atlanta papers. Their old promise of regional coverage (The *Journal* "Covers Dixie Like the Dew") was unfulfilled, and if these richest of the monopolistic big-city papers wouldn't undertake the task, the others weren't going to try it. In their Southern bureaus the wire services were probably even more bland and "objective" (ignoring any meaning in a story that might offend the politics or prejudices of client papers) than in the rest of the country. Certainly they (especially the Associated Press) were weaker in their abject dependence on the reportage of the local papers because these were so generally bad. The wire services were, of course, caught in a dilemma on such a matter as racial news, between the racist inclinations of their Southern clients and the demands, quite strong during the early 1960s, by the Northern press for coverage sympathetic to civil rights in the South. They were not above tailoring stories to suit both ends of the wire. Equally as damaging as their abilities to serve racist Southern journalism has been their willingness to serve the needs of anti-Southern prejudice in elements of the Northern press.

The thing Southern papers were good at was providing long and detailed accounts of the flavor and specificity of the region, whether in stories about local and state politics or about barbarousness in the never-ending dealings of police and banditry or, not unusual, in exposing local corruption and graft and, increasingly, in honestly telling the story of poverty. From such fine journalism that resulted from the honest work of reporters in the worst as well as the best of the Southern papers, the wire services borrowed nothing, hewing to their own peculiar, colorless professionalism and to their objectivity.

The Southern press was capable of betraying the fine reportage, too, like this from the Atlanta *Constitution* editorial page, generally considered to be the most liberal, most courageous in the South:

MORE FACTS IN WORTH

> On December 4, 1968, the *Constitution* carried an edi-
> torial entitled, "Obscenity in Worth County." We re-
> ported that two schoolgirls were removed from class-
> rooms and carried to a juvenile detention center, and
> that their parents could not discover where the children
> were.
> We now have information that the juvenile court service
> worker made four trips to the parents' home, but was
> unable to locate the parents. That puts a different light
> on the subject.
> We also have new information that the words "damn"
> and "goddamn" were not the only obscene words used.
> Our statement regarding "such medieval, stupid efforts
> at repression" is retracted and we apologize to the Court
> because we had no intention of impugning its motives
> and integrity.[15]

The children in question were Negro; their offense had
stemmed from school desegregation and a contretemps
over where they might sit on a school bus. Massive demonstrations ensued. One *Constitution* editorial-page writer
who resigned shortly thereafter was said to have done so at
least in part because of the editorial. Eugene Patterson,
Pulitzer Prize winning editor, had resigned a short while
previously in disputes with General Manager Jack Tarver
and James Cox, Jr., of the ownership (the Cox chain),
over managerial interference with news and editorial independence.

The big-city press, then, was bland and sanctimonious
and full of an offensive self-satisfaction in the face of
failure to perform even the base function of providing
accurate information, let alone the higher duty of serving
democratic processes, or providing honest leadership of a
city or state or the region. Actually, there were some better
papers in the region than Atlanta's—the Chattanooga
Times, Arkansas *Gazette,* Miami *Herald,* St. Petersburg

[15] Atlanta *Constitution,* December 19, 1968.

Times, maybe one or two more. The best regional coverage has been by the two Southern bureaus of *The New York Times,* the bureaus of the Wall Street *Journal,* and more recently those of the Los Angeles *Times.* But these made no attempt at comprehensive coverage; they lacked the manpower. At the height of the civil rights movement, Claude Sitton of *The New York Times* was alone responsible for covering all eleven Southern states. Later, from two to four men in two *New York Times* bureaus and two in the two Los Angeles *Times* bureaus were trying to do the job. The news magazines had similarly small staffs and the usual problem of good men trying to wedge the truth into the special treatment such publications give to the news.

The *Texas Observer,* published fortnightly in Austin, Texas, was probably as close as any publication in America to the high European standard of informed reportage and commentary. Its concerns have been almost exclusively Texas politics, economic and social conditions, but it has applied to this coverage the kind of intelligence and responsibility that should be the norm for American journalism instead of the extraordinary exception to the rule that it has been. Alone of Southern papers, it has consistently and diligently sought to reveal the *Realpolitik* of Texas (possibly more blatant and ruthless than in any other American state), the vital connection between business and politics which is ignored in the rest of the Southern press as studiedly as sexuality. That this kind of journalism emerged in Texas was probably a result of a combination of factors, including the rawness of the politics and the longevity of the state's liberal movement, approaching by the 1960s that state of maturity which marked the movement in the North, a kind of disarrayed ineffectiveness and schism. The art evidenced in the White House by Lyndon Johnson of destroying liberals by co-opting them had been developed over the years in Texas. The *Observer* developed what al-

most might be called a school of free-swinging, sometimes superficial but always on the mark of reality, word-
loving writing that in such practitioners as Ronnie Dug-
ger, Larry King, Robert Sherrill, and Willie Morris has
spread across liberal journalism generally a new liveliness
and honesty.

Otherwise, the most hopeful, honest journalism in the
South of the 1960s was a variety of underground press,
born of the civil rights movement but continuing in the
darker days of struggles with poverty and black power rationale. These were little Negro community papers, usually mimeographed, crude, unprofessional, but capable of
telling, often poetically, the truth. They filled that vast
gap created by ignoring all Negro news beyond crime and
agitation that was still the rule with most of the Southern
press in the late 1960s. Concessions to demands for something better usually amounted to an occasional photograph of a bride from a prominent Negro family or of an
athlete (though not infrequently Negroes recounted bit-
terly such things as a black winner of a track event not
getting his picture in the paper while a white runner-up in
another event did). The movement community papers
also provided exhortative leadership and often wise editorial advice to readers, and in this were far ahead of the
conventional press. This dispatch from the Freedom Information Service *Mississippi Newsletter* probably conveys
more of the truth of certain Southern conditions than any
material the conventional press carried during all of
1967:

Marion County News

We are all up set in Marion County. Mr. Willie Daniels
was hit by the white professor of Improve School. Mr.
Daniels' children was put out of all white school for a
week. He went to see the professor to get what the children had done. So the professor got angry, hit Mr.
Daniels, then told the laws Mr. Daniels curst him. The
laws put Mr. Daniels in jail just for nothing. We need
something done about that.

We T.C.C.A. workers are yet trying to carry on without funds. We need help. The poor people are yet neglected in Marion County. The poverty program is not helping many poor people. If you are not miss who I am you can't get help at all. Please help T.C.C.A. help poor people.[16]

Reporter—Mrs. Lucille Dukes

These assertions, both from the same issue of the *Low-country Newsletter* of Johns Island, South Carolina, exemplify the flavor and tough intellectual grasp of black militantism at Southern grassroots:

It was a great weakness to go through all the legal channels that the white man had available to black people. We knew that these legal channels were not going to get us anywhere, but we wanted our people who believe in the Federal Government to see that the government is not on our side. This belief was one of our people's greatest weaknesses, but now more and more black people have become aware of where the government stands . . .

—Black Militant Group of Charleston County

There are many black people today that are willing to pay the final note for freedom. We as black people have made the down payment on freedom years ago, and we have been paying notes ever since, not knowing what the balance was. But now we know, and we are going to pay the price and receive the title to our freedom or make sure that nobody else in America is free.[17]

—William Saunders

What more might be said?

There were some more formal units of the underground press, including the *Southern Courier,* a project run mainly by Harvard students who had been involved in the 1964 Freedom Summer, started the paper in 1965, and closed it up in 1968, despairing that it had not in that time altered conditions in the Black Belt of Alabama. It was a

[16] December, 1967.
[17] November 4, 1967.

weekly with standard format, press-printed, of news of Negro Alabama, a service to those people and perhaps an even greater service to people outside Alabama seeking details of its racial affairs. There were a few of the New Left sort of papers, the best of them *The Great Speckled Bird,* published in Atlanta by young whites, some of whom were veterans of the civil rights struggle. It had its own Southern flavor and was capable of criticizing the New Left for calling policemen "pigs" on principles both of human dignity and of pragmatism (urging that poor whites, police and the like had to be proselytized, not further alienated). Older, country-raised Atlantans who bought it under the misapprehension that it would be a fundamentalist religious journal (from the hymn, "The Great Speckled Bird Is the Bible") were shocked at its contents.

The low state of Southern journalism at its big-city best, along with the bad education, poor information, and ugly indoctrination that blocked any political effort to remedy the South's basic ills, was part of a national problem of vital importance. The South would want, should it miraculously begin to develop a responsible and intelligent press, to do better than *The New York Times.* But in this, it had very far to go, even to catch up with the sorry state of affairs in the rest of the country. Not only did its newspapers not perform their basic function; most of them in big cities and small ones did definite disservice.

VIII

As for the varieties of art and artists, even with regionwide notions of renaissance in the 1960s, there was a regrettable tendency to irrelevancy—if not to frivolousness, then to a luxury status in an economy unable to support the basics of existence, in a society long given to repression. Repression of art was not, of course, a main activity of the segregationist system. Rarely, an artist would get in trouble for making some direct comment on race. But the more pernicious effect was upon the spirit of the artist, on the creative impulse, by the mere act of residence in a region of repression. At least the soul of the creator must remain free. The basis of Southern tolerance for the eccentricity of the existence of the artists—and it is genuine tolerance, extended to all manner of deviants, from the town atheist to the village idiot, so long as they are white—has been racial intolerance.

This was evident, for example, when white Atlanta chose to forego hearing fellow Atlantan Mattawilda Dobbs (she refused to appear before a segregated audience) until theaters were desegregated in 1962. They seldom heard in the local press about her world-renowned career though all the while they attended many concerts of local white singers of far less stature (upon whom the press lavished vast attention). Similarly, Leontyne Price's incomparable voice was heard by few whites in her native state of Mississippi until 1967. And that was the year one of Atlanta's high society parties celebrating local performances of the Metropolitan was held without the customary attendance by the cast when Miss Price was substituted at the last minute in one of the lead roles.

So the arts, cut off from the bloody yet beautiful soil of the South's racial reality, its prime reality, have mostly been playthings of the rich and powerful in their more frivolous, harmless moments. They have been caught in systems of dependency, not unlike those of education, and have moved easily into the less arbitrary, less ignorant systems of national foundation grants and federal and even state government subsidies. They have little relevancy to the life of the South or to the mass of the people and, as under the old system of private patronage, have continued to lack spontaneity and originality and have gone on being bland and tame and given to authentic imitation. There were brave efforts in nearly every large city and many of the small places to break away from such a pattern—independent, experimental theaters, dance groups, musical efforts, painting, the like. But these were overshadowed by such pre-emptive moves of public and private power as the craze for massive and expensive "culture centers" and by such degradation of public taste as the high priority placed by governments on sports arenas. Atlanta, setting the pace for the region, exhibited both fallacies fully in the 1960s.

The city's construction in 1965 of its $18 million sports arena at public expense was indictable not only for its raw assertion of priorities—the fun of the well-off was deemed more important than the plight of the poor and the education of the children. Such criticism was answered by proponents of the project—notably, Mayor Ivan Allen, Jr., the single-minded chief of them—in terms of all the wealth the thing would bring in which in turn could be applied to the more serious needs. This, of course, took time that the poor and the children didn't have, and, besides, a precedent in the ordering of priorities had been set.

There was deep damage of another kind in this. For the construction of the stadium clearly reflected the long-range ideal role of the larger cities of the South, as conduits, as service centers, as the places to which most people would be attracted—but not necessarily as places to live. The cities would be places to use, to be serviced by, to travel to from home and back, streaking along the superhighways slapped down across the South as elsewhere, in the federal government's own expression of a dubious value system, misplaced priorities. The cities could avoid the inhuman, insufferable density of those grown up before communication and transportation developments made a community of all America, and, with the barest of intelligent economic and governmental planning, Southerners could continue enjoying the peacefulness of the small cities. In touch with better parts of the metro civilization (again, developable with a minimum of intelligent planning), these small city dwellers could move out of provinciality and narrowness without having to give up the convenience and virtues of smaller places, traveling to and from a mini-metropolis like Atlanta for drama, concerts, art, culture.

But in its leadership role, Atlanta had asserted in its public policy a preference of baseball over the bozarts, and that would seem to sum up the unlikelihood of more rational, more civilized planning by the big cities. It was not, of course, that Atlanta wasn't also more slowly developing facilities for the fine arts—not that the large cities shouldn't offer both (as indeed Houston, Dallas, and Miami were doing with less raw favoritism of sports).

In fact, for once, the South was not lagging behind but moving along, mindlessly for the most part, in the mainstream of such activity—which unfortunately meant that it was concentrating on buildings, on material opulence rather than enhancement of the spiritual and creative aspects of art. In Atlanta, this amounted to public construction of a vast brick barn of a civic center for home shows, boat shows, and the like, and the larger-scale cultural events, including the circus. Atlanta also built itself a culture center through private financing. In the background of this was pathetic irony relevant to the rest of the South. In 1963, a group of 115 Atlanta art patrons off on a holiday tour of European cultural offerings were killed in a plane crash at Orly airfield, outside Paris. By all accounts, they were the more serious of the city's art and civic leaders, the workhorses. They were the kind who might have been expected to sustain an effort underway at the time of the tragedy (it, too, soon died) to involve the mass of the people in affairs of the Atlanta Art Institute. We tend in America, for all our mourning and memorializing, not to acknowledge the terrible effects to society, to civic health from the sudden death of leaders. Other cities had a chance of faring better. In Atlanta, the art institute soon reverted to being the private domain of cliques of high society, its museum unfriendly and intimidating to the mass of the people. Meanwhile, there was a subscription effort for a memorial to those who had been killed. Genuine interest in art would have invested in acquisitions, in faculty and scholarships for the art school. But in the name of the lost leaders, the Atlanta Art Institute elected to build a bigger building from which to discourage the public. It would house, in addition to the visual arts, the performing ones.

When it was completed in the fall of 1968, Ada Louise Huxtable, *The New York Times* architectural specialist, called it "ludicrous . . . backward-looking . . . Caricature Classicism . . . Running Scared Modern . . . a building signifying little except tasteful pomposity."[18] She told in detail the ways the original architect's design—intelligent, indeed imaginative—was eroded by cost factors and whims of important donors and lamented that, in Atlanta and elsewhere, "the design decisions are controlled by a respected and powerful generation that is completely innocent of the architecture of today. The last art that is being encouraged is the art of architecture." She pronounced the final judgment, evident from the beginning: "It seems quite obvious that when all of the resources for culture are being channeled into one monumental effort that can absorb more [money] than is available, the chance diminishes for support of other non-affiliated, more experimental, non-Establishment arts. These enterprises never break even. All they do is provide the talent, style, and new forms and meanings that are what culture is all about."

What culture was still mostly all about in the big-city South was demonstrated in where the heralding of the new center appeared in the Atlanta Sunday paper just prior to its opening—not on the portion of a page devoted each week to music and art, but on the full-color front page of the Society Section, announcing that "in an unprecedented step, Society will makes its formal bow to the city's

18 *The New York Times*, October 13, 1968.

new Memorial Arts Center . . . at a gala drama production followed by a champagne dance."[19] Here is how the paper a few days later described that gala drama production:

> Practically every theatrical art, trick, optical illusion or extravaganza will keep the three-act Seventeenth Century plot ["King Arthur," a fantasy based on a Dryden text] moving toward its opulent finale . . . Among the stunts: flying actors; props operating mechanically such as the "hell mouth" which swallows actors; trees that collapse into rocks or disappear beneath the stage; dragons puffing smoke; and stage settings which completely change in appearance, as if by magic, without benefit of a closed curtain.[20]

The opening night performance tickets were $100, not to help pay for the center, but for the production—which cost $250,000.

In controversy over the Atlanta sports stadium, statistics were produced to show larger total audiences for artistic events annually than for sports events. There were far more of the artistic events, however, often involving the same people in the audiences over and over. Most of the people, black and white, "common" or "nice," used television as their main source of sports and culture, and they had the other mass media. So the struggling little efforts at art, at culture (barn theaters popping up in unlikely little towns, the outdoor exhibits of paintings, informal and attractive to the masses, the college-related activities), and even the culture center kind of thing were not only an important part of the South's struggle to free itself from its own distinctive ailments—its inability to think or feel wholly—but were also a part of a larger, little noted effort across America to resist somehow the influences of the mass media, standardizing and debasing adult taste, whatever their mystic and (if one may follow McLuhan at all)

19 The Atlanta *Journal-Constitution*, September 29, 1968.
20 The Atlanta *Journal-Constitution*, October 13, 1968.

organic effect on the young. In the 1960s this movement in the South was still fragile, almost as frail as when Mencken sneered at it in "Sahara of the Bozart" in the 1920s. Houston, with its oil wealth, came closer to possessing what all the South had lacked when Mencken wrote, but the rest of the big cities were without one or the other of a first-rate art museum, first-rate symphony, composers of any rank, real artists. Atlanta, for example, had no museum of the sciences at all. Its public library in 1968, after all the sports and arts construction, remained cramped in 80,000 square feet of space when it needed 200,000. It spent $1.90 per capita on its library system compared with a national average of $4.75. Charlotte and Knoxville were spending $3.25, Dallas, $3.75, and Memphis, $2.70—none were up to the national average. Atlanta's library director, Carlton C. Rochell, summed up the situation for most of the South when he said of Atlanta: "Tragically, public apathy has also been a direct result [of inadequate facilities]. Not knowing what a progressive library program can and should mean to the community, the public has no basis of comparison."[21] All the while, over all effort toward a free and full cultural development, there hung the knowledge that any expenditures, public or private, were, like the Atlanta stadium, at the expense of more basic needs of the people. Which was more important—an adequate library system or school system? First things had not anywhere in the South been put first.

The people reflected this in their own cultural predilections beyond the mass media. They liked all-night gospel sings, wrestling matches, automobile races, musical comedy. Atlanta's Theater Under the Stars probably came as close as anything to the level of "nice" people's taste in the South; it and numerous counterparts in other cities gave devotees long summer seasons of musical comedy's banal bastardization of all the performing arts, satisfied for them the national lust for celebrities in the presence of imported

[21] The Atlanta *Journal*, November 9, 1968.

leads, and gave them a sense of pride in the local talent
filling out the casts—all of this pleasurably presented amid
trees and the magic of Southern summer night. It was fine
for the family, toddlers to grandparents.

More traditionally or deeply, Southerners of all types
cherished local curiosities, like Atlanta's Cyclorama and
Stone Mountain. The former was a grotesquery of the
nineteenth century, a 50-foot-high, 400-foot-round painting of the Battle of Atlanta with plaster of Paris model
extensions of the painting being shot and bleeding all over
the ground. City-owned (and deteriorating from water
seepage), it was desegregated in the early 1960s for whatever black citizens wanted to view its pro-Confederacy version of history. (Yet, irony of ironies, as late as 1968, the
privately administered Wren's Nest, the museum home of
Joel Chandler Harris, creator of Uncle Remus, had not
been desegregated.) In the basement of the Cyclorama,
amid the usual bird nests and stuffed snakes, was the steam
engine "Texas," one of the two used in the Andrews Raid
adventure of the Civil War, cheapened by Walt Disney in
"The Great Locomotive Chase." (Nashville, from a past
welling of civic celebration, had itself a replica of the
Parthenon which, somehow, its creators had contrived to
make ugly and graceless. The Fugitive poet Donald Davidson was reputed to have cried every time he looked upon
it.)

Stone Mountain was a once awesomely beautiful hunk
of solid granite on Atlanta's outskirts, 1,683 feet high, in
ancient times sacred to the Indians and more recently a
trysting place for generations of Atlantans and the site of
many Ku Klux Klan meetings. Gutzon Borglum, before
going on to more ambitious things at Mount Rushmore,
defaced Stone Mountain around the turn of the century
with a gargantuan carving memorializing the Confederacy.
He became embroiled with the sponsors in some complicated quarrel and left the thing uncompleted, leaving
General Lee and his fellows and their horses footless, all

raggedy-edged and ghostly—a fitting symbol, some said. Vowing to complete the carving, the state of Georgia acquired the mountain in the 1960s, turned it into a Disneyland-like tourist attraction with exorbitant prices, and succeeded in what even Borglum and the Klan had been unable to do—robbing the mountain of its majesty and dignity.

These were the kind of places closest to the hearts of most of the people. And how different were these people from those who put on tuxedos and airs at the more high-falutin cultural events?

At the symphony concerts, actually, only a few men wore tuxedos and tails—most were in business suits—while the women were more splendid, showing off their jewelry and bosoms. Older couples, probably predominant, would be on the Maggie and Jiggs model (she fierce in the quest, he dragged along), but with variations, the best of them involving that Southern archetype, the doting husband. Beaming and beautifully genial, he came here as to grand balls, fox hunts, what have you, oblivious to content, just happy to be along with his beloved. Or so he seems. The old fellows nod and sometimes nap, tapping their black square toed shoes to the Mendelssohn; their ladies strain to the music as their mamas did to the preacher. The younger couples have their own models of these types but have also college-course familiarity with the music (seldom venturing, anyhow, into the unsettling departures from the late nineteenth century), and some will have their children along like flowers scattered through the audience, wistfully seeking something fine for them. The music, like the church service of the Southern past, is to be gotten through; the real fun (and often, there is real meaning) comes before the performance and during intermission and afterward, when the people can be together, greet friends, chat, gossip, laugh, admire and envy one another's getups. The lasting impression of such evenings is the set faces during the performance, not of course suffering or

enduring, just cut off from it, as from most of the tim
consuming minutiae of their lives—club meetings, busine
rituals, church. Their minds dwell on who knows wh
secret inner resources, or maybe dwell on nothing at al
having come to their own Southern versions (how ofte
the South seems touched of the mystical East) of medit
tive detachment, escape of the consciousness from boc
and mind. The old pink-faced gentleman with his fu
head of snow-white hair shows no sign on his face or in h
soft hands that life has ever touched him harshly or d
manded anything of him: tapping his foot, he smiles, wa
ing to a friend; his wife's hair is honestly undyed and h
face, similarly unlined, hints at the beauty of her past
with a fur, in the early spring heat, on her shoulders, s
bends forward, peering with opera glasses at—what? T
violin section, local folk mostly, moonlighters, sawi
gamely away? Bravo, bravo, at least one of the gentlem
will shout, showing he knows a thing or two, when a rou
ing rendition of *Scheherazade* finally is wound and twirl
through.

It is civilized, in a way pathetic, but pretty to see,
speaking the very best instincts, yearnings in the Sout
Under Robert Shaw, the Atlanta Symphony was attem
ing to attract broader audiences, including children a
black people. But despite such efforts, in the South ge
erally symphonies and the like seldom touched even t
struggling middle-class of young people one might find
such evenings in larger cities elsewhere in the nation a
as sadly true across the nation, had nothing whatsoever
do with the life of the mass of the people, not merely t
poorest, but the majority of the population. Those g
people hovering precariously just above the poverty li
are most in need of the touch not only of the music, w
its hint of grandeurs of the past, but of the dignity a
civilized decorum of such an evening—its imparting a f
ing of having done something worthwhile, enriching, a
beyond this, for the more alive, the primitive pound

pure joy of the music that makes you when you walk out throw back your head and laugh, or catch a tree branch.

IX

The South had a penchant, always had had, for leisure, and maybe that touch of mysticism one keeps sensing. But it seemed unlikely that it would emerge as a center of original, creative art, or even as a leader in mass appreciation of fine art, unlikely that it would somehow show America how to break the evil spell of television, lift national standards and taste. And yet . . .

The only truly original innovation in art to emerge in America came out of the South—Negro jazz. Close to it in spirit and continuing vigor was another distinctive Southern art form, country music.

The enormous influence of jazz—not merely on the music of the world, to the highest reaches of serious music, but on world culture, with its pervasively freeing, energizing effect on people—has not been fully celebrated by America somehow, certainly not fully recognized by the mass of people. Likely a measure of prejudice has been involved . . . and snobbishness, and that arrogance summed up in the term, "culturally deprived" as automatically and undisputedly applied to Negroes, to Southerners. Related to this has been the watering down of jazz, cheapening it for mass consumption, not in response to the public but out of contempt for it—part of that ugly assumption in much of pop culture that Americans are incapable of enjoying genuinely good music or movies, books, entertainment, what have you. That jazz not only survived this but kept developing on its own has been testimony to its strength, living as it did an almost underground existence, always fraught with danger because it was integrated and despised for its drug use and dress peculiarities long before these became the focus of generational battle, cultural crisis. It is testimony also to a strength of taste in America, that same strength to which the underground movies and similar institutions paralleling the mass media came to appeal.

Country music was a kind of precursor of these parallel institutions, existing on its own first in Atlanta, then in Nashville with record and sheet music companies, responding to, respecting public taste rather than debasing it. I have heard it all my life on Southern radio stations and jukeboxes; we called it hillbilly and "nice" people scorned it, preferring the watered-down jazz. Like jazz, it has survived and developed with its integrity intact, and the two musics have come together as most of the basis of the psychedelic and rock music with their distinct literary tone.

In the late 1960s it was still possible to travel the backroads of the South and to find old Negro men playing guitars, twelve-string guitars, banjos, more fanciful homemade instruments, and singing the old songs, some religious, some the field hollers, some the street songs and blues that the black troubadour beggars used to sing in the cities—Blind Lemon Jefferson, Huddie Leadbetter, all part of the prime source of early jazz. Old early jazzmen, their instruments put away or sold, were to be found too, only too happy to get to the music again, given the chance. One of the unseen tragedies of the South was the small amount and the haphazard, unsystemized quality of recording not only of music, but of the tall tales and folklore and wonderous varieties of speech, of dialect out of the past still abundant across the South, but dying as the older people passed on, never to be available again.

Part of the origins of country music were out there too, a little more extensively collected, in the mountain songs, hoedowns, and country ballads of the whites. Country music, more than any other, has kept close contact with the conditions of ordinary life in contemporary culture, singing of jet airplanes, billboards, the PTA, truck driving, mini-skirts. Negro music has centered on emotions, states of feeling. "You can't jump a big jet plane," sings the country song. But the blues talks about: "I'm goin' back to the Delta where that I have got no fear . . ." The one music has been sociological; the other, psychological. But they have been akin in their shared concreteness, stubborn authenticity of language, vividness of imagery, and, most of all, faithfulness to the reality of the human condition. Humor in both tends to be heavy-handed, tending to sexual double entendre in jazz, to riddle-song surprise endings in country (like the man whose great-granddaddy cut all his kinpeople out of his will and left all his fabulous wealth, described in great detail, to Sally who loves only the singer—Sally finally turning out to be a lovely, brown-eyed cocker spaniel). In both musics, the Southern penchant for the specific and for the feeling for place is strong. "And I looked down on the house where I used to live . . ." And both are heavy on the basics of life, of love and all its joys and tribulations, of marriage and childrearing, of sickness ("I've got the tee-bee blues"), of death. Johnny Cash laments in one of his country songs, "Mister Garfield's been shot down, shot down, shot down," getting into the words all the helpless, shocked outrage of decent people at the senseless killing of humane leadership, and into them, too, the deeper theme of man's appalled knowledge of death. The ability of the music to probe the basics of life may be akin to the Southern love of gossip, another outlet for generalized statement about things not discussed in the specific by Southerners.

Protest has entered into both musics, neither as a dominant theme nor faddishly nor even topically, but as a natural expression of one part of the lives of the people they reflect. Bessie Smith asks the rich man where he would be "If it wasn't for the po' man." Johnny Cash almost snarls, "Call him drunken Ira Hayes" . . . the lament of his degradation by prejudice and sordid death denouncing not only the disgrace of America's treatment of the one Indian among the six men raising the flag at Iwo Jima in the famous World War II photograph, but of its treatment of all Indians.

They have borrowed from each other, too, the two musics, the blues heavily influencing, for example, such a country song as "Detroit City," a hymn, a requiem for all those Southerners, white and black, dislocated and lost in the trek North after a better life, with that never-ending sigh of the transplanted Southerner perfectly rendered: "Oh, Lord, I want to go home." Surely the most sensational acknowledgment of the common bonds of the two musics has been the emergence of Country Charlie Pride, a country music singer who happens to be Negro. His musicianship, his enunciations, tonal qualities (including the nasal twang) have made him not some curiosity on the Grand Ole Opry circuit, but an acknowledged favorite. A person who was on the scene told me whites came flocking to the Ernest Tubb music shop in Nashville to buy Country Charlie's first album, having heard it on radio, but when they saw on the jacket the color of the artist's face, many of them flung the album down and walked out, angry, betrayed. But as they kept hearing him sing, they began coming back, ultimate acknowledgement of art and their own devotion in the command, "Gimme that album by that nigger country singer . . ." It was unlikely that all the combined forces of civil rights organizations, church, government, or even integrated athletics had worked as much good for race relations on the whites of the South most in need of it as had Country Charlie.

Such music has served Southerners in the way that well-wishers have wanted the more conventional forms of Western culture to work—intimately, deep within their private and public life. What will you do at your peace vigil, the excited voice of a network announcer asked a Florida delegate to the 1968 Democratic National Convention, and, drawling amidst the debacle of that event, the delegate replied out of all his good white liberal, innocent experience: "Aw, we'll probably just come back here in the hall and sing."

Negro music and country music in two of their developments, church singing and labor songs, came together to provide much of the spiritual force of the civil rights movement of the early 1960s.[22] Much of the South's paradoxical plight, the kinship of the cultures of the two races, the artificial antagonism, was apparent in this intermingling, this true integration of their music. Much, too, could be seen of the differences in style, in psychological tone of the two cultures in their differing treatments of the same songs. I remember listening to an SCLC field worker lining out the flat words and singsong tune of "We Shall Not Be Moved," derived from an old hymn, at a mass meeting in Albany, Georgia, in 1961, and hearing it transformed into a swelling, polyphonic paean by the Albany Negroes, pouring into it all kinds of subtleties and slynesses of rhythm and tone and intonation.

It is possible to make too much of the phenomenon, but this kind of integral, deep-rooted role of music (art) in the life of Southerners has been a remarkable thing for our age. It was suggestive of what art might really be: not the imposition of self-conscious "folksy" propaganda songs or paintings on situations of Southern life and not the pitiful and pale things produced out of the perversion of art into snobbery, but the real, the powerful thrust of art through the bodies of individuals and society and events, a great energy, an ennobling influence.

That other strength of indigenous Southern culture, the great outpouring of writing that has occurred since the 1920s, was more a part of national than of Southern culture, a participation in a freeing of the creative impulse

22 See "Hear the Music Ringing," by Glyn Thomas, in *New South*, Vol. 23, No. 3, Summer, 1968, pp. 37–47. He traces development of songs from country music and Negro hymnals to their labor union versions to their civil rights versions, including, "We Shall Overcome."

that was international in scope. One reason Southerners were able to participate in this national renaissance was because writing has a national financial base; evidence that dependence on the Southern economy inhibits a writer, hampers his freedom, is presented in the problems of Southern journalists.

The Fugitives were as close as the South has ever come to developing a formal, self-conscious literary movement. They were a group of writers, poets mainly, who banded together at Vanderbilt University in Nashville, Tennessee, from the late 1920s to the early 1940s. They included John Crowe Ransom and Allen Tate, leaders of the group, Robert Penn Warren, Donald Davidson and Caroline Gordon. Their movement, however, illustrated the national rather than regional thrust of most Southern writing. The main thing Southern about it was that its members were born or were working in the South; much of their material was Southern, but their treatment of it was in national and international vogues. Their criticism was even more so. It was only when some of them (with varying tenacity) moved into social and quasi-political theory, the Agrarian nonsense, that they became intrinsically Southern. The mark of this was surely the suicidal Southern ability to choose the most ruinous of institutions, in this case a hopeless system of agriculture, as the foundation upon which to try to preserve the best of Southern traits—independence, individualism, close human touch with nature, with humanity, not to mention that grand foreshadowing of SNCC, New Left, Marcusian, Birchite ideology, decentralization. Their Agrarian Movement was the failure that it deserved to be, and in this they were more Southern than in anything else; the Southern willingness to fail, to be defeated, comes from having tasted the gall of defeat and knowing it can be endured. It makes one capable of risking it again and eventually, maybe, of winning.

Indeed, such was their literary movement—eminently

successful, influential, popularizing, if not inventing, the
principles of the New Criticism, and founding such important literary magazines as the *Fugitive* in Nashville, the
Southern Review which later became the *Kenyon Review,*
and the *Sewanee Review,* and indirectly inspiring the
Hudson Review. They were men of great literary ability,
but it was in the national, not Southern arena that they
achieved literary success. The contemporary Southern
group with whose sociopolitical ideas their Agrarian fan-
tasies greatly contrasted, the Regionalists (Dr. Odum, Dr.
Johnson, *et al.* at the University of North Carolina), was
also rather than a unique regional phenomenon, the
Southern expression of the national mainstream—oriented
to the New Deal, liberalism, sane planning. Theirs was a
great achievement, indeed the model for any distinctive
future development of Southern culture, whether in tourist attractions, race relations, or literature—not something
entirely different from the rest of America but something
which is an intrinsic Southern version of mainstream
thought, technique, theory. The Regionalists loved the
virtues of the South and the people of its vices fully as
much as the Fugitives, and their abilities, maybe even
their literary abilities, were equally great, but they poured
their efforts into the plodding prose of the social sciences.

In the days when it flourished in the South, the civil
rights movement attracted much journalistic attention and
some important serious writing. Unfortunately, much of
the vast amount of informal writing from within the
movement has been lost—letters, diaries, field reports,
poetry, school work of youngsters in the Freedom Schools.
Perhaps, in the fast action of historical event the bulk of
all such writing, all that expression of the immediacy, is
lost. Even the accumulations of records and reports, photographs and tape recordings that SNCC once had seem to
have been scattered. CORE's collection happily remained
intact. (Efforts to gather together movement materials

have been underway, the most notable the Martin Luther
King, Jr., library in Atlanta, formed as a memorial after
the assassination.) It was not a self-conscious movement;
indeed, it lost much from an inability to show itself in its
true grandeur to a nation, a press at the time eager for
material about it. Of the writing from within the movement that did get published, among the most authentic
were: *Letters From Mississippi,* from volunteers in the
1964 Freedom Summer, reflecting its mood and spirit, collected and sensitively edited by Elizabeth Sutherland, and
I Play Flute, a haunting book of poetry mainly of Mississippi movement days by Jane Stembridge, formerly of
SNCC.

Most of the writing about the movement was done by
whites. Of Negroes who were too busy participating in it
to write until later, Stokely Carmichael (with Charles V.
Hamilton) in *Black Power: The Politics of Liberation in
America,* drew less than one might hope on the details, the
feel of his Southern experience, his knowledge of the
greatness of the Negro people he worked with. Something
nearer to what he might have done was Julius Lester's
Watch Out Whitey! Black Power's Gon' Get Your Mama.
Endowed with a real writing (as well as photographic and
musical) talent, he has come as close as anyone probably
will to expressing the sound and sane aspects of black
power, to making the reader see events (with which he
might have been previously familiar) from its special, in-
furiated perspective.

But in the big Southern cities (and smaller places, too),
where momentous, haphazardly recorded history was occurring all around, it was not likely that such books as
were written about the movement—or any others—were
much read. The South has never contained readers in
comparable quantity to its proportion of writers. And its
level of taste was no better (nor worse) than the rest of
America's. If it preferred Harnett Kane to Faulkner, had
in the past doted over Frank Staunton, doggerel poet of

Atlanta who created "Mighty Lak a Rose," in preference to Georgia's other nineteenth century contribution to American poetry, Sidney Lanier, that was little different from the popular taste of the nation, choosing not Faulkner or Eudora Welty, but Atlanta's other notable contribution to American letters, Margaret Mitchell's *Gone With the Wind*.

X

What lay deeper down, more profound—integrated, abstract, totem expression of a people, their culture, their psychology? I went once on a cold winter's day, with a bottle of Jack Daniels sour mash whiskey for sipping among three of us, to a backwoods clearing, the turnoff from the dirt road marked by a dead hawk hung on a tree, to a clandestine gathering of Southern country white men who still persist in the illegal sport of cockfighting. There was a barn fitted out with grandstands and a cement circle, and there was a crowd of men, mostly in overalls, and there were trainers and owners, and there were the cocks, every ounce of them belligerent. I had expected to be sickened, to gaze once more in a new context into the depths of the ugly and demented side of the white South's psyche. I found something quite different. There was dignity in the people there, the dignity of *aficionados* (the cross-lingual reference is appropriate; what might the South be if its violence might be respectably ritualized?), and there was majestic seriousness to the undertaking, to the elaborate ritual of the actual pitting of the cocks against each other, and there was great decorum through the long day of the contests with its constant and impressively large betting and its equally constant whiskey sipping, and there was camaraderie, again dignified and decorous, among all of us there so involved together, and there was, most of all, the expression, abstractly, of the virtues of the crowd, of a people, a culture, expressed by the fighting cocks—the chickens, the crowd called them, "That red chicken's a game un"; "Git 'im yeller, git 'im yeller chicken": ferocity, braveness, endurance, stubbornness, stubborn refusal to lie down, to die, gallantry. I went expecting to scorn, to find the cocks in their ritual suffering, ritual death, of a higher order of animal than the men pitting them against each other, a reproach to them. I found instead a real bond between the men and the game cocks—the trainer gently, lovingly, picking up his downed bird and literally breathing life back into him, the limp head in his mouth, then thrusting, throwing the revived warrior back into the battle, neck arched, feathers ruffled all over him, silent and deadly purposeful, like as not, to win. The realization came early that the birds were bred to battle, delighted in it, had no other meaning. The realization came slower of all the care and love of this spectacle that was expressed even in the construction of the grandstands, the fighting pit, a feeling not to be found in the physical constructions centered on art and culture in the South. The final realization was a matter of years in coming, the understanding of why, in this barbarous, illicit setting, I had felt more rapport with, more respect for my fellow white Southerners than I ever had before, and more strongly experienced that old, gnawing wish—that somehow, somehow they might find the way to the true dignity and majesty of what they are.

XI

The city Southerner grows Bermuda grass with the same ferocious intensity with which the farmer Southerner fought it out of his fields. The city Southerner prides himself on his green lawn as the country Southerner did on his bare-dirt, broom-swept yard. The origin of these efforts was the same. The South was no longer rural but not really urban, and the cities were something big and unplanned and largely unintelligent sprawling out over the ruins of the old, doomed agriculture. If the main inanities and dangers that festered in the more mature cities outside the South were to be avoided, if something better than them were to be developed, it would surely be out of the honest roots, the surviving good of the old South, like the love of land, of place, of home. In the yards and gardens, beyond ordinary American compulsion, and beyond the routine services of the yardman in those neighborhoods where still he trundled his hand mower, as ancient and patched-up as himself, city Southerners lavished work and skill on growing things; this love of digging in the dirt, of the whole miraculous process of germination and growth, blossoming and harvesting, was as fervent in the slum sections (tiny yards covered in every inch of sandy soil with bright-hued flowers) as on the professionally landscaped estates, and most fervent of all in the grim stretches of sameness in the suburbs. But was there any awareness that this was of a pattern of inherited virtue to be proud of and nurtured; was there any realization that the cock fights shouldn't have to be hidden, illicit?

In their public life, the large cities showed little inclination to draw on that which had been good in the past. In the early 1960s, Atlantans presumed that the rest of the country admired the city's performance in race relations, abhorring the racist displays in other Southern cities. But it became clear in subsequent years that the difference between the bad-image Southern cities and the major cities of the rest of the country, once these were face-to-face with demonstrations or racial disorders, was only that the Southern ones seemed mild by comparison. (Compare the fire hoses and police dogs of 1963 Birmingham with the run-amok rifle fire in Detroit and Newark, or the Albany and Jackson police with Chicago's at the 1968 convention.) Even so, by the late 1960s, the old bad-image Southern cities, having seen the error of their ways, having seen all the monetary advances Atlanta's good image had gained, had moved in tone to image-seeking super-respectability: Jackson and Birmingham were as greedy for good publicity as Atlanta had ever been. (Birmingham's state-supported extravagance in building a $34-million culture center was part of a campaign begun soon after the police dog disgraces to overcome that bad image.) Atlanta, ever attuned to the rest of the nation in such things as advancement into ghettoism, police overreaction to near-riot, arrogant contempt for needs and protests of Negro citizens —evident not yet at the heart of its city government but in branches of it, like the school board—seemed moving toward the uglier aspects of the worst of urban America. This was not pronounced, maybe not even permanent, just a sense of impending ugliness, rancor, the hints of it coming as swiftly and ephemerally but as real as all those jet streaks across the Atlanta sky at noon.

Atlanta's early success in image-building was mostly as observers had described it—the product of a rather more powerful and intelligent power structure than most Southern cities possessed. Power structure has become a term to conjure with in the South (not the least cause, overly literal interpretations of Floyd Hunter's book, *Community Power Structure*,[23] in which he described Atlanta's upper and middle-class rulers with disguised identities). There was generally a tendency to concede too much power to the power structures in all the Southern big cities, and crossroads hamlets for that matter.[24] The truth was that, in Atlanta and probably to a greater degree in the other cities, only in fits and starts, usually in some crisis, some threat to private interest, did the power structure function. Moreover, within power structures, there were feuds

---

[23] Chapel Hill, University of North Carolina Press, 1953.

[24] You have to hang onto your sense of humor contemplating the South. The power structure of one little hamlet fell upon evil days in late 1968. Almost within a week, the mayor was found guilty of thieving from the town bank the prodigious sum of $2,000, and the entire Democratic Committee was upbraided for refusing to turn back to the central party funds left over after primary election expenses from candidate entry fees. The gentlemen had split the few hundred dollars among them.

and disputes, conflicting views of what ought to be done. Certainly their rule, ragged and haphazard, has not been overly intelligent; they were not visionaries, these assortments of bankers, utilities officials, industrial managers, department store owners, with their intellectual lackeys and political hirelings. Far more of the explanation of a Southern city's success would lie in the abilities of the political hirelings, a man like Atlanta's William B. Hartsfield, mayor for twenty-three years, one of those last hurrahs of a political tradition which invested proprietorship in the elected chief official of a city and drew from his whole life a passion and love and jealous protection of that city such as other men put into the smaller social units of home or business. He told me once that in his every act, his every decision as mayor, he always kept in mind that Atlanta was the headquarters of the Coca-Cola Company (its president was one of his good friends) and that anything that would reflect unfavorably on Atlanta would hurt the company.

The mechanics of Atlanta's past political stability and leadership lay in a coalition of Negroes and "nice" people, the respectable elements, including the conservative rich. This kind of coalition was to become fairly common in Southern cities and all state elections eventually but began earlier in Atlanta than in most because Negroes had voted there earlier than in most (a stroke, largely, of Hartsfield's canniness). The pattern in the past of such coalitions was the delivery of the Negro vote by powerful old leaders in return for racial moderation in campaign speeches and other public utterances, and promises toward Negro goals delivered in private. Compared with gains that came later from direct action, the results were small: mainly a matter of better-than-average Southern police treatment, better separate schools, better city hall response to Negro business interests, a better tone in general to race relations where such coalitions were effective. The civil rights movement, of course, shook the ground out from under most political coalitions and arrangements. In the cities, new leaders, black and white, grappled for some new accommodation; in the small towns and rural areas, newly enfranchised Negroes and their leaders presented the white powers with similar problems of new accommodation. Probably in no sphere more than in politics, the disruption of the old order had not by the late 1960s developed any new firm patterns regionwide. There was great disarray.

If anything, with new Negro voting power, Negro political power had diminished. To be sure, the numbers of Negroes in city, county, and state public office had increased greatly—at least 375 held elective office in the South in 1968, including mayors and sheriffs and legislators, but no congressmen. Many others held appointive positions. But often Negroes had been elected, as in Atlanta and Memphis, through sacrificing citywide or countywide representation for district systems. Negroes were assured of representation from the districts where they lived, but they lost the moderating effect of white candidates having to seek their vote and the enhanced power Negroes would have if elected by citywide or countywide vote (as they inevitably would be through coalitions and slates). They sacrificed whatever good (and there was considerable) there had been in the coalitions, in which the whites were compelled, often not even knowing it, to consider Negro interests—which were usually the best interests of the community and especially of the poor, including those archenemies of such coalitions, the poor whites. Yet the preference of the Negro politicians for the bird-in-the-hand advantages of district representation was understandable enough. (In Atlanta, where city aldermanic posts were elected citywide and legislators by district, there was only one Negro alderman in 1969 while there were eleven legislators.) Where city or countywide elections were proffered in accompaniment (again as in Atlanta) with annexations drastically decreasing Negro voting power, Negroes were left with little choice but to insist on district elections or oppose annexation.

Also, with the falling away of the old Negro leadership and the old compulsions to follow that leadership, in most cities no Negro leader or group of them was able any longer to deliver a solid vote or, indeed, often even to turn out a large vote. Failures of moderates in gubernatorial and senatorial races were rife, and the humiliating extent of defeat, if not the defeat itself, was attributable, particularly in the 1968 elections, to a failure of Negroes to vote.

Part of this was out of disillusionment with the right to the ballot just won for many; part was the disorganization and ineffectiveness to be expected in such a situation; part out in the country was surely a hangover of fear from the old days of brutal white resistance to Negro participation in democracy. In Georgia, a Negro candidate running against Senator Herman Talmadge, whose very name was a symbol of ugly racism, failed to turn out a normal Negro vote in 1968, and a Negro candidate running against the racist Representative Mendel Rivers, in the Charleston area of South Carolina, not only failed in inspiring a large turnout, but did not even garner all the Negro votes. He also failed to get any (badly needed) financial help from the peace movement though his opponent was as much an enemy of its cause as of Negroes. There were evidences in both instances that some influential Negro leaders whose support of the Negro candidates was lacking had made their accommodations with the old white racist politicians —a mark, indeed, of a new day.

Most large Southern cities were, like Atlanta, beset with problems with the police and approaching the Northern pathologies of ghettoization and the related problem of the white exodus to the suburbs. Atlanta's experience with each was a guide to what might be expected in the rest of the South.

The Atlanta police—full of the prejudice and sentimentality of all American cops, with the cop's special knowledge of mankind's worst depravities and the cop's special belief (once mainly Southern but seemingly spread to all) that these were deepest and most widespread in the Negro population—had been, withal, the major instrument of averting disgrace during school desegregation and civil rights demonstrations. No Black Belt constabulary ever violated the constitutional rights of Negroes more thoroughly than did the Atlanta police and courts violate those of representatives of the American Nazi Party and other ragtag agitators attracted to the school desegregation. Liberals either applauded or did not protest too loudly. They were to see the same ruthlessness applied (when, as before, correct procedures would have accomplished more) to disturbances in Negro sections, including the two near-riots which were quelled with chilling overreaction.

Police Chief Herbert T. Jenkins, a tough and wily old warrior, more of a figure of municipal statecraft than most chiefs probably, a big and handsome man with silver hair and wrinkles around his eyes, with an unaffected rural drawl, had been in charge of both operations. Moreover, he had been on President Johnson's Commission on Civil Disorders and was noted in the preface to the Bantam edition of the Commission's report as having been among the most liberal members. Yet, once more, in the aftermath of national reaction to the report, when the very President who commissioned it was critical of it and the totalitarian connotations of the term "law and order" began to find favor in the majority consciousness, he adroitly dodged any serious political trouble from his role by such stratagems as selecting from the report in a speech to a civic club those precepts compatible with the "law and order" leanings of his audience. A wily old fox. The death of a man and injury of a boy during the second near-riot had occurred with his police using the lethal "double-ought" shotgun shells common to cops across the country, used in the Orangeburg shooting of students. While he was on the President's Commission, Chief Jenkins quietly ordered what should have been eminently reasonable for all police forces: that in the future bird shot be used in riot control.

The problem with police, perhaps particularly in the South where such low-standard matters as police pay were the lowest, was not in most instances the caliber of the chiefs of police. They were, like Chief Jenkins, literally public servants, tending to the best tenets of their calling, but subject to the pressures of majority opinion and capable of carrying out bad policy as forcefully as good. The greater difficulty was in instilling down to the rank and file of cops such notions as minimum force or the rights of American citizens in an arrest. In Memphis, in March, 1968, the then accepted, respectable, and enlightened method of riot control, Mace, a tear gas compound that irritated the skin so severely as to immobilize a person, was used so randomly and in such heavy doses against a nonviolent demonstration that police brutality became a major issue in that tragically ending civil rights drive.

Take a cop in a city like Atlanta, sullen and weary from moonlighting as a shopping center traffic director or a nightspot bouncer and tormented anyhow with all the fears and pressures of impecunious middle-class striving, his wife haggard with too much housework, too many children, the children a lurking menace of cop's knowledge of human depravity likely to come home; find such a man, ill-educated, with likely a below-median intelligence quotient, conditioned from babyhood in pop-culture violence (the cult of manliness as antidote to the dread fear of homosexuality was extra strong in the South), and filled with the conditioning to racism of the "common" sort; encourage all his worst instincts with John Birch fanaticism and national backlash racism overlaying his Southern conditioning, and put him to patrolling a Negro neighborhood or send him to quell a Negro disturbance bordering on rampage or riot, full of the old nameless Southern fear of slave rebellion, racial retribution, and then expect him to remember that the Chief doesn't want any unnecessary violence, that the image of the city these days demands an avoidance of violence. It asks too much of him; he is at once society's creation for carrying out its darkest secret wishes and, at the same time, scapegoat for hypocrites, liberal and anarchy-tending radical alike. "I hate cops," we say in all earnest rapport in the best of do-gooding and reform-society circles. Traveling together in the Deep South, a Negro man and I were nervous, for the old sense of danger hasn't yet departed such places. When we checked into a motel at a time of near-riot tension, we discovered it was headquarters for more than a hundred state police—they were everywhere, eyeing us with cold cop-eye hardness, hatred—and we struggled not with simple fear but with something stronger, a revulsion through our skins, and finally checked out and moved to another motel, more expensive, less convenient, but uncontaminated with cops, both saying, "I just don't like to be around them. I hate cops." As soon hate the most innocuous of American functionaries, bookkeepers or botanists, anyone, for being precisely what society has patterned him to be, incapable of being other.

In the matter of population of its central city, Atlanta had in the early 1960s proclaimed itself a city of a million people, describing a metropolitan area that took in five counties and countless municipalities. The official city limits, however, encompassed only some 400,000 souls, and it was within these city limits, because of comparative welfare advantages, proximity of jobs, availability of cheap rental property, and suburban segregation, that the Negro population burgeoned while whites, as elsewhere in the nation, moved out, newcomers settling on arrival in the suburbs. One heartening counteraction to this trend was a trek back to close-in neighborhoods by well-to-do young people, taking over and refurbishing the old houses, developers building luxury town-house complexes. But as in all Southern cities, such private expressions of good sense were at the mercy of heedless and mindless expressions of public policy: for example, the state, with the city's acquiescence, ran an interstate highway through the heart of one of the better close-in neighborhoods. (Out in the suburbs, they were planning a state highway that would destroy a hauntingly beautiful group of antebellum mansions in Roswell, including one which was Woodrow Wilson's wife's childhood home.)

The economic and social utility of making one city of the counties was as impossible in Atlanta as elsewhere; like other Southern cities it sought at most to combine city and county government functions. Experiments in metro government were as rare in the South as in the nation. In a hobbled way, Miami had tried it with mixed results. Jacksonville had annexed itself an area so large as to allow it to call itself the biggest city in the world. Nashville had combined city and county governments by popular vote in 1962. The results were not reassuring. For as numbers of well-off whites who had fled the city were brought back into the fold, the tax base increased but Negro power diminished, and those returned reactionary elements were a hamstringing influence. Nashville had experienced one of the South's few near-riots in 1967, and race relations there were as deteriorated as any in the South.

In such places as Memphis and Atlanta, Negro politicians, understandably, but elements of thoughtful, more disinterested Negro leadership as well, were talking against consolidations, talking of all-Negro governments of the inner cities. When plans were made by Negroes to run for mayor of Atlanta and other Southern cities nearing black majorities in the late 1960s, many observers thought they were making the move prematurely, with danger that the worst of racist and reactionary city government might reemerge. Negroes would need more than a bare majority to get along without white allies, and, sadly, the candidacy of a Negro for mayor of any Southern city was designed to alienate all but a fraction of white votes. Though such a

moderate white administration as that of Mayor Ivan
Allen had been given to lip service to Negro advancement
(as the only Southern mayor to endorse the 1964 Civil
Rights Bill) more than to acting effectively against disad-
vantages to Negro citizens, it was preferable to such racist
regimes as Mayor Allen Thompson's in Jackson, Mississippi. More than governors, mayors could make their
racism effective. Mayor Allen, announcing he would not
seek re-election in 1969, said candidly that it was good to
be able to speak freely without fear of being charged with
seeking the Negro vote. He then proceeded to tell Atlanta
it was failing Negro citizens economically and urged
whites to accept Negroes socially. During his term in office
he had acquired a sensitivity to the plight of Negroes and
the poor that he could not have learned from his previous
conditioning as the son of a wealthy local merchant, man
of the "nice" people. His actions during those tragic days
after the death of Dr. King—calling on the family and
giving the resources of his office to the grieving thousands
at the funeral—were a mark of the good that might come
out of the better traditions of the white South allowed
unfettered to influence its public life. For in these things,
he acted like the gentleman he was raised to be.

Negro mayoralty candidates would not long need white
votes unless population trends of inner cities changed.
What if an all-Negro municipal government did emerge in
the not-too-distant future in the South? It might not be the
nightmare most liberals, Negro as well as white, feared.
Through history, the voting records of Negroes across the
South have been consistently more responsible, more attuned to the general welfare than white voting records. So
it is not inconceivable that such a government would
emerge as America's first really rationally run, humanely
developed urban community, taking full advantage of federal money and programs, enforcing codes consistent with
human decency on such elements as slum property owners
and small loan firms, and perhaps with revisions of tax

structures, requiring suburbanites to support the city where they make their living and businesses and utilities to do so more commensurately with their earnings.

But there were places where Negro majorities elected white officeholders. In such places, given their first opportunity to vote, barred all those years by whites from the basic right of the ballot by the rawest subterfuges and cruelest force, these Negro majorities nevertheless were, often, by their own testimony, making their choices in terms not of race, but of genuine conviction of who might be the better qualified candidate, white or black. Even the Negro politicians, given to all the regrettable tendencies of politicians the world over, evidenced that the spiritual strain was still strong in their motivation. At workshops conducted by the Voter Education Project of the Southern Regional Council during 1967 and 1968, "veteran" Negro politicians constantly advised newly elected Negro officials to keep a close grasp of the needs of constituents, to shun deals that meant voting against what one knew was right. One Negro alderman in a large Southern city assessed his role in this way: "I grew up in the Negro community here. But there were individuals worse off than we were. I get a satisfaction out of politics. I do feel as an individual who comes from an ethnic group assumed to be disadvantaged, an ethnic group identified with the poor, that it is a contribution for me to say to seasoned politicians and power groups that these people have the stamina to stand independent and make decisions based on the good of the total community, that they don't bow to power groups." At the time, a vicious battle was raging in his city over a typically complicated budget procedure, and I had asked him, without thinking of moral implications, how he was using the battle to enhance Negro interests. His reply was neither naive nor reproachful, but indicative of a politics a little freer than most. He was making up his mind how to vote not on the basis of jockeying for immediate gain, but on the real question of what would be best for the city. It was a startling attitude to encounter.

In Tuskegee, Alabama, such leaders as Dr. C. G. Gomillion, of Tuskegee Institute, expressed a similar political philosophy in their efforts, dating from 1964 when Negro voting majority status was achieved, to maintain biracial rather than all-black city and county governments. A drive through the town in 1968 showed solid achievement in housing, public health, school construction, and other elements of civic responsibility and well-being. Few towns of its size anywhere in the South looked so well. Dr. Gomillion, a county commissioner at the time, gave a running commentary on the budgetary and political considerations involved in various of the projects; it was a treatise in responsible, conservative public administration.

But there was one flaw in the flickering spirit of a new kind of politics abroad in the South, insightful into the whole of American history. What had been done by some of the enlightened new Negro political leaders had been done *for* the people—not much with them or with their consultation. These Negro leaders were, in short, the founding fathers. They were imbued with a wisdom, graced with a selfless sense of duty and responsibility to the people, but their concept of politics did not take the people into the process. The people would grow accustomed to having things done for them. Then would come lesser men exploitative and unheedful of the needs of the people, and later, probably, men of more democratic leaning wanting not to involve the people in responsible government but to give them a share in irresponsible looting of the public wealth. Never entered into the reality of government whether by founding fathers or exploiters, the people would rise happily and ignominiously to Jacksonian waste and corruption and irrationality. Thus might history repeat itself in the promise of democracy in the South; certainly the condition of the cities of the South so long ruled by whites showed the sad end to which, full circle, the promise might come, Atlanta among the examples.

XII

Negroes, no less than whites, were home-centered in the cities of the South. Atlanta, in Collier Heights and other sections, had one of the most extensive, most lavish areas of high-priced Negro homes, but all the cities, large and small, could show visitors such sections, such estates. In most instances, the land and building costs were higher than for whites, and in many instances status-conscious Negro family heads worked two jobs and their wives a third to maintain them, even as so many home-loving whites had to do.

Housing desegregation, necessary base for a truly open society, that *de facto* bugaboo revealing racist fears in the rest of the country, seemed as unlikely to be attained in Atlanta, city of homes, liberal leader, as in the rest of the South. The cities had, to begin with, less than the towns of that casual proximity of white and Negro housing that was not really an anomaly in the South, because until the 1960s public segregation did not depend on housing. Where city housing integration once existed—in backyard and alley servant quarters in some of the rich sections or in settlements for servants near white homes—it was, with the advent of school desegregation and such, eliminated by urban renewal and private land development. Housing was integrated temporarily in those neighborhoods where Negroes (in 1966 occupying less than 20 percent of Atlanta's land while comprising then 43 percent of its population), like a choked stream, entered all-white neighborhoods near their all-black ones. The process of block-busting, so revealing of human indecency and treacherousness in so many different forms, so fully interracial, was an ongoing process through the 1950s and 1960s, but even here there was guidance by public policy, so that it was the neighborhoods on the South Side, repositories of the more rural, more overtly racist citizenry, who voted against the coalition of Negroes and white moderates, which bore the brunt of the pressure for more Negro living space, and not the benign North Side, home of the Negro's ostensible ally. Southern racists have been seldom wrong in assessing the meaning of the racial changes thrust against the altogether wrong social system they support. "It'll be us pore folks," they said, "not the rich 'uns wantin' it, who have to send their children to school with niggers." This was accomplished in Atlanta, as in most Southern cities and towns, by various buffers and barriers, confining and guiding the flow of Negro population, utterly dishonest in the reasons given for it (the need for an expressway here, a graveyard there), sneaky in execution, municipal management on the same degrading and self-defeating level as educational administration, involving at its cynical worst, skillful location of urban renewal. The other part of urban renewal's scandal, the uprooting and pushing of slum-dwellers into ever worse, ever shrinking slums, replacing the slums with immaculate, segregated institutions and businesses, providing no alternate land or dwellings for the slum people, was prevalent over the South, an enthusiasm of the smaller cities perhaps more than the large. Very little desegregation occurred in federal housing projects in the South, evidence again of the difficulty of securing federal policy through administration by Southern citizens who disagree with it. But on this matter it was 1968 before the federal government brought its first suit challenging a Southern city—against the Memphis Housing Authority.

Urban renewal demolished 21,000 housing units, mostly occupied by blacks, in Atlanta between 1957 and 1967, according to newspaper reports. During the same period, the city constructed only 5,000 public housing units. The rest of the people squeezed into the slum areas that were left or, with the aforementioned guiding of the flow, created new ones. Housing segregation increased from 91.5 percent in 1950 to 93.6 percent in 1960, and probably even more during the next nine years. Newspapers told the same story in the other cities. In Nashville, a black city councilman objected to the deliberate ghettoization involved in a proposal to place 5,000 new public housing units in a black neighborhood already possessing 400 of them. In New Orleans, more than 10,000 families, again mostly black, were unable to obtain public housing and were squeezed into high-rent slum areas. In Charlotte, an average of 1,100 housing units were demolished each year from 1965 to 1968, and were replaced by only 425 public housing units during the same period. And so on, across the South.

Only in the most degraded, desolate areas of Southern urban dilapidation (never, remember, as ugly or squalid, nor as advanced in decay or density as in the North) did one find any degree of permanent housing desegregation, and here among whites it was only one more reminder of having sunk so low. And yet—not always. In a Louisiana city in a neighborhood resigned to desegregation, I talked with a family whose children had attended a desegregated Head Start school and who had received some harassment from white neighbors about this seemingly unnecessary move further into degradation. The father, a painter with the painter's predilection for drinking and the poor man's unabashed ability to acknowledge having to be hospitalized occasionally for it, said, hell, he didn't have anything against niggers, he'd been in the Army with 'em and in the V.A. hospital there, bed alongside bed with 'em. He had come from a farm home in the northern part of Alabama (the TVA section, sparse of Negroes), and had partaken of the old Populist memory of solidarity with Negroes and of a more personal bond of the poor, the insistence of his mother that the family share food when times were hard with the people who happened to be black on the next-neighboring farm. His children were one of those year-apart, stair-step sets of dismayingly large number, tow-headed, pasty-faced; his wife in a shapeless dress was fat and fair, Anglo-Saxon, looking like some ancient barony's queen, gone to seed. The children, he said, have a hard enough time; anything that might help them, he was for their having, and the Head Start school, niggers and all, with its one hot meal a day, was helpful. A boy of five attended, with a boy of seven accompanying him, to "take care of him." "There's lots of whites worse than niggers," the father said, including those who had been harassing him (this last in a loud voice for the benefit of neighbors on the porch next door, who, he said in the same loud voice, were behind most of the harassment). "Bunch of prostitutes and bar-flies," he said and repeated it, to be sure they heard. The trouble had started, he went on, with Reconstruction; they should have had forty acres and a mule. The trouble has spread now, he said, to both races. A friend of his stopped by, an older man with his right hand disfigured, mutilated to a claw, victim of his trade, sawmilling. He agreed that niggers weren't the problem, that it was things like his hand—no recompense for the loss, and he was no longer able to work because of it and was on welfare, old, defeated. The younger man's face was thinly, even fragilely handsome, that same somehow despoiled evidence of Anglo-Saxon stock, blue of eye, straight of nose, hints of the quiet strength of frontiersmen in his face, but the eyes weak, shattered, defeated, and disappointed. "Don't worry," he said as I was leaving. "The boy'll keep going to the Head Start. It's a chance for him."

What might it take to reverse the ruinous public policy that stubbornly resisted such keys to social health as integrated housing in the cities of the South? Not the self-conscious, well-meant workings of the little liberal groups in the upper-middle class white neighborhoods to encourage Negroes to buy the big expensive homes there, and then make them welcome when they did. I canvassed for the group in my own neighborhood, which by 1968 had bravely come to the point of doing an opinion survey of all homeowners on the question of whether to obey the new housing law. On a block of ten homes, I received one affirmative answer on the question and, to be honest— though inevitably this entails complexity—wasn't sure whether the old gentleman spoke out of conviction so much as from his long-standing antagonism for the neighborhood civic club which—as I say, it's complex—he mistakenly believed to be against the proposition. But of the nine nay-sayers, none was hostile to my obvious support of the notion. Most gave rationalizations—property values, concern for what the other neighbors believed, the like. One quite old gentleman, partially paralyzed from a stroke and cupping his hand to his hearing aid to hear me, sat a long moment and then said: "I know that what you're asking is right, and has got to be. I know all about that in the. ." gesturing to the television, carrying a special on Negro riots. "I was born in North Carolina, and we were better about it up there, and I've lived all my life in the South. And I am old. I know it's right, but I am old, and I just want to let it pass me by. I can't say yes." I shook his hand. If there can't be respect, regretful respect for his wish, there can't be either, ever, the open society America must have. At another door, a fat, bustling sort of woman in her fifties whooped after I had urged her to come out for compliance. "Why I'd ruther go live in a cave than have 'em in here. Boy, you look warm. Come on in and let me git you a glass of water." No, the main difficulty of the little groups was finding Negroes, first, affluent enough to buy such homes, and, second, among them finding one or two brave enough to reject the new proud concept of black separatism.

The answer was not here, nor even with the hard-put little middle- and lower-middle-class groups with grim practical stakes, struggling to maintain a balance against the inroads of the blockbusters in a neighborhood where Negroes had moved in, the whites seeking to salvage investments, or merely their love of the neighborhood, wanting to stay. They learned much of race relations in the process, from initial resigned resentment to overreacting niggerloving to final, for most, respect and realization that these black people are like other people, no worse, no better either. But they lost out, the pressure of real estate agents of both races relentless; the attrition might be slow enough for some to hold on for several years, but eventually the right price would be offered, the fear of finding oneself a lone white in a whole section of blacks would become overwhelming—whatever works on people, all these things. One Negro grandmother who moved to such a neighborhood (and whose appearance was as white as her new neighbors') went out to get the mail one of the first mornings and met the nemesis, cheery and friendly, saying, "You better sell now, before they take over completely." She was so startled, so uncomprehending, and then so angry she couldn't reply, could only laugh in the eager, friendly, greedy face.

If the answer were to be found it would be, somehow, as with the painter and his towheaded boy in Head Start. It would, in the simplest terms, make living in every part of a city so advantageous that the suburbanite would want to come in, that the suburbs would be forced to join or at least keep up, that the whites in the transitional areas would be so well served that staying where they were would be more important than getting away from Negroes, normal attrition rather than panic controlling, and that, instead of upper-middle-class whites recruiting Negro neighbors, they might—everything else, schools, transportation, shopping, equal—move into upper-middle-class neighborhoods of blacks to be near a job, for some such convenience, and that the poor, black and white, always before fighting each other instead of fighting together for their desperate interests, ever the same, might find opened to them so much of creative and joyful good, so much of opportunity, so much of affluent-age goodies (all of which would in sane perspective take so little) that it would be worth it to bury the hatchet, or, more likely, become irrelevant to their needs any longer to hate.

This, of course, speaks to government, not merely city, but county, state, and federal, to its most basic function and duty. Why, why—the question by the late 1960s had turned to gall for those who had asked it so long and thought for a time, finally, the answer had come—why could not the society of the South, the people of the South in the formal organization and functioning of their governments meet the basic needs of all the citizens, summed up and symbolized in those bedrock basics recognized and at least wholeheartedly strived for the world over, simply to feed, to care for, to educate the children? Why not, in the name of God, in the South?

CHAPTER 5

I

FOR A TIME, it seemed that we would change, would indeed overnight come to new governments capable at last of performing the minimal functions for which governments are established. The admission of Negroes into political participation in the 1960s was a fundamental procedural reform transforming the very basis of government, with profound implications for change of the basis of society. It was accompanied by that other fundamental political reform, almost as profound in effect and potential, reapportionment. The two things coming together amounted to—in the loose way of using the term—a revolution in the region's political system. More than ever before, the South had begun to approach democracy.

Southern liberals explained and rationalized the South's major problems prior to those two reforms by attributing most ills and most evil to the previous palpable political imbalance and disenfranchisement; with the reforms, they hoped, would come alleviation of all those manifest ills and evils. But the millennium did not immediately arrive. Indeed, in the elections of the years just following the reforms, the political climate seemed to deteriorate, and the caliber of men elected to the higher offices—state officials, congressmen—certainly showed no great improvement, if not also deterioration. The only immediate gains were the considerable ones of numbers of Negroes in lesser offices and what seemed a slight improvement or at least alteration in tone of campaigns and governments. No great breakthroughs toward the solution of the perenially pressing social and economic problems were perceptible, and the problems were all the while worsening.

Why had the reforms not achieved more? Obviously, supporters of the reforms had expected too much or, more to the point, differing things. Some liberals and Negroes may have seen utopia coming, but the main body of voters in the cities and towns were after something else. For one thing, they were out to wrest control from the farmers, who, as their power increased almost geometrically with the wane of their numbers, were obviously the main beneficiaries of the old malapportioned legislatures and congressional districts.[1] Here, practical American self-interest asserted itself for once in the South. Governments which had logically and satisfactorily in the past accommodated a rural, agrarian society and economy just had to be brought into some kind of line with the change to an urban, semi-industrial reality. The most powerful of power-structure figures had monetary interests in the matter, and we have noted that where such interests are involved—be it in desegregation or ghetto rioting—nothing else, not even sentiment or prejudice or justice, matters.

Not *all* the evils of national farm policies can be assigned to that period of the history of the South when it

[1] In Georgia, the system was complete, with rural control of the executive branch of state government and the election of U.S. Senators assured by an ingenious set of rules for running Democratic primaries, the county unit system. Counties had from two to six unit votes to cast, as in the electoral college by majority rule, in statewide races. As the large counties grew larger, and the smaller ones smaller, the disparity between the power of individual voters became ludicrous, one voter in a small county equaling thousands in Atlanta's Fulton County. The system was one of those anti-democratic stratagems of the post-Reconstruction period, this one designed in part to disenfranchise Negroes, but also in part to offset the stealing of elections by city machines, a noble aim not irrelevant to our own times, but a laughably unsatisfactory method. This involves familiar ironic history. It was the Populists, in Georgia led by that romantic hero, Tom Watson, democrat turned in defeat to rabid racist, in their good Southern period of trying to weld the black and white poor together, who were most often bilked of their rightful election victories by the city machines. To complete the irony, bought or otherwise controlled Negro votes were not the least of the agents of the larceny.

elected congressmen so beholden to a small number of big farmers, because the Midwest and West did about the same thing, but *much* of it can because those Southern congressmen had disproportionate power in the U. S. House as a result of the seniority bestowed on them by the South's one-party system. Southern city dwellers came to varying degrees of animus against these agrarian interests, but the sad fact seemed to be that they thought of the farmer as the one-horse fellow remembered from childhood, not the agribusiness giant who had taken over the countryside. So when balance was restored, it seemed likely that the legitimate interests of small farmers in the South would still be passed over, and unlikely that the South would make any real demand that the nation eliminate the worst inequities of the various subsidy schemes designed to make rich farmers richer and drive the poor ones off the land.[2]

During the time they were discriminated against by malapportionment, Southern city and town dwellers paid considerable lip service to the virtues of democracy, and many even developed real feeling for the principle of one man, one vote. So when the Congress applied the notion to Negroes shortly after the Supreme Court applied it to white city and town dwellers, many whites genuinely rather than grudgingly conceded that it was only fair that Negroes be allowed to vote with everybody else. Yet part of the willingness of the small counties to accept reapportionment without the kind of ruinous resistance and general discrediting of the American system of law that accompanied decisions on school desegregation and school prayer, must surely have been out of awareness that the other reform was on the way, too. They didn't want to see their own disproportionate influence in state affairs fall into the hands of Negroes who were near or in a majority

---

[2] Again, greatly influenced by Southern congressmen. No one, strangely, has ever called these Southern friends of the farmer in Congress on their ignominious sellout of the small farmer, the "pore farmer" whose virtues they continued, all the while doing him in, to praise.

in those rural counties of small white population more than any other places.

Of course, this fear of Negro rule, haunting the South since Reconstruction, was at the base of most of the anti-democratic practices in the region's history, from the white primary to the poll tax, areas of sparse Negro population acquiescing in the demands and worst prejudices and practices of the whites in areas of heavy Negro population, Black Belt racial harshness setting the tone for all of the South. That reform came no earlier, that the demand for it was no more vociferous can be attributed to the same fear. By the 1950s, following the Black Belt had become habit. The worst demagogues elected under the various situations of malapportionment and Negro disenfranchisement were often an embarrassment to the more urbane Southerners, to the "nice" people, but they were considered a necessary evil. In Georgia, there had always been the opportunity to get out from under the embarrass ents of the Talmadges, the Marvin Griffin sort, by the imple expedient of running a more moderate man in the general election where the county unit system did not apply. In 1952, then Governor Herman Talmadge threw the full weight of his considerable prestige behind a constitutional amendment attaching the system to the general election and was roundly defeated.

But no one saw enough possibility of victory from the same majority of voters to put up a moderate slate in the general election. The majority was against the system, but not necessarily against the men, most of them anti-democratic and reactionary to the extreme, that the system put into office, and this applied more or less Southwide. The people of the cities and the towns just wanted their share in naming those men, bad as they might be or good or indifferent, and of the time-honored rewards and influence resulting—their thirst for democracy was not nearly so much founding-father Jeffersonian as it was Jacksonian. Though this was not nearly so true of Negroes who fought their moral and spiritual battle for the ballot, it was not altogether lacking from their motivation. The best ethic of black power in its Southern origins and development, indeed, expressed little other than this.

So grand expectations of the liberals and idealists were, in the nature of things, delusive. When they pictured a practical coalition of liberal city dwellers and Negroes, they had not computed relative scarcity not merely of liberals but of city dwellers. Power had shifted from the farmers and hick-town courthouse rings to the big cities, but it had moved also into the small cities and larger towns and to the suburbs of the cities. These suburbs, more than in most urban areas, were populated by people just entering urban existence, at its fringes from the towns and, yes, the farmlands as well, a process C. Vann Woodward termed "rurbanization."[3] (Some of us had simply believed in people, Jeffersonian belief, mystical, saying that if the South would just let all of its people have a say in the governments, the governments would be better. To understand why this faith was not rewarded would be to realize fully—as we shall attempt to do—not just the South's, but the nation's, chief debilities and gravest, most dangerous problems.)

The highest hopes for a new day in Southern politics came with the civil rights movement of the early 1960s in the South. In the two years between 1962 and 1964, voter registration of Negroes increased as a result of concentrated drives by civil rights organizations more than it had

[3] C. Vann Woodward, *The Burden of Southern History* (New York, Vintage Books, 1961). He uses also the graphic imagery of the "Bulldozer Revolution" to describe a meeting of urban and rural that has happened faster in the South than elsewhere: "The symbol of innovation is inescapable. The roar and groan and dust of it greet one on the outskirts of every southern city. That symbol is the bulldozer . . . The great machine with the lowered blade symbolizes the revolution in several aspects: in its favorite area of operation, the area where city meets country; in its relentless speed; in its supreme disregard for obstacles, its heedless methods, in what it demolishes and in what it builds. It is the advance agent of the metropolis. It encroaches upon rural life to expand urban life. It demolishes the old to make way for the new" (p. 6).

in all the ten years previously. In states where administrative trickery and/or intimidation were still practiced rigorously (roughly, the Deep South states—Alabama, Mississippi, Louisiana, South Carolina, Georgia), the registration drives availed little, but in the other six states, Negroes had increased their registration enough to become a formidable power a year before the voting rights act was passed. Much was made of the fact that Goldwater was prevented a victory by the Negro vote in four and probably five of the six Southern states which he failed to carry in 1964, the very states with powerful percentages of Negroes registered. The other side of that coin—that in ten of the eleven states (all but Johnson's home state of Texas) the majority of whites had voted for a racist candidate—was less considered. After all, moderates like Carl Sanders in Georgia, Frank Clement in Tennessee, and Paul Johnson in Mississippi had won governorships. The passage of the Voting Rights Act saw sudden shifts from blatant segregationist politics to more or less moderate stands by such worthies as John McKeithen in Louisiana and the backlash pioneer, Orval Faubus of Arkansas. But then came the putdowns of a new crop of moderates seeking governorships —Richmond Flowers in Alabama, William Winter in Mississippi, Ellis Arnall in Georgia, John Jay Hooker, Jr., in Tennessee, Robert King High in Florida, Richardson Preyer in North Carolina. With distressing regularity, the old standby segregationist senators and congressmen continued to be re-elected, often without opposition, reapportionment notwithstanding.

By 1968, Negro registration was above 50 percent in all eleven Southern states, but once more, Texas alone gave its vote to the man (however mistakenly) considered in the South as the spokesman for liberalism and humanitarianism, Hubert Humphrey. Five of the others went for Wallace and five for Nixon, who was considered generally in the South (assured so by Dixiecrat diehard Strom Thurmond) a Wallace with a chance to win. By then, most high hopes and illusions about the new reforms were gone. If anything at all, the results of that election showed an increase in the majority of whites who were voting racist.

One question to ponder was why it might have been that, alone in all the nation, for two national elections hand-running, the South stood as the *only* stronghold to that date of those forces of anti-intellectualism, anti-humanist, indeed, totalitarian impulses summed up in the disgrace of the Republican nomination of Goldwater and the candidacy of Wallace. The old liberal temptation would be to blame it on the small cities and towns, to say that they had come to be the balance of power and to say that racism was more central to the bundle of beliefs and interests by which they lived than in the big cities of the South, and more advanced in its grip on whites than in the rest of the country. Or maybe outside the South, there was merely a better grasp of political reality. I encountered enough specimens of the small city and town Southern mentality in 1964 to believe that most of those who supported Goldwater really thought that he would carry the nation. It even seems likely that most Southerners who supported Wallace had more than a wistful hope that he, too, would sweep America, a delusion shared by how many frightened Northern liberals? Even more than most Americans, Southerners have the compulsive need to support and vote for winners, out of the sad past when for so many, the courthouse-ring largesse of jobs and patronage (not merely for oneself but for all one's kinfolks) was a desperate necessity.

But we cannot say that, since the balance of political power in the South had come to reside in small cities, towns, and suburbs, that the Southern predilection for the hobgoblin candidates for President was merely a reflection of both men's appeals to the seedily sanctimonious, piously patriotic, shabbily sentimental strain in the small-city, small-town mind, as much as we might want to avoid laying it all to racism. For there were enough counterparts of the South's smaller urban units across the country to have made a great difference in Wallace's and Goldwater's popular votes, even to have carried states for them in the West and Midwest, had the rest of the small urban units taken the two as seriously, loved them as much. It is better, if we are to avoid racism as the answer, or the whole answer, to consider that racism more closely.

The examination would begin with those moderates upon which liberalism pinned so much hope in the first flush of the double reforms, and the question would be whether under such men there had been any significant degree of difference in the lives of Negroes than in those states ruled by the raw racists? The answer would have to be only to the degree that their abstention from rabble-rousing might have cut down on the amount of that continuous violence by whites to Negroes that is the easily overlooked leitmotiv of Southern racism. (Even here one must not overestimate the influence. Some of the worst Mississippi murders occurred while the more or less moderate Paul Johnson was in office, and a Klan revival was underway in the upper South, including Virginia, while moderation reigned in the state houses.) In the basics of desegregation, things were little or no better, indeed could be worse under moderate governors than under ultra-racist ones, and the same might be said of the conditions for poor people, black and white, and of the exercise of the bedrock duties of the state to provide decent education, health services, and economic opportunities.

George Wallace, when he was governor, was the movement's example *par excellence* of the recalcitrant segregationist who, by forcing the federal government to act, did more to advance the Negro cause than the most fervent of civil rights advocates. In the late 1960s when he served as governor by consort, Alabama was the first state to go under an all-inclusive federal court order that said integration's meaning included white children's going to formerly all-Negro schools, real abolishment of the dual system. Sadly, what became most clear during the little time of transition when moderates seemed in the ascendancy in the South was that all the federal forces, charged with enforcing the sweeping social law to pry Southern society open, wanted from the states was mere lip service to that ideal, absence of publicity-creating confrontations of state and federal power. Thus, if holding onto as much as possible of the old system of segregation was the main purpose of Southern racist voters, they were better served by men who caused Washington no trouble, who in effect conformed to national hypocritical standards on race, mouthing equality but doing virtually nothing to achieve it, allowing ghastly conditions to fester on, unseen. One would think the voters would perceive this, would not require a politician to be a ranting racist, or even a conscious racist because it hurt their cause, but would ask only that in his administration of policy and law, he maintain racism. Perhaps men who did this, and the nation, itself, allowing such scandalous evasion of law and duty, were racist. It might have seemed in 1964 that Southerners, white Southern racists, would have known in their bones, just by the very sound of his nasal intonations of certain words, that Lyndon Baines Johnson was more thoroughly, more fundamentally racist than Goldwater—whose nervous-talking speeches showed unfamiliarity with the idiom of racism, with even the first subtleties of it. Indeed, it is difficult to say what Johnson was on the question, having moved in his political postures along every inch of the line from segregationist to integrationist, back and forth, or even what he was unconsciously, subconsciously, ideologically or psychedelically. But the performance of his Administration, its nearly complete failure to achieve any of the simple goals of desegregation, was racist, maybe more completely so than Goldwater's might have been. Lester Maddox, rabid in his racist talk, has far more of desegregation in Georgia under his administration (especially in such matters as Negroes in state jobs) and more concern for such interests of the poor as welfare and prisons than the moderate Sanders who preceded him. There appeared to be, maybe there was, maybe there wasn't, diabolical political purpose among the men who paid lip service to equality and administered their offices so as never to move toward it: maybe they responded to the big-city cynicism, sophistication, hypocrisy of the majority of whites in the nation, and what was eventually to be the majority in the South, and were shrewd enough, crafty enough to carry along with them, to fool for a time, majorities of Negroes and either to fool liberals or placate them by indulging their fixation on means rather than ends—programs, methods, technique, never mind that they never achieved anything. The racist John Bell Williams had no sooner gotten into office after defeating the moderate William Winter for governor of Mississippi than he found his administration saddled with actual financial involvement in a vast foundation-supported program in the Delta to train displaced Negro farmworkers for a new life in industry. The wily liberals had more or less tricked him into it (or, horror of horrors, maybe he was a new breed of wily racist politician who had caught on to the fact that liberals weren't interested in anything beyond setting up the program). It is likely that Winter might have avoided the thing altogether, would have been considered not needed to be tricked into anything. Or maybe he would have taken it, too, a part of moderation and lip service. If so, the result would have likely been the same as under Mr. Williams—few Negroes even entered into the program, fewer trained for anything real, lots of jobs for white friends and supporters.

Perhaps it is too harsh a judgment to say that the moderate politicians responded to big city hypocrisy, and that the big cities of the South were deep into the mainstream of this hypocrisy. Our main concern now is with racial predilections of the smaller cities and the towns—why they preferred Goldwater and Wallace, why so often in their state and local races they almost invariably took the outspoken racist over the moderate whose ability to forestall integration was either proven or implicit in history, and lacking a racist, seemed almost always to incline to the less effective, more unsavory of two moderates—Fritz Hollings over John Bolt Culbertson in South Carolina, for example, or Republican Howard Baker over Frank Clement, who had defeated Ross Bass in the Democratic primary in Tennessee.

We have already noted that Southern political communication became muddled and murky with the advent of the Negro vote. To the extent that even the racist candidates have had to adopt code-word communication, Negro voting had improved the political climate. Even in the Deep South, the old, raw niggerbaiting would likely not any longer be acceptable to the majority of voters. There had emerged a more subtle style of racist politician, a more frightening brand, smarter than before, like John Bell Williams, Claude Kirk, Howard Callaway. In the upper South, most notably in Tennessee, a tendency had developed to avoid the race issue from either side, and this was the most hopeful sign, for it would eventually maybe force the politicians to talk about the real issues. Nevertheless, amid all of these indications of flux and change, it was possible to know that some candidates were loyal to the old racist creed, indeed still believed in it, and some were not, and almost invariably when given a choice between the two, the majority of white Southerners preferred the racist.

Is it too easy on these white small city, town Southerners, and too simple-minded to suggest that, rather than racism, it was loyalty that they were asking out of their candidates and that racism had become the shorthand code for loyalty? In 1964, they spoke of Johnson with real loathing and the burden of what they said was not in the specific terms of his civil rights apostasies, their impact and effect on the places where they lived, but was the whined or outraged or anguished cry that he had betrayed the South, had been a traitor. When the racists came home with their tails between their legs after one of their spectacular defeats, Wallace under more and more severe court orders, Wallace even after his schoolhouse door stand (utterly defeated in practical terms), Ross Barnett from the Battle of Ole Miss, Stennis forced by wily liberals to introduce legislation actually to feed some of those starving Delta blacks (never mind that it would never likely move any food to any mouths), there were no vociferous criticisms, no political repercussions. Instead there was sympathy, and headshaking awe for the perfidy of the enemy, and gratitude, real and deep, for their men having fought the good fight.

In most classical analysis of the South, the discussion would end here, almost automatically attributing the voters' attitudes and actions to that deep strain of the romantic lurking illogically in the mind and psyche of the South. Undoubtedly, this is a major part of the phenomenon, but maybe there is another more important part. Maybe, just maybe, in demanding loyalty from their politicians, they were asserting that other strain in their souls, that redeeming one, of honesty, that, even if only unconsciously, they were rejecting a dishonesty in the nation and its politics. Maybe unconsciously, with the old Southern preference of the frying pan over the fire, they were saying they had just wanted no part of a politics, liberal or conservative, which had come to a complete cynical disregard for any human, any real consideration in the calculations of election victories, that they wanted to be no part of electorates completely willing, on the one hand, to acquiesce in hypocrisy even where self-interest was involved, and increasingly unable, on the other hand, to be able to perceive whether a candidate, a program was or was not in one's own better interest. If there was a good old boy talking the old-timey politics, coming right out and saying he didn't like all that civil rights mess, or condemning a race by lambasting particular members of it, leaders usually, Dr. King while he lived a favorite target, then the whites would stick with such a fellow. Maybe it was merely the simple-minded matter of projecting the old honesty, of assuming it existed in their politicians—that, in short, they meant what they said, that you judge a man by what he says instead of, as the more advanced notions of psychology and philosophy had informed the sophisticates, by what he does. If so, they were far behind the Negro South which had as long ago as 1964 in SNCC when it disavowed the Democratic Party, and in the intervening years with the increasing disillusionment of the general black public, come to discount almost all of what whites (politicians and otherwise) said and to judge entirely on the basis of concrete results, or the lack of them, on the basis of the sad realities of their lives. The Negro South was coming to discount for the most part American democratic idealism and white liberal ideology because there was so little evidence in real life of either's working. The white South of the small cities and towns seemed to have, as at least part of its rejection of the moderates, an unwillingness to lend themselves to the same hypocrisy, maybe a plain unsophisticated incapacity for the subtlety necessary to judge Johnson not by what he said, but by what he did. Or maybe those whites were just saying (as blacks had through all their long struggle against racism) that they wanted desperately a feeling of being important, of being something, and racism remained the pitiful core of an old bundle of corrupt, indeed, irony of all ironies, totally dishonest political oratory which gave them that feeling. Maybe, like the Negro Southerner and mankind everywhere, they just wanted dignity.

All of this has been in the way of reaching out beyond conventional and classical analysis to find some better explanation than the slur (partaking of superficiality and overgeneralization, faults of racism itself) that racism and

a kind of half-crazed romanticism explain fully the phenomena of Southern politics and Southern society. The
effort may be as much out of a sentimental desire that
one's own people be better than that as it is out of the
profound fact that such simplistic explanations of complex
phenomena had come to be applied fashionably by the late
1960s and even officially (in the report of the President's
Commission on Riots and Disorders) to all of America,
even to all Western Civilization. But more than wishful
thinking or even tortured analysis can be found to sub-
stantiate this reaching out for other explanations. Encountering the small cities and towns themselves, their institutions and functions, and the blacks and whites within them
has not always been pleasant, and there have been times
when I was as ready as any to apply the epithets racist and
fascist and worse. But even then, and more often in normal
encounters, there was always the evidence of good among
so much evil, often with the total absurdity of *Dr. Strange-
love,* good devoted wholeheartedly to the worst of evils,
but good nevertheless, not just pitiable but tragic. Maybe
we have come in the South, in America, to so sad an end
that the lesser of evils is not only our only choice in everything, but has come to seem to represent some positive
good. Nevertheless, let us look closer at these small cities
and towns of the South to see if there might not be alive in
them elements of human good that—if somehow they
could become untwisted from the evils inherited from a
bygone day and from environmental reality—might serve
the large cities and save them from immersion in a mainstream that is polluted not with past but with brand-new
evils that are perhaps even worse than those still-crippling
ancient ones.

II

Andy Griffith's Mayberry, on television, stands as the
symbol of that mixture of old and new that has come to

reside in the downtowns and the close-in old homes and, God help us, suburbs (treeless, graceless, crowded together, often, as in any land-scarce megalopolis) of the small-town, small-city South. Mayberry is the myth, the dream, the South as the white South sees itself, a town upon whose sidewalks black people never walk, and on whose streets exist no Negro shanty or warehouse or other ugly site of hard work, ditches being dug in slithering red mud, where black labor, cheap labor is yet required, no kitchens for that matter presided over by forehead-sweating, lowly paid, Negro women, but instead Aunt Vi, fat and jolly, motherly archetype of a white Southern womanhood that never was. For shorn of the black shadow of niggertown across the tracks, Mayberry is all that the whites of the South have the potential of building a town to be; freed of the darknesses in their souls of cruelty and guilt that has ever been the terrible price of the Negro's presence and position among white Southerners, the people of Mayberry are all that the white South might be, charm and good-heartedness and foolishness and fun-lovingness allowed full play, unhindered and without the darknesses and shadows that so often make ugly these lighter, brighter aspects of human character as they are so shrilly manifest in the South. "It looks like Mayberry" say my notes on one of the countless little towns that look so much alike across the South. "Broad streets, clean, bright-painted stores. The courthouse sits a little back from the sidewalk on a corner—without much grounds, no square. Old men silent, stolid on green benches. In transition from county seat-farmer town into part of an area of cheap industry (mostly textiles). Rural virtues (minding one's own business, honesty, respect for individuals) recurred in interviews. But so did a sophistication and the new sense of being part of modern times that might not have been here ten years ago. (Interviews were with leaders, white and Negro. Less of this would show with average people probably.) The pretty, quiet town has a three-block-long main street with business streets going a block in either direction off it. From the main street you can look down one of the side business streets to where it becomes homes or tapers off into countryland. On the main street is a knitting mill—an old brick structure that may have once been stores: it has windows bricked in. It was owned by a prominent family from the capital city, but was sold to a chain which was unionized. It is thus the only union shop in the county—whose 'industry' includes one large textile plant (2,400 employees). 'Unions don't get to first base because the people are pretty satisfied,' said a leading citizen. 'The one in the main street plant doesn't make much stir; you wouldn't know it had a union,' he said. 'It is just a bunch of ladies in there. . . .' "

From another set of notes, a small city: "Not a pretty town, though many hills and winding narrow streets. A harshness here. On a summer morning, the main wide downtown street is full of cars, the sidewalks full of people, busy, prosperous feel. A pall of papermill stenching smog is down heavy, almost at rooftops of two-story stores, this all the way out into the countryside of woods and green fields for a good ten miles, and then suddenly you run out from it, into sunshine. The paper mill and a General Electric plant give the city a diversity in industry that other nearby ones don't have, and this one didn't used to have. What it used to have was cotton mills, and these it still has, including a plant that used to make rayon but dropped that because of labor troubles, wildcat strikes, with lay-off this spring of upwards of a thousand people, many of whom had worked there most of their lives, are too old to learn something new, and too young and poor to retire. . . ."

The power that controlled the South in the late 1960s resided temporarily in these places. It would not do so long. The superhighways which they liked so much were, as much as anything else, the catalyst for change. People no longer did major shopping in the little locally-owned

stores on the town squares; they could reach a big store, a
Sears Roebuck or Belk's, or a big city's variety of them, in
about the time it would take to walk downtown. (These
were the people possessed of cars, of course; the poor were
still dependent on the main street and neighborhood
merchants, not incapable in their adversity of outrageous
over-pricing, this a particular problem where federal food
stamps were in use, grocery items doubling in price when
the stamps came in.) Small cities were beginning to grow
together, or to consider themselves one community, its
being about as easy to visit a friend in the place twenty or
thirty miles away as to visit one at the other end of the
town. Greenville and Spartanburg, South Carolina, had
institutionalized the process by locating a jointly used
modern airport exactly halfway between each other on the
interstate, a half hour or less from either. States themselves
were becoming communities, their limits as accessible as
those of a county in horse and buggy days, no point more
than a day away. A high school championship football
game 250 miles away from a small city could draw a crowd
of 15,000 to support the home team, the round trip in the
same day no great strain. In whatever new configurations
of urbanization this additional revolution in transportation would create, the little cities with their smog and
exploitation of labor would grow into bigger cities, maybe
keeping, maybe losing their virtues (such ones as the feeling for honesty, individuality, minding one's own business
alive in them, too), maybe becoming, maybe resisting
what the big cities had already become or were becoming,
that nameless ugliness we sensed hovering over Atlanta,
that likelihood in *them* of continued increasing density,
expansion, rather than becoming the more sane mini-
metropolises that they might be. The little towns, looking
like Mayberry, would either become little cities and then
bigger ones, or they would fade away, as the little farms
and the plantation system that once nurtured them had
faded away or drastically changed.

Lurking about these places is the evil ability of the white South to project false myths, to convince us of a romantic conception of all the South, either all good or all evil, and of the white South to delude itself, to see itself as Mayberry where actually there is still a niggertown never honestly confronted, never fairly dealt with, never expiated. (We will enter these beguiling, treacherous places as I force myself to act as a reporter, full of the knowledge that I am as ignorant of them as the freshly arrived Northern reporter is ignorant of the city South that I know well. His weakness in the city is to think that, in talking with people, he is finding wondrous and amazing truth, while I know the patterns of untruth and half-truth and rationalization and romanticism that cling to and often choke the truth that is in what the people say to him. The task for the reporter [and perhaps for America if it is ever to learn to trust itself] is to strike some balance between believing everything people say and not believing anything, dismissing people whose very lies might be the truth we are seeking, dismissing them as one more duplication of an exact same pattern when in reality there is infinite variety, as in all nature.) To sit in a small-town lawyer's office—works of literature among the law books to the ceiling on his shelves, the shelves in harmony with the graceful, old-fashioned furniture of this old office, marred by a plastic and chrome table thrust in, a Rembrandt on the wall, and alongside, framed, "Objectives of Rotary"—and know that what this man says is flavored and influenced by the fact that he was raised in the Black Belt, where racism was rawest, and attended one of the better Southern city colleges at a time when its liberal predilections were given full sway, then moved to a small city to begin his law practice and soon decided he preferred the pace, opportunity, and companionship of an older partner, in this small town. To hear and chuckle but not miss the real point of the story told by the white member of the little-town school board which had, when the federal government got bossy and enforced the letter of the law about integration locally, got bossy in turn and enforced the letter of the law on Negro adults, forbidding them the use any longer of school buildings for their club meetings, the white giving the old Southern self-depreciating laugh and saying, "My aunt has a cook who is an official in the AME Zion Church, which used to have all kinds of clubs meeting in those schoolhouses, and I couldn't eat with them for months without getting blessed out by her." But to hear the tone of pride in that same man's voice and know all the ambivalence in the South that he represented when he said that the Pony League baseball team in the town had been integrated, and then added: "The schools' doing what they did more or less led to all this other. It's been accepted by the majority." To hear the same note of pride in the middle-aged white woman's voice in a small city where before 1965 Negroes by and large were not allowed to vote tell the vastly efficient and convenient procedures she has helped to establish for the registration process, including the taking of the books to any church or school, Negro as well as white, that requests it. To feel a whole unknown history of small-town racial accommodation in the story of how the Presbyterian church in a very small town allowed colored members of the faith to attend services in the balcony because there weren't enough of them to build their own church, this in years past, the last of the colored Presbyterians by the time of the telling, "dead now" (in the way of Southern saying it, one word, carrying its own commentary. "He's dead now," the afterthought ending to so many anecdotes.) To know the horror reading a news story from not the ghetto wilderness of the North nor even a city slum of the South, but from a small city that is a garden spot, noted for the number and beauty of its antebellum homes: "Police attributed the death of an 89-year-old bedridden [Negro] woman Thursday to bites from a huge rat . . . Rat tracks found on the pillow of the bed showed a big rat had attacked her and no doubt caused her death." To see in such a story, not in the small town's probably prejudiced newspaper, but in a United Press International dispatch, which one must understand is based on the integrity and intelligence of that very same home-town newspaper, the statement that an eighteen-year-old granddaughter "said to be living with" the deceased "was apparently not at home when the attack occurred," implying somehow that it was her fault, not the society's which allowed rats to exist so prodigiously in a garden spot. To hear, in the middle of a niggertown of more than usual demeanment, with rows of houses made of corrugated tin, and outhouses in back, in a little town whose government had skipped over this section with water and sewage lines to build its little white suburbs, this recital of racial progress in the year 1967 from a Negro leader, a tough and resourceful old lady: Are restaurants and theaters desegregated? "Noooo––No. No." (Most sadly spoken.) What about the poverty program? "There's no food stamps, no commodities, no poverty program. They had a hand-picked, all-white board, and they turned down everything last year." Is there much poverty? "Ohoooh— Lord Jesus." The roads? "You saw 'em." Sewage? "The majority of Negroes that have bathrooms have septic tanks. Yet they get charged for sewage on their water bills." Schools? "They're separate and unequal. The desks and typewriters are handed down from the whites. I have a friend whose daughter was smart from the beginning to finish of school. She was valedictorian. Then went off to college and wrote back that they classified her as a tenth-grade student. The girl who lives above me went to Indiana to improve her children's education." She said that it was only in 1942 that they quit having three-month school for the children of Negro farmworkers in the county. "It's not the brains of our children; it's just what their brains are exposed to." Are there any whites in the town you can depend on? "Let me get that question straight, now. Are there any whites we can depend on? If there is—I don't know him." Then she added that, yes, well maybe there was one man, a crook, but helpful sometimes. What hope was there? In voter registration, she said, Negroes were slowly moving toward a majority of registered voters, had the majority already in some wards. "We've worked hard, hard. The tree is beginning to bear a little fruit this year. So that there will be more next time." A pause, and then: "Sometimes we haven't known where we were going. But we just keep on going."

To hear the many stories of little-known, brave white men, like the "Christian gentleman" who built a manufacturing plant in a small town, hired an integrated work force, put a Negro engineer in an office larger than those of some of the whites, and found one morning that the Ku Klux Klan had blown the front of the building up. He went to the sheriff and said we can't have this, arrest 'em. The sheriff reported that he just couldn't find who did it. So the man said, all right. I'll close the plant. It was a large payroll in the little town. That night the culprits were locked up.

In short, to sense all the shiftings to good, to evil, trying to know what will become certain, solidified, and to accept the surface superficialities of nothing, to make judgments, to hear a small-city white leader and to try to understand him: He is aware of a lack of communication between Negroes and whites. "So I try to discuss things with the colored people I come in contact with in my business. And as far as I know there are no sore spots, nothing to cause real trouble." This is not quite the classical, "they're happy." This is a man, though, who is subtle and sensitive enough to find trouble spots, if he really wanted to. There is the hint of a deeper layer of prejudice speaking. Throughout his comments on race, there is a contrast— fair, measured assessments, intimations of good will, and then judgments that fall into the clichés of racism, put a little more sophisticatedly than usual. He, like other whites of the small city, speaks of Negro friends. Says they never eat together, but do visit in each other's homes. He cannot be called racist and, indeed, is closer to the norm of these small-city, town leaders than the outspoken racist. Try to understand events in terms of this man.

In towns more often than cities the most hideous violence has occurred over the years—retaliation, intimidation through all the phases of racial change, continuing strong in the late 1960s in the struggles over school desegregation (which only began to be felt forcefully in these smaller places after 1964). Whites and blacks in one such place still remember the night thirty years ago when a Negro man was clubbed to death by the sheriff on the courthouse lawn: his screams for mercy were heard all over town. Official violence, private violence in these places: the two civil rights workers who were murdered in Lowndes County, Alabama, three others tortured and murdered in Philadelphia, Mississippi. In a small city, riding the new current of subsidized industrial plants, developed that first, self-conscious, grassroots paramilitary organization of Negroes, the Deacons for Defense and Justice, soon to fade from view but for a shining moment an inspiration across the South to beleaguered blacks; perhaps, too, they provided symbolic motivation in the Northern ghettos, and influenced the sad, slow shift from nonviolent redemptive love to black power in the thinking of the young men and women who worked longest and deepest in the ugly underside of the pleasant little towns, pleasant small cities, challenging the most fundamental points of their public policy.

It is not Mayberry that we enter now. But it is no camouflaged system of complete totalitarian, psychopathic rule either—no Dachau. Neither of these, it contains elements of both, the seeds to become either or neither, to become merely like the rest of America.

III

They had their own versions and varieties of the dominant forces and institutions of the cities, their own power structures, law enforcement, newspapers, political traditions, art and culture ambitions and pretensions, educational hierarchies—not so much miniatures of the city arrangements, but different configurations of them, with different degrees of emphasis.

Power structures were, for example, generally described as more cohesive, more powerful. A power structure might consist of one tyrannical old man: more often it was the old-family business and property owners, Snopes or Sartoris as the crucial case might be, with inroads from such newer influences as the industries, the mushrooming colleges and junior colleges, occasionally a doctor. One of the keys to the character of the little cities and towns was whether or not the power structure wanted to keep things as they were, usually with an interest in maintaining a surplus of labor for the advantage of their own cotton mills or lumbering operations or the like, or encouraged, in the self-defeating ways we have encountered, the proliferation of new industry. Rarely, there might have been a balance, men in control who wanted economic growth but were unwilling to sacrifice all of the old to it.

The Negro power structures in these smaller places tended to be restricted to those whose economic or (as in the case of preachers) community situation allowed them freedom from the pressures of coercion and intimidation—professionals where they existed, dentists often assuming the mantle of militant leadership, businessmen. Undertakers were the mainstay of the older patterns of Negro power structure, at least one to every hamlet, a statewide network of leadership still in the late 1960s actively in touch with each other in a state like South Carolina where the NAACP remained strong. The civil rights movement while it lasted, the poverty program and other token outposts of federal good intentions provided a newer kind of leader, a sort of professional militant, as important for pushing and goading the older Negro leaders, the under-taker and preacher varieties, as for confounding the white power structures.

Invariably, the white power structures in these small places would be described as conservative, and this in an environment where mildly moderate social and economic views tended to define the limits of the left. Usually, the term applied chiefly to economic conservatism, and what was meant by this, more often than not, was a projection in their minds of family budgeting or small-business prac-tices to the Keynesian complexity of governmental finance. It was to such ignoramus notions about economics among the men of power in small places across the country that Goldwater made the most respectable part of his appeal, and Wallace, too, as far as he was able to move from his monomaniacal concern with race. Among many of the small-place people to whom racism might have been anathema, there was genuine response on economics. Con-versely, it might also be proposed that many to whom both Goldwater and Wallace appealed enormously in their stated economic and racist views nevertheless withheld their votes because of another part of their economic con-servatism, a better part, their unwillingness, indeed in-ability, to trust with vast amounts of money men who were obviously damn fools.

At any rate, the economic conservatism espoused by many of the power-structure (and for that matter man-on-the-street) Southerners included thought and feeling and superstition that was bizarrely primitive and fancifully unrealistic.

An ugly part of the economic conservatism resulted from the persistent delusion that the free enterprise system in pure classical form still exists, that *laissez-faire* is still some rampant reality, functioning perfectly, with jobs and boundless opportunity for all deserving them. This has been a national hallucination especially among people just emerged from the lower economic situations to a precarious position in the middle class, and since the South has proportionately more of these as a result of its past economic difficulties, it has a more than ordinary amount of the hallucination. Goldwater played upon it with endless dishonesty (or maybe he believed it, too), and so did Wallace in his racial slurs against welfare, all the while working the other end of the street with Populist promises of increased old-age insurance. (The general Southern practice was more generous treatment of the elderly than of dependent children, whites having greater longevity in all the states, Negroes more children.) The worst manifestation of the economic delusion was the conviction—deepfelt and blind to all contradictory evidence—that any person without work, lacking middle-class affluence, was himself totally to blame, too lazy, too corrupted by welfare to get out and take advantage of all the opportunity awaiting him (translated in specifics often to the plaint that you just can't get a yardman any more, not even paying the exorbitant $1.25 an hour minimum wage). The outrage and scorn was mostly invoked against the Negro, but was not spared the poor whites, especially in areas where there were more of them than Negroes. All that rioting up North was, as part of the view, nothing more than an expression of the pure cussedness, depravity of these lazy ingrates. It was frightening to hear such talk, largely by the generation salvaged from bread line destitution and saved for private capitalism by the frantic welfare stratagems of the New Deal. (A younger variant, innocent of the Depression, was described often with great loathing by Democratic politicians in the South as the source of the upstart new Republican strength. Actually a creature of both parties, this was the GI-bill educated and housed young businessman, convinced that his good fortune was self-deserved, contemptuous of all less blessed.) And yet . . . For all the wrongheadedness, indeed paranoid quality of the concern over welfare, there was in it at least the dim awareness that something was in need of correcting, as indeed it was—but in the opposite direction from their thinking.

The power structures, on another level of concern with racial problems, were engaged over the South of the 1960s in one of the truly original innovations in the social order, the biracial committees. Usually *ad hoc* groups (often considered concessions to Negroes—ends, not means), occasionally given official status by ordinance, they amounted to a new governmental branch, or better, new form of governmental body that frankly reflected the power of power structures where conventional forms tried to cover it over. They attempted to deal with, ameliorate, handle the startling changes in relations between the white part of town and the Negro part, and problems thereof after the 1954 school decision. These committees were most numerous in the small cities and towns, in some as genuine efforts to find a mutually satisfactory new balance, in others as candid, frantic efforts to stave off demonstrations and other causes of ruinous publicity, including white violence.

Two Florida sociologists, viewing these remarkable phenomena across the South in 1964, concluded that the committees were not the instruments by which real integration might come to the South. They saw it coming, not in Dr. King's mystical vision of reconciliation through redemptive love, but in the time-honored ways men learn to know and respect one another through honest opposition, erasing racial antagonism through the reconciliation of conflicting positions about the ordering of the society.[4] Certainly, the white men who served on such committees came to the first crucial step of losing prejudice; they came to see the black members as individuals. Indeed, they studied these black adversaries, knew their strengths and weaknesses, as they would know busi-

---

[4] Lewis Killian and Charles Grigg, *Racial Crisis In America: Leadership In Conflict* (Englewood Cliffs, N. J., Prentice-Hall, Inc., 1964).

ness rivals, political foes. In the cities, the Negro power structure from which members of the committee would be drawn (even though the effort was always to get the more "reasonable," which is to say docile, people) contained skills and personalities and even power and money that were a match for these qualities within the white power structure. Thus, there was reluctance in some of the big cities to get involved with a committee; former Mayor Hartsfield in Atlanta wouldn't touch it with a ten-foot pole, saying it was better to work things out informally. Outside the big cities, too often, the odds were just too great against the Negro members. In one small city, for instance, white members included the president of a bank, two executives of manufacturing plants, a furniture company owner, and the executive secretary of the Chamber of Commerce while the Negro members were a house painter, a barber, a retired Army man, a retired business-man, and a Negro insurance company executive. One of the Negro members concluded: "We can sit down and dis-cuss things. But there is no unified Negro structure. There are just a few people who can petition and be heard. The committee will discuss what we propose, and then the whites will either intercede in whatever the situation is, or we have to go it alone. The committee's real purpose is just to keep an eye on the racial situation." Whites tended to regard the fact that the black and white members met together in public places (after 1964) as one of its major achievements.

The quality of Negro leadership in the small cities and towns across the South was not as high as the vast gains it made in the 1960s would lead one to believe. Negro progress too often depended on whether a given locale had independent men of the courage and drive necessary to push the white power structure to its limits of change. The smaller the place, the less the likelihood for this because it was most often young leaders who had the vision and stamina required, and the young left the small places usually as soon as they could. There were, of course, incredible exceptions like Mrs. Fannie Lou Hamer in little Ruleville, Mississippi, the best known of a number of tough-minded, resilient grassroots leaders in little places in that fearsome state—others were Mrs. Unita Blackwell, Mrs. Victoria Gray, Howard Taft Bailey, and Amzie Moore. In Williamsburg, South Carolina, was Virgil Dimery, a funeral home director who had worked for local Negro rights more than half a century and had founded the town's Negro Voters League, which was involved to the hilt in the registration drives of the early 1960s. (In 1962, he sat in the shade of a big tree in the yard of his funeral home with a representative of the Southern Regional Council's Voter Education Project puzzling over what a grant from that organization might be spent for—the only equipment needed was paper tablets, and the young people who did the canvassing surely didn't need to be paid. In 1968 the town was near the final goal of majority Negro registration. "We work in vain if we don't train our young people to take over . . . ," he said. And: "If an official will work, I don't care what color he is . . . I'm not ready to burn things down. There are good words there, the Bill of Rights there—it's just never been executed." In a small city like Durham, North Carolina, emerges a leader of the eminence of John Wheeler, president of the Farmers and Mechanics Bank (though Negro-owned, not located in the Negro section nor limited in clients to Negroes), a member of the President's Economic Advisory Board during the Johnson Administration. One of the nation's most prominent Negro businessmen and a militant integrationist, he has been an able behind-the-scenes adversary to the Durham white power structure and served as president of the Southern Regional Council. When he was in his fifties, he went out in his business suit and joined the students in their first sit-in in Durham.

But obviously out of a leadership situation so fragilely dependent on chance, the pattern of racial progress in the

small places of the South has been extremely ragged, ranging from near-zero dismalness to full, if not always har-
monious, sharing between the races of all of the public
sector and as much of social integration as in most of the
big cities.

The warning not to attribute omniscience to the power
structures of the larger cities applies not equally but
strongly to the small cities and towns as well, despite a
tendency to the fallacy discernible in the foregoing. Where
there is only one bank or only one doctor or only one of
the other necessities of modern life, obviously, there is
more power to control, to intimidate the people dependent
on these necessities. And in the smaller municipal units,
where not much is happening, it is easier for one or a
few men to know more of what is going on, and to
exercise strong influence or control. But once again, except
in the misfortune of a population to have fallen into the
hands of a tyrant, a fanatic, the control by the power
structure in these smaller places has not been unrelenting,
nor concerted nor planned—but mainly the reactions,
haphazard and inconsistent, of private interest, private
gain.

Probably the nearest the power structures of the small
urban units came to the kind of concerted and galvanized
unity that is associated in the popular mind with the term
was in the heyday of the Citizens' Council during the early
1960s. Here was as near as the right wing has come in
America to a real movement, replete with strong local
organizations, a regional superstructure, a central office for
general strategy and propaganda and, unlike the Birch
Society in its national attempt at the same, solid citizens
rather than fringe-fanatics and lunatics as officers and
members up and down the line. The thing was more
effective and widespread in some states than others and
by no means all-inclusive in any state, but it had strength
in all of them, and it was in the small cities and towns
that it was strongest. It was a frightening thing to go into

a small city and to realize that not merely the semiliterate poor white gas station attendant, but also the bankers, the mayor, the editor, even some of the preachers, all those who are personages in such a place supported it fervently.

The collapse of the Citizens' Councils with the passage of the 1964 Civil Rights Act did not come about just because this had been the signal that respectable resistance could not prevail. It was also a result of a differentiation somehow strong in the minds of these solid citizens of the small places between the validity of law as promulgated by the Supreme Court and law enacted by the Congress. Said one: "We fought the Supreme Court in 1954, but when Congress acted in 1964, we knew the ballgame was over, and it was time to go home." The main effect of the congressional action was a calming one, he added. Perhaps their sense of loyalty and respect for their congressmen carried over into respect for the entire body even when it defeated their men. Anyhow, the Citizens' Councils lost many of its respectable mainstays in its fight against the law of the land, once that law gained congressional sanction.

The Councils were petering out by the mid-1960s, and the organizational expressions of racism for "nice" people were more diffused. Enough politicians and preachers still talked it to allow the most respectable of institutions to serve those whose need was only verbal; even local civic clubs (often with their choice of speakers) and some churches of the standard denominations served this need, as did, in diffused fashion, the John Birch Society. (One whole evening of a Deep South Birch public speaking was devoted to the intricacies of foreign trade as they related to the Cold War, the function of wheat in American diplomacy—a rather tame contrast with even civic club racism and beyond comprehension of most of the nevertheless rapt, rigid audience. One had to be adept indeed at code words to make any sense at all out of some of the harangues.)

The fearsome force of the racists and the rightists should

never be underestimated. The "hard-core" resistance to
the civil rights movement in the early 1960s was as frightening a manifestation of anti-democratic, totalitarian tendencies as probably America has seen. There was administrative resistance—recalcitrant administration of simple
rights to Negroes, as in voting or welfare, or outright refusal. There was police resistance—failure to enforce laws
or protect constitutional rights, false arrest, police brutality, jail beatings, illegal trials, false imprisonment.
Courts, juries, police forces were all-white, a situation not
greatly improved in the late 1960s. There was economic
resistance—jobs lost, mortgages foreclosed, evictions, essential services refused. There was private violence—sluggings,
beatings, fires, bombings, shootings, even aircraft strafings.
And murder. These things did not usually come singly;
they came concertedly. Seemingly, a whole white society
(all of a town, a county, even a state) was pitted against
Negro advancement, against freedom. Not all whites, of
course, participated, but by intimidated silence or indoc-
trinated acceptance or, worst of all, paralysis of will so
deep that it appeared to be indifference, the whole society
would be implicated.

SNCC and CORE bore the brunt of the resistance, were
with and among the people who suffered; more than one
black power spokesman took years of this while nonvio-
lently seeking the simplest rights of democracy. Yet too few
have considered this in explaining the black power phenomenon. And few have admitted that here was the great
triumph of the racists—not in stopping the hated new laws
nor the court decisions, but in destroying the most effective organizations and strategy for fighting racism, for
making the procedural reforms won by the civil rights
movement real in the lives of the people.

And the Councils were not extinct. In the Black Belt in
the late 1960s, the Councils were still referred to with some
respect by friend and foe alike—ominously with the recur-
ring phrase "The Citizens' Council mentality." In the hey-

day the Councils were intrinsically Southern, like George Wallace, but, again like Wallace, with borrowings from and extensions into the rest of the country's far-right pathology. The center of their credo and program was racism, resistance to Negro equality. But there were tinges of anti-Semitism, of superpatriotism, and more than a little Communist witch-hunt hysteria. Indeed, one of the achievements in semantics was to instill in many an automatic connection of integration with Communism. In the late 1960s, a preacher with contacts in churches across northern Louisiana noted as one mark of improved social climate a decline in the willingness to call anyone not segregationist (or in disagreement with other facets of majority opinion) a Communist. The charge is not made lightly by such elements. The emergence of the hippie movement and campus revolt stirred anew the concern over conspiracy; I have been assured more than once in the most serious of tones that "the Communists are behind it, every bit of it."

Should there be some comeback of the Citizens' Councils, it would likely be in collaboration with such a sinister political movement as Wallace's, making the old version, as evil as it was, seem innocent by comparison. The main difference would be that the new manipulators of it would likely be far more pragmatic than the old. There was always about the old operators a faint sense of medicine-show profiteering, but never a hint that they did not function out of pure conviction. Since the logic of such conviction pushed them sometimes into extreme stands and tactics which repelled members who were "nice" people of the power structure and since it eventually ran them into the stone wall of the popular regard for Congress, the old operators were to that extent handicapped by conviction. The new ones would suffer no such debilities, as Wallace did not in his move to the national arena. Meanwhile the small-place power structures stood athwart the new federal law in fine disarray, most of them against it in principle but bound by law and order to support it and, indeed, often finding themselves enforcing it against the popular sentiment, even facing sometimes in pure poetic justice the old Citizens' Council tactics of anonymous harassment.

IV

One element of small place society, a remnant of the old social order, that has been far less touched by the intrusion of the malenforced new federal law has been law enforcement itself. No better description of ᵗhe function of law enforcement as a component of the old racist order may be found than the following from a 1965 Southern Regional Council report:

> It can be said without unconscionable exaggeration that the southern system of justice suspends the Negro in . . . a state of torment and obligation. Because he is black he is continually subject to caprice. In a manner of speaking, there is no such thing as "definite acquittal" for the Negro. His color carries with it a presumption of hard luck in the white man's court; a given Negro is automatically a poorer risk than a white man at the bar of justice. That is a statistical certainty that hovers over every Negro and makes him never quite free.
> But . . . the Negro is not without a fretful, worrisome kind of hope. He is reminded constantly that he can buy insurance against the harshness of the system. One thing that most Negroes learn early is that a "good nigger" fares better in times of trouble than a "no 'count nigger." By debasing himself systematically, a Negro can earn a reputation as a "good nigger" and assure himself favored treatment should he be called to account in a court of law.[5]

Though federal law reforming jury selection practices has alleviated the situation a little, the local, state, and federal court structures across the South in the late 1960s

[5] "Southern Justice: An Indictment." Published by the Southern Regional Council and Southern Regional Office of the American Civil Liberties Union, October 18, 1965.

were still virtually all-white, and the above assessment was still generally true.

Civil rights workers, union organizers before them, troublemakers through Southern history knew the terrible clamp of the small-city or town police state, which in the early 1960s possessed most of the trappings—electronic phone taps, torture instruments—and all of the criminal contempt for human rights, for justice, indeed, for law that have terriorized our age, from Germany to Russia to South Africa to, one deeply fears, the major cities of America. However, these Southern police apparatuses would be more aptly compared to the cavalier and capricious police arm of dictatorships in some of the lesser republics of South America, rather than to the cold, rigid organization of the rest of America. Often Southern policemen seem ludicrous—one would laugh if it were not so fearful— in a Keystone Cop fashion: louts casting about on motorcycles full of the joy of all the noise they make, swaggering with the power of the pistols bouncing on their hips. One tiny town hired a dozen or more of these young toughs to increase city revenue with traffic arrests of unwary tourists, but also used them in a local political squabble to push people around (one was inspired to place tacks on roads traveled by the political enemies).

The terrible legend of Southern police and the feared sheriffs' departments as chief agents of lynch-mob lawlessness was still alive in some of the towns and small cities of the South in the late 1960s, an example once more, the list of them wearisome, of a neglected Southern problem highlighting in its crudeness, rawness, a more widespread one in the nation. At any time one begins to feel sanguine about the South, comfortable that its times of racist terror are done, he has only to sample a couple of weeks of the regional press to note how many acts of violence, including killings, by the police are recorded. (Probably the same sort of shock would ensue from sampling any similar-sized segment of the American press.) The stories chill.

The following are from an informal file of the Southern
Regional Council, based on news clippings, labeled, "Race-
Related Deaths."

ELTON BRAYBOY (N) Columbia, South Carolina. The
State (Columbia, South Carolina), 7/6/67. An inquest
jury charged a white policeman with murder, ruling that
he "did shoot and kill Elton Brayboy in a willful and
felonious manner." Brayboy was shot five times; twice
after he fell to the floor.

ROBERT E. TOWNSEND (N) Okolona, Mississippi. *Delta
Democrat Times*, 10/3/67. A white Okolona policeman
was freed by a three-man justice of the peace tribunal.
He was charged with murder in the pistol slaying of
Townsend, who was handcuffed at the time of the shoot-
ing.

ROBERT LACEY (N) Birmingham, Alabama. *Southern
Courier* 2/4-5/67. "Holy Jesus, They Kill My Child For a
Dog." Robert Lacey, the father of six children, was shot
to death last week by a Jefferson County sheriff's deputy
while members of his family watched in horror. Lacey
had been charged with failing to take his dog to a veterinarian. ". . . 'Please don't shoot again,' I [his wife] said,
and my little girl came running to see what was happening to her daddy, laying there, bleeding, and I said
again, 'Please don't,' and that's when they shot him
through the head."

What they did to the people in the secrecy of their police
cars, back alleys, and jails was sadism allowed full sway,
expertise in the breaking of the human spirit. From the
"Race-Related Deaths" file:

JAMES EARL MOTLEY (N)   Montgomery, Alabama. New
York *Times* 12/3/66. "A state autopsy report made public today confirmed that James Earl Motley, a 27-year-old
Negro who was taken dead from a Wetumpka, Alabama,
jail November 20, died of severe head injuries. (Negro
friends of the man have said that he had been beaten by
a white deputy sheriff and state troopers a few hours
earlier.)"

Frightening in another way were the stories told by student activists of the early 1960s, middle-class teenagers for

the most part, of their treatment after arrests for sit-ins and
the like—threats designed to terrify, and such provocation
as the turning of heat up high in summer or off in winter,
beatings, solitary confinement. In the small places where
there was no Negro lawyer, the youngsters might spend
weeks in the jails waiting to be bonded out. (I remember
one sit-in leader in a small Louisiana city who spent sev-
enty-eight days in jail, fifty-seven of them in solitary confinement.)

On the other hand, more than one civil rights worker
who survived the Southern jails came away with tales of
kindness furtively done by jailers and their minions, or of
such men coming slowly, gradually to friendships, or at
least to serious hearing and discussion of the idealism that
had landed the activists in their custody, black ones telling
such stories, as well as white. And let it be said that there
were some police and sheriffs, through the harshest of
Southern racial confrontations, who acted for the real
meaning of the law, protecting civil rights of demonstrators,
coolly quelling white violence, often fighting down their
own prejudice and their partiality to friends in the white
mobs. Orangeburg's chief of police acted with consistent
responsibility during events leading up to the tragedy
there, twice over objections of the owner closing the bowling alley that was the scene of confrontation, trying to
protect rights of students to peaceful protest. (The shots
that were fired at the defenseless students were all from
state police.)

Certainly, in the days of the most numerous demonstrations there was never anything in the South like the police
riots in the Northern cities. Southern police, where they
operated honestly, did know how to keep the white crowds
from gathering and were capable of keeping hostile camps
separated. It was not that the ugly and lurid reputation of
southern police and jails was not well deserved. But for all
their bad reputation, they were no worse, often not as bad
as their counterparts the country over.

The courts, the lawyers in these smaller urban units had only a slightly more blatant record of injustice and discrimination than those in the larger units. The Atticus Finches, the perfect Stoics, of the South existed, but perhaps less in the legal profession than in any other until one reached the rarefied domain (relatively free from political pressure) of the federal judiciary. Even here was the well-known, sorry record of the Democrats, with their custom of allowing Southern senators to choose who in their state will get to be federal judges. For most of the 1960s, almost the only agents of the federal government who seemed to stand as a bastion for the laws against discrimination (while many, including federal judges appointed by Democrats, actively opposed them) were Republican-appointed federal judges—men like Elbert Tuttle and Frank Johnson and John Minor Wisdom. The Fifth Circuit Court of Appeals more than once salvaged the system of law, and American decency, from complete discredit in the eyes of Negro Southerners. J. Waties Waring was one of the good judges who, for more years than one likes to think, bore not merely the spite of fellow whites in Charleston, but also the special contumely of its aristocracy from which he derived. When he died in 1968, few whites attended his funeral, but Negroes from all over South Carolina and beyond, in a great outpouring, profound tribute, did.

Not the least of the sins of the Southern bar was refusing the duty to represent the unpopular client, or worse, representing him in a way that violated his rights, that placed the defending attorney in collusion with the prosecution. Negroes arrested for rape or other crimes most outrageous to white sensibilities were advised, regardless of the facts, to plead guilty on the hope that a judge would give them less than the death penalty that an all-white jury was sure to deal out. Patent jury discrimination was seldom challenged, its results a continuing crime.

Again from the "Race-Related Deaths" file:

LARRY WAINWRIGHT (N)   El Dorado, Arkansas. Arkansas *Gazette*, 3/4/68. The prosecuting attorney charged that a 17-year-old white youth, "obsessed with the idea of killing Negroes," had shot Wainwright, 19, from a moving automobile after "boasting that he was going to throw a Negro off the Ouachita River Bridge." Warning that failure to convict would "show the futility of the courts," the prosecutor said, "your verdict will determine the conscience of the community." The all-white jury found the accused not guilty.

CURTIS INGRAM (N)   Little Rock, Arkansas. Arkansas *Gazette*, 7/25/68. A white prison trustee was found guilty of involuntary manslaughter (defined in Arkansas law as "accidental killing of a person without intent"), in the slaying of fellow-prisoner Ingram. Ingram was beaten to death.

The influx of Northern lawyers and law students with the civil rights movement of the early 1960s in such organizations as the NAACP Legal Defense and Educational Fund and the Lawyers Constitutional Defense Committee had a salutary effect on the courts generally and the legal profession specifically in these small places, forcing them— if out of nothing more than professional pride—to more honorable attendance to their duties. The Negro civil rights lawyers of the 1940s through the mid-1960s, a part of the NAACP history of forcing change through the courts, were quiet heroes, seldom recognized. Often only one or two of them to an entire state, they fought tirelessly all the discrimination and discourtesy of the white system of justice, most of them earning eventually the grudging admiration and respect of the better sort of white lawyers and judges. By the end of the 1960s, the increase of opportunity for Negroes in Southern law schools, the entry into the South permanently of Northern Negro and white lawyers interested in civil rights, and the establishment in 1964 of the Southern office of the American Civil Liberties

Union under Charles F. Morgan, Jr., had alleviated their situation somewhat.

The other professions in the smaller places performed little better. Physicians and dentists were in short supply. Negro ones, of course, were more scarce than white, but both were critically needed. Towns would sometimes try to lure a doctor by building and equipping a clinic. I spent a day once with a wild young man, just out of medical school, who had come to such a set-up in a mountain town and was making his rounds on impossible mud roads in a Model A Ford, working himself into exhaustion with frenzied enthusiasm for the people and all the vast and exotic variety of pathology their long medical neglect had engendered. Public health services were inadequate in the larger cities; in those smaller places, they amounted to little. Even after theoretical desegregation, hospitals had their own shameful history of discrimination, even against those at death's door, and small charity. Negroes and poor whites sick enough to require hospitalization often had to hie off to a charity one in a city or to die. Midwives, herb healers, faith healers, what-have-you, witchcraft and voodoo were still common in the late 1960s, filling the vacuum of the scientific age's neglect.

"People say they'd rather die than go to the city hospital," said a young Negro leader in one small city. "It's humiliating for them." He told horror stories of a kind familiar across the South (and perhaps to all charity hospitals and both races)—of a quite sick man waiting from eight-thirty at night until four in the morning before anyone would see him, of another who was refused admission and died two days later of uremic poisoning. The hospital's Southern style of compliance with desegregation law amounted to the replacement of discriminatory signs with a big white guard in the middle of the two waiting rooms: his presence dictated for most Negroes that they would go to the "Negro" room. "There was an old lady the other night on the edge of the bench in the white part, and the guard's eye was hard on her. After about ten minutes of that, she got up and left—never got treated." He went on that attendants called Negroes "aunt" and "uncle," "boy" and "girl," used rough language to the kin of sick and injured Negroes, and even pushed them when they were slow to understand a direction to a ward.

As for that old American legend of the wise and kindly country doctor, the sad truth was that, like most of the other country legends, he had descended into mediocrity, a fellow too old to be elsewhere (not exactly having kept up) or a man of not much skill—scandals continuously involved their illegal sale or personal use of drugs. Like the most of their brethren in other regions, they tended to the most stupid and implacable of far-right intolerances and intransigencies. But doctors who were dedicated to social and racial justice did exist in all parts of the South, and they were uniformly extremely hard-working and effective in the cause.

V

Newspapers were as dismal as their counterparts in small cities and towns the country over. One of their chief debilities, especially of the small-town weeklies, was surely worthy of congressional rectification: thralldom to the county political powers for legal advertising, often the mainstay of steady revenue and not to be jeopardized by any suggestion of criticism of the county political powers. Timorous attitudes toward other sources of revenue, mainly merchants with all their tentacles into power-structure and political affairs, was a problem shared with all American journalism but was probably more pronounced here, at the mercy of more whims and zanier prejudices.

We have cited the papers, the Jackson *Daily News* and the *Clarion Ledger,* as likely to be among the worst newspapers in the world. (Their headlines were famed for a sort of defiant dishonesty, classical examples the proclamation in the largest of type that Goldwater had won, only the smaller type distinguishing that this was in Mississippi, not the nation, and announcement that a Californian had been arrested in the murder of Medgar Evers, the story eventually revealing that the suspect had in childhood briefly resided in that far state but otherwise was a Mississippian.) Their editorials could be placed at the bad end of a spectrum of taste and intellectual integrity while the Charleston *News and Courier* deserved a place at the other end. Papers of both towns were outspoken examples of the general social and political outlook of the preponderance of the South's small city and town journalism. Herewith, a brief but savory sample of the style and mental processes of the Jackson approach:

> In the death of the Reverend James E. Reeb of Boston, the Unitarian minister who died in Selma, racial agitators have found themselves a martyr over whose body they can pass the collection plate.
> We were sorrowed by the brutal death of Rev. Reeb and think the persons responsible should be punished for an unthinking crime. . . .
> Normally we would think it the better part of judgement to let the Rev. Reeb rest in peace but since memorial marches are still being conducted and since an Air Force jet plane was summoned by the President to cart the remains of the Rev. Reeb to his resting place, more insight into the minister may be appropriate.
> According to an Associated Press story of March 12, Rev. Reeb was in Selma working for the American Friends Service Committee.
> What is the American Friends Committee?
> It sponsored the World Youth Congress which has been cited as a Communist front. It sent a delegate to the World Youth Festival, held in Prague in 1948, a pro-Soviet and Communist-sponsored affair. . . .

This was in the *Daily News* of March 18, 1965, under the headline "Rev. Deeb—Dead Martyr." The rest of the editorial continued the distorted attack on the eminently respectable American Friends Service Committee.

The following are from the *News and Courier* of July 30, 1964, and July 21, 1964, respectively:

FACTS AND FICTION

In its July 17 issue *Time* Magazine rattled the bones of William Faulkner, an alcoholic genius, to promote its racist line against sinful white Southerners. The cover story was a skillful tribute to a great author and an equally adept exercise in regional prejudice. In a forthcoming issue *Look* Magazine will print another installment of axmanship by one of its staff—a former Georgia boy—entitled "A Southerner Appeals to the North: Don't Make Our Mistake!" These articles were prepared before the riots in Harlem, Brooklyn and Rochester. They now seem strangely out of date. The eggs that agitators laid deep in Dixie are hatching north of the line.

Nothing that *Time* and *Look* and all the rest can say can blur the vision of those who have seen the jungle erupting in their own home towns. The people of Cleveland and Detroit and Los Angeles and many another city outside the South also are learning the hard way what to believe and what to disbelieve.

CORRUPTION DEVICE

Sen. Strom Thurmond has properly called attention to the need for defeating the Johnson administration's so-called War on Poverty. . . .

The Legislation has a two-fold political aim: 1) to implement the Civil Rights law by establishing integrated labor camps in rural areas and 2) to purchase votes for Mr. Johnson in carload lots.

The legislation has many provisions. One alone is sufficient to establish the need for killing the measure. It would give $1,500 to every needy farm family. The Poverty Czar created by the legislation would determine who was in need and deserved a $1,500 hand-out. The answer to the question is simple—anyone who would vote for L.B.J.

The day-in, day-out, decade-after-decade effect of such as this, the only window to the big world for many citizens of the small places, reveals the disservice of such a press, the terribly serious problem behind its grotesque absurdity.

Of course, the Southern public was reached by other sources of information. In the larger cities readers enjoyed no less an abundance of reading matter, including hard-core pornography, than New Yorkers—if there may be found any comfort in that. But in the smaller places, the very magazine racks sometimes seemed to have been censored, either in anticipation of prevailing tastes or with more diabolical purpose. *Time,* with its peculiar distortions of reality, almost always penetrated and, more welcomed, *U. S. News and World Report.* (*Newsweek* was less available—too liberal.) But the real journal of popular acclaim in these small places (and in the lower middle class of the cities and the suburbs as well) was the *Reader's Digest.* Here, for any who would study its pages, was the key not merely to the mind of the small place South, but of majority America.

Then, too, there was the influence of national television, as central to the lives of Southerners as it was dismally to Americans everywhere: no conglomeration of aerials (some of them rising three stories above a simple shack) was too arduous to bring its death-flicker into the most remote places. The towns were served by the network outlets from the cities and some small cities, these otherwise dependent also on the cities. None, in large or small city, was a distinguished station; WDSU in New Orleans came probably closest to what the Federal Communications Commission ought to demand in local performance. What it ought to demand of the networks was, of course, a national problem of incalculable importance, worsened in the South by the general tendency of station managers toward only the lowest levels of the already lamentable programming, and by the practice of hiding from their audiences those few documentaries promoting racial sanity and other social advance. (In some of the small cities, such as Jackson, Mississippi, even broadcasts of national news were deemed unpalatable to the audience.[6]) Of course, nothing the managers could do diminished television's most profound universal effect (for good as well as evil): the display to startled white and black poor of all the opulence that the rest of American society enjoyed, and the demonstration to Negro Southerners that their black brethren around the world had advanced beyond them.

Radio was to the Southern extremity of television's wasteland as a ragtag street-corner evangelist to a most pious high-church reactionary bishop. In the South, it spewed out an incredible, dismaying jangle of pop music of every screeching variety, camp announcers, fundamentalist evangelists and a constant harping of the worst know-nothing, right-wing propaganda (all the Billy James Hargis's and Carl McIntyres and Life Liners and others surely heard nowhere else in the world), reinforcing the effect of the papers by making them, often, sound moderate and sane. Every little city had a band of stations, and every town at least one station, and to drive through the countryside from one broadcast range to another was a sobering experience. What the FCC might do here merely to establish norms of minimum taste would be vast; what has gone into the brain cells of Southerners from this blather to help explain their voting patterns alone would be a good subject for the most serious, most concerned sociological research.

The few good stations were mostly in the big cities—talk stations of varying degrees of responsibility, a hopeful development in a few places. Most of the "Negro stations," which were mainly devoted to varieties of Negro music, were white-owned, brutally exploitative, and, of course, little involved in the thrusts for social change. The better ones did provide news coverage of direct Negro action, though, and in some of the small urban units were the only source of full coverage.

[6] A famous weather report there forecast cloudy—with demonstrations.

Certainly, the media served the small places of the South even less well than the deplorable cities, and therein lies much of the explanation of voting patterns.

And yet . . . some of the best, the most courageous journalism in all the nation has been produced in the exceptions to the general failure in professional duties in these small places of the South. Mississippi was blessed with a curious abundance of courageous and intelligent small papers including the Tupelo *Journal,* the McComb *Enterprise-Journal,* Hazel Brannon Smith's Lexington *Advertiser,* and, by its contrast with most small city dailies, Greenville's *Delta Democrat-Times.* The latter, in the second generation of Hodding Carters, was characterized by a kind of studied and purposeful liberalism, typical of most of the select few good Southern papers, but was still staunchly true to the high standards of intellect and honor set by the elder Mr. Carter. Good papers, here and there across the South, knew the literal fear of bombs and death, year in and year out, and this threat had not completely abated as the 1960s neared their end. And more than anyone in the world they would despise romanticism of their role, a crediting of their occasional brushes with threats and violence above the more common courage and agony and crises of integrity involved in standing up to power structure condemnation and the hurt of old friends over their telling the truth, and the human ability (who is without it?) sometimes just to give in, to compromise, but never to give up. These papers achieved a level of good sense seldom attained by the muscle-bound giants of the big cities and not even imagined in the consciousness of Madison Avenue. For example, this editorial from the Asheville (North Carolina) *Citizen*:

> Americans are troubled about the apparent breakdown of restraint in their polite society. They deplore the evidence of increasing crime and "violence in the streets." We doubt, however, that is their prime worry and if it is, their values may be misplaced. . . .

America is in trouble at home—and violence is one of its problems—but America is in greater trouble in the world. . . .

Much of our woe is attributable to the war in Vietnam, but the end of that war will not end global animosities. The truth is, we haven't been very smart. We have attempted to buy international friendship while boasting of our riches, and we have subsidized dictatorship while proclaiming our love for freedom.

We haven't fooled anybody; we've grown fat on a myth. . . .

Things will turn out reasonably right under Nixon or Humphrey; the United States is a nation of great recuperative strength.

It seems somewhat a shame, however, that neither of these spokesmen—both of whom know what the problems are—has felt free to discuss them frankly.

Maybe next time.[7]

How sad that such was the exception that proved the rule of general failure in the South to develop an informed electorate. How far the institutions and the men of the small urban units were from the fundamentals of democratic theory was summed up in the casual comment of a member of the power structure of a thriving small city. "Yes," he said, "A fellow from the *Wall Street Journal* came in here and did a story about our town and he sure treated us badly. He tried to make out in his story there were two sides to things here."

VI

We have already noted low educational standards and resources as an often-cited, catchall explanation for the South's manifold failures and miseries, including the vagaries in the voting patterns. This explanation was a little better than blaming everything on the former restrictions of democracy, as long as one kept in mind the difference between real education and mere sophistication,

7 October 28, 1968.

and the realization that nowhere in America was education what it ought to be.

The towns and small cities were at the median of Southern performance in public school education; maybe even more than in the large cities, their strivings were to reach the inadequate level of the rest of America. These strivings amounted mostly to improvement of buildings through state and local bond issues, and increases in teacher pay. Neither activity, even if both reached the nation's highest standards, would of course answer the needs of the children.

The tone of the schools in the small places was below even the essentially anti-intellectual one of those in the large cities. At worst, this meant inferior imitation, particularly in personnel, men and women trying, with much posing and pretense, much juiceless heartiness, to project the sterile images of professionalism they had admired in teacher's colleges or at the big-city education meetings. Like their big-city cousins and the breed the country over, they concentrated their educational association activities and their graduate studies on the goal of higher pay—needed, God knows, but not the ends, really, of professionalism, not related to erudition. The struggles of the states each year to push teachers' pay a little higher (the money usually sweated out of the iniquitous sales tax) served chiefly as a holding action, to keep them from moving on to where the pay was better, rather than as a means of replacing them. Actually, replacing them would not solve the basic problems which had to do with the national scandal of inept professional training and with the inadequate methods they had to use against insuperable problems relating to the society and conditioning from which the children came. The teachers were energetic, capable people for the most part; what they lacked was the kind of training that would impart excellence and true love of learning to their teaching, and a proper program for this. Little was said in these schools of libraries; the Cold War emphasis on scientific training had created some fervor for laboratory equipment. But the gymnasium and the football stadium were the physical focus of pride: sports, bands, pageantry for the parents—these were the main emphasis.

In a small-town high school, which housed the city school superintendent's office, sitting before a window with a view of the charred ruins of a grammar school that was recently burned, it was suspected, in protest of desegregation, I listened to one of those inferior-imitation, small schoolmen with a bad haircut and not without his own problems of grammar. He told of the trials and tribulations of his system, not the least of which centered on desegregation, and of progressive things going on, special efforts in reading instruction, a new program of "manual arts" for the "unteachables." A phone call interrupted, and it was some man he was trying to hire as a band director, and this superintendent of a small school system showed all his familiarity and skill with the uses of small power: quickly, he pressured the fellow to come to work for less money than he obviously wanted. Then the superintendent went on to tell me of the "language problem" with Negro children newly enrolled in desegregated schools and then of dropouts and the causes, including parents who had never gone beyond eighth grade and could see no reason why their kids should. Silent a long moment and with none of the caution such a skilled small-schoolman should show, he said in a quiet, worried voice something that obviously had been much troubling him. "They sit in these classes and they know they will go to work in the mill when they get old enough, and they know there is no connection between what goes on in the classes and what they know faces them."

Very little innovation was going on, little that promised the South might avoid the country's mistakes. Four Atlanta professors of education drew up a blueprint for what a real educational institution, attuned to environmental problems and assets, might be in a typical Southern town. They based their plan on study of two counties, one in Georgia, one in South Carolina. They used plausible-sounding new ideas about curricula and theories of learning and emphasized such things as flexibility, extensive pre-school training, and low ratios of pupils to teachers, recommending extensive use of high school students as teachers' aides. The children would live at the school during the week, removed from homes that might cripple their learning capacity, and associating with representatives of a more sophisticated world in which they would come to move. There was also the suggestion that they spend a quarter of each year in a large city for the environmental experience and training. The report estimated that the cost of such a program would be not quite double per pupil expenditures for education in the two counties studied. The authors even suggested ways of raising the extra money, including federal grants that might be obtained.

"The educational problems of these communities ramify into the problems of the whole social and economic context," the report said. "We have tried to suggest that the transformation of education in some sense calls for the transformation of a community. We think such a transformation can be brought about in the South only with the help of genuine local effort and concern."[8] During the next three years, no community attempted to put their ideas into practice.

The Child Development Group of Mississippi was the most attention-attracting of a number of Southern Head Start programs which attempted to make real breakthroughs in pre-school training. CDGM was founded on imported notions of child psychology and what seemed a pure form of Deweyism. Especially in the first year, these achieved some spectacular organizational results and of-

8 Donald Ross Green, James A. Jordan, W. J. Bridgeman, and Clay V. Brittain, "Black Belt Schools: Beyond Desegregation," Southern Regional Council, November, 1965.

fered heartening physical evidence of efficacy in the bright faces and articulate voices of the children themselves. These were Negro youngsters from Mississippi's depths of poverty, particularly severe in the rural areas and small towns; by the end of the second year, after the Office of Economic Opportunity and internal stresses had watered down the original vision, one could still encounter in these three and four-year-olds a remarkable brightness instead of the normal hand-over-mouth shyness and lethargic dullness of eye and response. CDGM introduced Little Golden Books in shacks where the only book before had been the Bible, and mothers who could not read sat with their preschoolers in that patient posture of the conscientious middle-class parent, pointing a finger to a bright-red drawing, saying, "What is that?" and the child chirped the exaltation of his dawning cognition of symbols: "B'loon! Balloon!" To know the emptiness of verbal content in the lives of such children theretofore (not emptiness, of course, of other important things, like closeness to nature) was to know the miracle of such a scene. CDGM laid great stress—against the wishes of the Office of Economic Opportunity—on having the parents of the children (many of them unlettered, few with any formal training in teaching) as the teachers and officials and boards of the schools. This obviously moved the educational experience into the home; not the least of its effects was to impart new respect (both self and filial) to the parents, and it showed the children the connection of their learning experience with their environment. Not the least of the tragedies of the situation—and these included CDGM's insecure position, ever fighting to stay funded, with the schools going on with no pay to anyone during the unfunded times of fighting, and the increasing use of the program as a political issue—was that the brightened-up little boys and girls with their big eyes and alert faces moved into the dreariness of first grade in the regular schools and soon disappeared into the dullness of response and role that was their norm. Again, tragically, much of that alertness and brightness noted in the CDGM schools was the result in large part the introduction of the children to an adequate diet, the meals served at the schools.

Higher education, where it was available in the small places, was largely the patched-up, stamped-out variety of state colleges and junior colleges thrown together in a losing effort to keep up with increasing population and aspiration of the young. The kind of exaggerated importance of Negro educators as an intellectual elite was attached to a lesser degree to the white faculties of colleges in the smaller places. Certainly, the existence of a college, white or black, made a difference in the tone of a town, more of one, maybe, than outside the South because of such basic things as its just not occurring to parents and children to think about going to college in the small places where colleges did not exist. People who otherwise might never see live theater, hear a lecturer, or even visit a library, gained access to them. But it should not be assumed that the existence of a college in a small city of the South might have the same progressive, liberal effect that it would in, say, New England. Not a few of the private institutions waited until the public schools desegregated before making the step.

One administrator confessed that his college had not had "large numbers" of Negro students. There had been eight the first year of desegregation, "twelve or fifteen" the second. They got "good reception." Also "lots of ignoring." They participated in all activities, though none had yet made the basketball team. The older faculty members didn't like it, but they were "professional" about it. The younger faculty members, the majority, had wanted it sooner. There had not been one complaint from Negro students about faculty or student treatment.

At another small college in 1963, a group of students from an all-Negro college spent a night on campus to attend a meeting with white students, and, though the experience created thoughtful reassessments, challenging the assumptions of (in the words of the college president) "young people from homes where there was great resistance to Negroes, competition with them," i.e., poor whites, it also set off repercussions. The Klan and Citizens' Council threatened the president (he stood up to it), and about sixty students, some armed with chains with razor blades welded into them, marched on his home. (The march was broken up by other students.)

Aside from such early discouragements, one reason Negroes Southwide did not attend the formerly all-white private and even state universities in as large numbers as one might expect (colleges in the small cities often had to recruit their token desegregation strenuously) was that they came out of a tradition that saw the all-Negro institutions as the height of aspiration. Long before black consciousness gave an ideological base to it, the average run of youngsters preferred the cultural familiarity of the black schools. And those with an above-average educational or social motivation for getting into a formerly all-white college generally tended to think in terms of the big Northern universities.

The South's struggles with college and public school desegregation—lasting over a decade for the colleges by the late 1960s—had confronted the public schools of the small places directly only with the fumbling efforts of the Office of Education to administer the 1964 Civil Rights Act. The act was an administrative impossibility, containing the contradictory mandate of Title Six—that dual systems of white and Negro schools (a Southern condition) be abolished—and the prohibition in Title Four against affirmative action—busing—to overcome racial imbalance, a Northern condition. Nowhere was the irresponsible capriciousness of Congress more evident, and nowhere the effects more devastating, than in Southern education. For it was obvious that a major factor in the continuing, inexcusable debilitation of Southern public education in the

1960s was the amount of energy and resources of educators and boards of education diverted from the overwhelming problems of education to the skirmishes and strategies of desegregation—either to evade the law, to circumvent its intent with tokenism, or in some rare cases even to obey it conscientiously against strong public opinion. This was evident in the amount of emphasis people in individual schools, colleges, or school systems placed on desegregation when one asked how things were going with them. What was on the minds of teachers and principals and school board members was not all the exciting new knowledge of ways in which human beings learn but, rather, the continuing battle with guidelines or the delicate social adjustments of fitting a few Negro children and teachers into an environment of white children who had been raised implicitly racist.

"We have lived one way, and now things are changing," said a young politician in one small city, himself full of the ambiguities of racial attitudes summed up in the new Southern tendency to pronounce "Negro" four different ways. His summation and that ambiguity were the psychological setting for the great social experiment of Southern school desegregation that seemed doomed from its start by the dishonesty of the law which compelled it. "You know," said a thoughtful small city educator, "a lot of white people have been surprised and pleased that their children and Negro children could go to school with each other without any trouble, and that they could have PTA meetings together." That was part of it.

But consider the implications of an occurrence at a different meeting—when officers of the white state education association convened with officials of the Negro one to discuss the National Education Association's weak-willed dictum to merge. (The Negro bureaucracies of the state associations have generally lost jobs where the mergers have taken place, a cause of Negro acquiescence in the South to white foot-dragging.) Negro delegates to the meeting found themselves seated separately from whites, and when they went to the rest room, they found that one of their white professional colleagues had scrawled with a black crayon in big letters over the urinal: "Black Power. LBJ Niggers. Watch Dem Niggers. Dem Smart Niggers."

Where in one town a teacher might be surprised and delighted with her reception as the (timorously volunteering) only white in a Negro school, another in the same situation comes home weeping in frustration and anger at the appalling conditions she finds in the school plant—including bad ventilation and a highway so close that motor noises make normal classroom discourse impossible. A Negro teacher in the reverse situation, the only black on a white faculty, is invited by white parents to attend a picnic for teachers, apparently an annual affair in the spring. It is far out in the country; the old fears (rational and irrational—it might be a trap) consume her, but she forces herself to go. "It was so good. These are poor people, mostly. And they were just so genuinely gracious and kind. I learned so much that day—including that you can't keep on holding things against them."

From large city and small, the resistance to the law had been disgraceful. State officials and congressmen fought year after year against each scheme of enforcement, no matter how paltry. Nearly all state and local education officials resisted as much as they could the compliance requirements, did as little as absolutely necessary to keep from losing federal funds, and kept up steady complaints, carpings, and attacks on the federal officials trying to enforce the law. Slowly, they pushed the federal government back. From an inadequate but at least clear-cut set of guidelines enforced for two years by a special branch of the Office of Education, there came a retreat to far more flexible enforcement under general auspices of the Office of Health, Education, and Welfare. After a year or two, Negro children gave the most eloquent expression of the success of the resistance by refusing to return to the unpleasantness of a desegregated school. The cruelty of children is peculiarly merciless, and they know when they can get away with it. There were instances in which teachers goaded white children to commit cruelties against Negroes, and many more in which the teachers themselves inflicted the cruelty.

Acts of racism can become so terrible as to defy empathy, and be all-defeating. A teacher in a Black Belt town, "liberal" by its standards, has in her class one Negro child. She takes an interest in him, finds the problems that are hindering him scholastically, helps him overcome them through a special class in the school system. Then she tells how, on the last day of school, as always, she has the class of little second-graders come by her desk, one by one, for a good-bye hug. "And do you know—that little colored boy came too, holding his arms out to me, just like the rest. And I just had to push him away. All the other children were there watching. I just had to. Can you imagine him doing that?" Even without cruelty, the white schools had higher standards than Negro ones; without harassment, just catching up could be an ordeal. A classroom teacher, like a state judge, is an unrestrained power. If she wants to fail each black child who comes under her, no one can stop her or say she has been unfair.

The American Friends Service Committee during the first year of school desegregation under the 1964 Civil Rights Act had a Southwide program to encourage Negro parents to send their children to the previously all-white schools. After the anguish of that first year the program was cut back—not as usual by bureaucratic edict in headquarters, but at least in part because of the bitterness of field workers. Family after family was severely hurt by the thing they had encouraged (jobs lost, welfare cut off, homes bombed). After one high school senior girl had endured a year of low-grade unpleasantness, the year book came out with her picture captioned: "I pays my money and I takes my choice." An egg was hurled at her evening dress at graduation. One of these field workers summed up: "I won't ever encourage another Negro kid to go through that." (The next year, the Friends increased emphasis on providing financial aid to families hurt in efforts to get what the law said Negroes should have.)

Letters the Southern office of the AFSC received from these families tell their own sad story of the relentlessness of persecution.

A woman trying to get on welfare wrote:

Then I said, I know the reason you want help me, then she ask why, I said on the account of my childrens, then she said to me, Well, why don't you take them out of the white school . . . Well, my childrens are back in school so i don't know what are going to happen, the reason I say this they will not give me a job. And won't let my children work on their farms, or rake their yards, So Mrs. Curry, you might know what i am up against. And that is why i can't explain the happiness i have over the gift the Service Committee sent to me, Any way, all i have to give in return are my prayers and a millions thanks. Oh by the way. you asked about my son eyes. Well i am sorry to tell you this, but the doctor told me the 30th of Aug. that one of his eyes were gone, I ask for help when it first happen, but they turned me down. So thats the way it is. I were born here, but they all treat me like a stranger, except for one family . . . Honey, I don't know, Because my waye are so dark, it don't any one knows but God. So this are all i can say for now.

A woman from Mississippi:

. . . School have started. Now the kids going back to school. My baby going. Ruth didn't want to go back. I am sorry about this but she get sad when we talk about her going back . . . A white man came to the car ask Matthew [her husband, taking the children to school] had he prayed to the Lord about what he was doing. didn't he think it right. did he think our kids was any better than other Negro kids. He went on to say we were payd to send our kids to this school and our kids can get just as much education in the Negro school. My husband

said he were afraid, being the only Negro there. But he
did say no one payed me to send my kids to this school.
The Freedom of Choice papers what he went by. he said
them pappers didn't mean anything. My husband said
he told the man and you don't have to tell me what kind
of education the children will get at the Negro school,
because he had five to finish there . . . be sweet . . .

P. S. My husband was told by a friend that the mayor
here said he would die and go to hell before he hire my
husband.

There are hundreds of such letters on file, telling much
the same things year after year.

Most of the national publicity and much of the Southern writing about the school desegregation adventure have
centered correctly on outbreaks of adult violence, persecution of desegregating Negro children. But among the "nice
people" majority of white teachers and administrators and
school board members was a tendency in the opposite direction, at its least admirable simply the neurotic Southern
desire to avoid overt expression of real emotion, the abhorrence of a "scene," and at its best a growing feeling
among the whites for the humanity of the Negro children.
This didn't imply any widespread agreement with the
philosophy of the Supreme Court school decision (that no
child gets the education he is entitled to in a discriminatory school system) or even any confidence that the dab-
bles of token desegregation would in the long run succeed.
Indeed, there was often an implicit and explicit sense that
the white school people were going through the motions of
token desegregation as a demonstration, a proof that it
couldn't work. But there was the desire in many of the
small places, maybe in most, that it not be disgracefully
violent or cruel. Voices would drop in the seriousness of
calculating the dangers or of retelling the close calls. Much
of the attitude was characterized by the words of a small
city superintendent: "We desegregated peaceably here,

with the help of Providence and substantial citizens who were determined to hold together a school system, even if they had to integrate to do it."

By 1968, of the pitifully, disgracefully small total amount of public school desegregation in the South, more of it (not merely numerically, but in percentages of black children in school with whites) was occurring in the smaller urban units than in the large cities. This was largely because most of the city desegregation came about under court orders before passage of the 1964 law and had not been achieved under the pressures of the various Office of Education guidelines (with percentages that were not binding, but were often misinterpreted to be so). If there was any hope in the sorry situation, it was that Southerners' sparse experience of one another's humanity on the level of the classroom would, in the years to come, culminate in the change of white habits of thought and emotion that full and firm enforcement of the law might have produced in shorter time. There were some heartening indications that this was occurring.

In the smaller places, far more than in the large cities, for example, there was less ability to segment the desegregation experience, to make it a schools-only thing. It was interesting in some of the towns to hear white and black adults speak of integrated teenage canteens and school dances. The Negro children keep to themselves; they are not going to do anything that would cause trouble, a white parent says assuringly. "I wanted to ask my nephew about the senior prom, whether they mix-danced," said a Negro woman. "But he didn't offer to tell, and so I didn't ask."

A liberal white couple had their faith shaken by discovering their child's desegregated classroom was almost entirely Negro and debated whether to have him transferred to a school with more balanced desegregation. Then the little third-grade boy came home the second day of school to tell what a fine friend he had made in his room. Was the friend white or colored, they eventually asked him. "I don't know," the third-grader answered. "I forgot to ask him." They decided to let him stay where he was.

As for the other areas of desegregation in the small urban units, there was more in public places and probably less rancor overall in this and the other comings-together of white and Negro than one might imagine. On the social level of the ten cent store, in big city and small alike, there was really remarkable accommodation to the new order— among the white and black women working side by side behind the counters, at the lunch counter where people of both races served people of both races. Among the employees, there was probably not ever much thought to visiting one another, social integration as the people in the small places called it. But in their day-to-day working together, there seemed completely natural relations, the small cooperations necessary to getting such work done, the small talk of babies and illness and acquisitions that was the evidence of their shared way of life, and none of the condescension or subtle animosity that too often characterizes the interracial relationships of better-off people, theoretically more enlightened. In the more expensive restaurants, especially where the main highways and interstates come through, and in the motels, the few Negroes who sought service, travelers and the local Negroes who could afford it—a middle-class matter—were served with the same cold impersonality as whites.

Movie theaters sometimes became a focal point for demonstrations during the struggles of the 1960s but seemed not much of a problem after passage of the 1964 law. Perhaps one reason was that fewer people of either race attended them because of television, and there were always the drive-ins. In one town, the new law's abolition of the old arrangement whereby whites sat downstairs and Negroes in the balcony of the only theater resulted in an immediate, gleeful taking over of the balcony by courting young white couples.

Housing ranged from the extreme of shacks on mud alleys, the conventional niggertowns where most of the black people, often a majority or near it, in the small places lived in crowded squalor with empty land so near, to the older sections of middle-class Negro gentility, sometimes the same as in the city, formerly white abodes, here dwelling the older aristocracy of teachers, undertakers, preachers, and then to the new thing of ranch-house, suburban splendor for the emerging younger middle class, the affluent older people, smaller replicas of the big-city Negro Gold Coast areas. This was a minority in all the places but something that hadn't been there at all before, a small sharing at least in the general, middle-class prosperity since World War II, greater than any the South had ever known before. The houses were as distinctionless and well-equipped as those of the white suburbs; the only difference was that they cost more and were harder to finance. The proliferation of them in subdivisions and Negro suburbs were in many of the small places the beginnings of housing segregation, of physical separation.

Many of the small places boasted good, but very seldom desegregated, public housing. This was a part of the enthusiasm for federal funds (like those for highways) that suggested progress and enhanced a town's industry-luring appeal (as opposed to those like the food stamp program or welfare, which merely helped poor people) and a part of the zest for urban renewal. Hardly a town and surely no small city (except those places one occasionally heard about where a crank in control announced a policy of accepting no federal money, soon passing on) had not torn out great chunks of close-in niggertown squalor and replaced them with industrial sites, parks, public buildings, what have you. I talked once with a professional planner whose firm contracted with small places across the South to draw up the elaborate proposals necessary to getting urban renewal grants. In not a single project that he worked on, he said, was there not at least some element in the planning of developing or perpetuating housing segregation, and in many it was the chief purpose.

The one public gathering place that was not desegregated in most places was that symbol of the white South's murkiest racial fears—the swimming pool. When all else had fallen, even the churches, the pools remained segregated. Some towns and cities closed their pools; some sold them to private interests which used their own extra-legal methods, the private club subterfuge, to keep them segregated. Some built their first "Negro" municipal pool and trusted the good judgment of the Negro community to keep to it. Negroes in the small places were remarkably willing to do this, maybe with their own sensitivity, squeamishness about being with whites where so much of human flesh was bared. Across the Southland, for whatever psychologists would make of it, there was very little interracial swimming.

I once watched (furtively, lest I give away the momentous test about to occur) as a lean young Negro man, his wife, another couple, and the first couple's little boy, a toddler, got out of a car and quickly confronted a bathhouse attendant, who, having been warned and instructed what to do, accepted their money and let them enter what had been ever before the white sanctuaries of the locker rooms. A few minutes later, these black bodies emerged in stylish swimming gear and moved together toward the water. Few people were about; no one seemed to pay any attention. The sun was bright and glaring. A couple with Northern accents remarked upon the scene, having asked a policeman and having been told what was happening. "Why, it's one of those desegregations," the woman said. Sure enough, out across the wide, white glow of the sandy beach the brave little party advanced, dots now in the glare of sand and sun, their color not discernible, as they waded out and then dived into the blue water. They were —and I have never felt the absurdity of segregation more strongly—integrating the Atlantic Ocean.

The computations, scheming that go into the skirmishings over desegregation were incredible in their complexity, and complexities and contradictions never ceased. These were almost as apparent in the late 1960s as in 1964 when Mississippians literally believed the Freedom Summer college kids coming to live among Negroes would be hordes of gangsters and Communists come to rape the white women, to burn and loot. In the smaller places, the fear and animosity for outsiders was more pervasive. The true story is told of an innocent shouting of one of its more innocent forms, a white fan at the annual North-South college football game the first year that both teams had Negroes in the line-up, yelling after a hard tackle, "Look at them niggers roughing up our colored boy."

In one little town, everyone remembered the fearful day in the summer of 1965 when a carload of Northern Negroes drove onto Main Street and all got out and ordered lunch at the drugstore counter. Some thought they were the dreaded CORE, others that they were something worse; no one seemed to have even entertained the thought that they might have been hungry travelers who had paused at this small place for lunch. Local Negroes had already "tested" that lunch counter (a ritual in many of the small places, particularly the towns, where, after careful beforehand arrangements, the local NAACP branch would march a group to a lunch counter at which they would sit and stiffly eat, trying to appear laughing and relaxed, dignified old preachers and the like, showing that it could be done, and then leaving, the counter likely not to be used by one black person afterward, but available to Negroes—if only in theory). But after the invasion of the foreign hordes, the owner of the drugstore took out the stools to his lunch counter, never to replace them.

The element of panic in the white fear of the outsider

doesn't permit differentiation between varieties of outsider. In the late 1960s whites still seemed not to know the
world of difference between the moderate NAACP and the
old CORE and SNCC or that the last two, as far as the
South was concerned, were really no more and, where they
did exist, had changed drastically. It was as though the
whites, having felt their control over "our colored" weaken
immensely, dreaded to see any reminder of this. Smart Negro leaders could play on this, on the fear of outsiders.
More than one had threatened to bring in CORE, bring in
Dr. King, with desired effect. Black power was even more
clearly a threat. Where things were seeming hopeless, most
often there would be the ultimate threat, to bring in
Stokely—something that chilled the most liberal of whites.
Often there was the strong suggestion that power structures took voluntary actions for desegregation or improved
facilities for Negroes with no threat to goad them, only the
gnawing fear of outsiders, or even to express appreciation
for their absence. Many places acknowledged that bad outsiders could come from both directions. "We're still not
doing what we should do on education and jobs," said a
young white leader in a small city. "You can't change in
two years what has been going on for one hundred. We can
do it though if we can keep Stokely Carmichael and Calvin
Craig [a Klan grand dragon at the time] out. If we can
keep the radicals out . . ."

The skirmishing would continue in all areas and varying patterns of adjustment would be reached, broken up,
built anew, ever new configurations emerging. But the
most important thing was school desegregation, and where
it all had begun earliest and where the results were least
encouraging, the sensible and sane solutions were becoming clearer. The good and beautiful thing that could, with
good sense and sanity, happen to the children showed itself
occasionally, rarely, with tantalizing fragility.

A pretty Negro high school girl in a desegregated school

in a small town talked freely of her experiences and impressions:

> If you get friendly with a poor white, really get acquainted, you find them more easy to be friends with than the rich whites . . . In chemistry class, the whites were all my friends because they could call on me for help . . . In two of my classes I am the only Negro, and they have no choice but to be friendly with me. They couldn't just let me sit in a corner . . . If there are just one or two white kids against you, they have to come around in order to get along with the rest. Now when I'm downtown, white friends yell at me across the street. They don't stand back on speaking, even if their parents are with them. Today at the grocery store, a white girl and I were laughing and going on and kidding each other . . . The children are easier to accept new things than their parent. A white girl at school got married and another white girl came up to me downtown to talk about it, about her picture in the paper and all, and she introduced her mother to me after we had talked. Her mother had been listening and she could tell we were together about things, and she was all right. She was nice. I wish more children would introduce their parents . . . I used to never smile at a white person. Now I can—and mean it.

This was what should have been going on universally, might have been with rational law and enforcement. The sadder thing that seemed to be happening was that as whites, in the ways described by this gentle and sympathetic young woman, began their slow moves toward the great distance they had to go (the moves heartening in consideration of the greatness of that distance), Negroes were recoiling from their old, patient wish for integration because of the very slowness of the moves, and such other reasons as the fact that whites were not the paragons they had pretended to be, familiarity breeding contempt. "There is a reservoir of good will," said the white man who had observed white parents being pleased that their children could go to school peaceably with Negroes. "I hope we will not lose it. But I'll tell you—I feel less and less welcome in Negro groups every time I am in one."

Certainly, as each year passed, fewer Negro children were eager to enter the token situations of desegregation, and with good cause. In many instances, they were encouraged in this by the Negro teachers, some fearing loss of jobs, some indignant over the evils of tokenism, some feeling that transfer of the best students to white schools reflected on their own schools and teaching abilities. Whites liked to point this out and to say, as several did in a town which was one of the very few in the South to abolish Negro schools altogether and fully integrate its system, that the Negro community had felt a sense of loss, a lessening of community spirit, at no longer having their own school system with its own events to function as a social focal point. What happened to the town was a commentary on federal law enforcement failure; it had taken the intelligent action it did toward immediate full integration out of the belief that all school systems would have to do this in a short time and that it would be better done quickly. The bitterness against federal enforcement and the political repercussions against those who had urged the action ("We believed in doing what was right," said one of these; "if anybody don't like it they can vote us out") were understandably great when it was discovered that tokenism seemed on a permanent basis in other systems.

The real meaning of the deepest implications of that seemingly simple edict of the Supreme Court in 1954 continued to unfold in the South. For when the little town closed the Negro schools to facilitate full integration, even this was hurtful of the real goal of integration, as evidenced by the sense of loss felt by the Negro community. The principal of an all-Negro school in a small city voiced the ideal solution when she said, "If only we had just one white family of stature in the town that would put their children in my school. Then some of the others would follow." In 1967 I talked to one of the attorneys who had been involved in much of the school desegregation litigation, and only then, after long and arduous thinking through the realities of Southern experience in the matter, had he been able to come up with the same answer—whites attending formerly all-Negro schools as well as Negroes attending formerly all-white ones. By 1968, the courts had advanced almost to the same point, declaring that the legal sanction against discrimination would not be satisfied until there was an end to dual school systems.

But there was, in the first feeble steps toward implementation of this decree, again the notion of closing Negro schools. In Swanquarter, North Carolina, a school boycott and demonstrations protested such closing of Negro schools under an HEW integration plan. Beyond the hurt to the Negro community, there was the old Southern penchant for waste in the shutting down of any facilities in a region with the highest ratio of school-age population to adult population anywhere in the country. Eventually, there would have to come a crisis of decision in the South which would determine once and for all whether real integration would be realized, with racial designations of buildings and attendance become meaningless and children going just to schools. It would be either that or, from tokenism, a retreat and retrenchment into the ruin of racism. Only with real integration, the end in practice of dual school systems, could the South get about the business of real education of the children.

VII

A small-city main-street merchant, not more enlightened than many, a moderate, believed the answer to the race problem in his town was education, not necessarily desegregation (even as black power advocates had come to talk), but simply improving the quality of the schools. "The right direction is upping education so colored boys and women can get better jobs. That's more important than sitting on buses. If they would just raise the colored people's standard of living by 10 percent, it would be a boon. I am for it selfishly; think what it would do for my business."

The connection between education and jobs was, thus, clear to most. Less certain were the connections the whites and blacks of the small places were able to make between the overabundance of the labor supply in the South and the struggles to adjust to the new law and government-contract pressure for ending discrimination in employment.

On the main streets, in the stores which often depended on Negroes for most of t trade (particularly the poor Negroes with no cars), there nearly always had to be pressure in the form of boycotts or picketing to gain jobs as clerks and cashiers for black people. The man who had spoken of the need for upping education was fairly typical on the job proposition, though the pressure had come to him from another source. Sears Roebuck had asked all the locally owned stores to hire at least one Negro clerk because it had to do so by orders from on high. He promoted "a girl" who had been in the receiving department many years. This was at the suggestion of the other clerks. They didn't think much of having a Negro on an equal footing, but if it had to be, they would like to see the woman they all knew (and in the weird way of it, probably loved) get a break. Customers, the merchant said (and this was true generally), didn't seem to mind. In fact, after awhile, there were a lot of white people who wouldn't let anyone else wait on them. He was training two other Negroes in receiving for similar advancement.

(This man happened to be a Jew—"I'm Jewish; I know what it is to be a second-class citizen." No main street was without a store or two with a Jewish name, usually an old and respected one in the place, but no preponderance of Jewish people were in retail trade or any other endeavor in

the small places because they tended to be scarce. The
general rarity of Jews or first or second generation immigrants of any kind ["foreigners"] has been noted as part of
the explanation of the South's provinciality and that lack
of leftist radicalism that so surprised Myrdal. Small wonder
that they shunned a land of such lurid reputation for intolerance, and such limited economic opportunity. But
because they were so scarce as to pose no threat and because the emphasis of intolerance was so strong against the
Negro, "foreigners" tended to have little trouble in the
small places as long as they—like the artists—accepted
things as they were. In the Delta of Mississippi, there were
a number of Orientals, who probably stayed on here after
helping to build railroads, well-fitted into the white world.
The Negro anti-Semitism that developed in the large cities
against the presence of Jewish small grocers and the like
was not a problem in the smaller places, no more than any
rampant anti-Semitism by whites. Temples were blown up
in various locales, but this was the work of white extrem-
ists and was always accompanied by great outpourings of
sympathy by most of the whites. This was not always the
case when Negro churches were bombed or burned, but
there were stories like that of the little town where hood-
lums broke into a Negro church and smeared paint in the
sanctuary, and the townspeople reacted with distress and
anger and sent white teenagers to clean it all up, not allowing the Negroes to help. Jews and the "foreigners" were,
of course, suspect on race and the like; one of the sadder
phenomena across the South was the figure of the lonely,
fearful Jew who sought to outbigot his white neighbors,
not merely a member but a leader, often, in the Citizens'
Councils when they were going strong, with their own anti-
Semitism. With recent changes in immigration laws, the
tendency of naturalized citizens to be more to the right
than to the left might, in one more irony, mitigate the
South's lack of a cosmopolitan population; like the Cuban
refugees in Miami and other Southern coastal places, they

might find the political climate more compatible than almost anywhere else.)

Local government employment of Negroes in the small places was not great. The Negro policeman had emerged in many as early as the 1950s, not without his own unsavory legend, in small city as well as large, of being more brutal, unfair, often, with black people than his white counterparts—again maybe a matter of overcompensation. The extensions of the federal poverty programs into the small places, little offices in the Negro business district often, were usually all-Negro, or Negro-dominated. Whites who worked in these places, hometown people for the most part, tended like whites in the big cities to move deeper and deeper into sympathy with the Negro cause, the more they saw of the effects in abject poverty of discrimination, this often, touchingly, reflected in their determination to endure the hard looks and whatever else might come from the superficial gesture of eating lunch each day with their black co-workers. (It was one thing for an all-Negro party to seek service in the shopping center diner, another thing for whites and blacks together, and something else again if sexes were intermingled as well.) Otherwise, the federal bureaucracy in small places was generally all-white or tokenly desegregated and, what is worse, was often, as in the outreachings of the U.S. Agriculture Department, a bastion of racist feeling and perversion of policy.

The pattern of "equal opportunity" in industry was as in the big cities—real efforts to hire Negroes in the newer plants, even tokenly at the managerial level, and slow compliance in the older plants, usually in some arrangement of attrition, replacing leaving whites with so many Negroes, so many whites. There was often low-grade harassment of Negro employees in both situations by their white co-workers, but little organized white effort to block Negroes from the ever-scarce jobs. This was true even in areas that might have a small plant or two, but not enough jobs to go around, so that whites often had to commute to nearby cities for work, even into adjoining states, spending hours a day driving back and forth. It was one more remarkable instance of the inability of whites to act, even unconsciously, for their own economic interests, in this instance even their harassment of Negroes to no such purpose.

A well-educated, middle-class Negro woman, presiding when she was not at work over a lovely home, told about conditions on her job at a recently desegregated older plant. Of 2,400 employees there at the time, thirty were Negro. All were on the third shift, late night to early morning, the least desirable. Of five people in her production unit, she was the only Negro and had the worst job. There were no difficulties, she said, for her or the other Negroes at the plant with white fellow workers. Management attitudes in those older plants, some locally owned, more often though branches of national firms, were discriminatory toward workers of both races: "Hell, we took these people out of the fields and trained them. They ought to be grateful and happy. They never made so much money before. The union shouldn't be making demands." (It was the Southern rationale, surely, that was different; the paternalism was the same the country over.) In one area, various people from different vantages on the economic scale spoke of a cotton mill owner who bragged that he would not hire kids right out of high school. "Let them go try somewhere else," he would say, "and get beat down and fail, and then let them come back here with the right attitude and I can make good hands of them." Even some of the working-class people, though resenting this, indicated agreement with its reasoning. Not so a well-to-do farmer: "I don't agree. What kind of employees would you have, browbeaten like that?"

Labor was, of course, no great force for progress or, considering its failure ever really to get hold in the South, its diminutive numbers, anything else. Labor in one little city, not considered helpful on race, splintered in politics, was blamed by businessmen for lack of new industry, for closing of one old plant. If a town got known as a "bad labor town"—one where unions have been rather militant —industry shunned it because there were so many places with no unions and docile laborers, and because of the low-grade kind of industry, in the first place, the South kept seeking to lure. The racial apostasies of the rank-and-file— among other failings of national labor (which by the late 1960s seemed nearing fatal)—had long been in clearer, sharper focus in the South. Heedlessly unions forced their own wages and working conditions up with no concern for the plight of the non-unionized, no real effort any more at new organizing, no concern for the unorganized except the compromised and pauperized minimum wage legislation. In a land of a buyer's market for labor, the resulting disparity had been evident for years in the South in the pitiful difference between the economic condition of the union man at, say, the local phone company, and the non-union wretch at, say, the local sawmill. Neither was what might be called prosperous, but between the one and the other was the difference between some hope and security and a losing battle against bills and the dread specter of sickness. A recent exception to the failure to organize was the impressive effort of the American Federation of State, County and Municipal Employees (AFL-CIO) to unionize garbagemen and the like, mostly black, across the South.

The AFL-CIO state headquarters staff, personified in most of the states by colorful, brave, and wary old warriors (like Hank Brown in Texas, Claude Ramsay in Mississippi, and Barney Weeks in Alabama), had the prodigious job of somehow reconciling these manifestations of the local labor movement with the liberal stances and occasional actions (as the call for unions to join in the big civil rights demonstrations, like Selma) of the national office. It was an impossible job; it took men possessed of a considerable optimism (which in the South sometimes seemed misplaced) not just about human nature, but about the ability of organizations to change, to improve. Probably the most effective, most successful of these state-level leaders was Victor Bussie in Louisiana, who wielded the power of a more or less deliverable labor vote of 100,000-plus to gain considerable influence in a state administration like that of Governor McKeithen in matters considered the concern of labor. Among these, sadly, were the outposts of the poverty program which in various ways, including whether the governor approved them for federal funding or not, were beholden to labor and its state politics, a newer form of patronage power. In sum, labor was in its small power in the South much the sad thing it had become in its larger power in the rest of the country, a dabbler in its affairs, a manipulator of its power, largely a part of the status quo. The brave battles of the past still haunted the hopes of those who sought real change, including Negroes. (Yet there was no more abject figure, no sorrier fellow, than some of the old-timey Negro labor kept-men, trotted out to show tokenism, devoid of independence.) Those past battles still bothered the power structures, preferring the absence of unions, ready as ever to fight them, believe them to be Communist and other deplorable things. In the conservative world of the power structures, where they sometimes tried to manuever, unions were ineffective because they were still suspect. In the efforts of the liberals, they were often a hindrance, a conservative force.

I attended the rump convention in Georgia that sent the "challenge delegation" to the 1968 Democratic Convention. (The regular delegation was appointed by Governor Maddox, whose loyalty seemed leaning to Wallace.) It was a stirring affair, bringing together young people and Negroes in a real new-politics feeling of cohesion, nearly all of them, a majority of the delegates, for Eugene McCarthy's candidacy. Arrayed against them was a force which had organized the Convention in the first place, largely labor, and largely ineffective people, "delegations" from each county come to dutifully be appointed as Humphrey delegates to the national convention, and go home, older Negroes, sadly, among the most of them. The labor people hadn't expected the influx of young enthusiasts who had been organized at the last minute by McCarthy workers and who put to shame and shambles the rigged and essentially feeble thing labor had constructed there—labor's petulant walkout harking back to other futile Southern boycotts of political due process, Julian Bond emerging from the fray the leader of the young people and surely the most attractive figure at the Chicago Convention.

A measure of the difference between the North and the South was that most people in large cities and small considered the advent of new manufacturing plants, no matter how exploitative, an unalloyed, positive good. Air pollution in a paper mill town might have reached degrees of unpleasantness beyond even that noxious mixture of gas and garbage breathed in the more intensely developed industrial megalopolises of the North; in such things as pollution and exploitation and ugliness, some of the larger Southern cities were approaching what had happened to much of the industrial North. But such problems were not even acknowledged, let alone measured against the social and economic utility of the industry. Considering what had been the mentality of the cotton mill owner before and the continuing relative shortage of jobs and capital, one could at least understand the general rejoicing over more and more new industry in the large cities. The difference between the large cities and the small places was that the good of the lured, new industry probably did outweigh any evil in the latter. Consider a small city with the kind of ultra-reactionary power structure we have discussed, with newspapers and radio blathering racism and far-rightism day after day. Consider its politics.

One young politician of some sophistication viewed small-town political life in this way:

We've had unstable politics around here for many years.
There are too many factions. The Labor Council is in
disarray; it amounts to each union being able maybe to
carry its membership and no more, and no agreement
between two unions. The [court ordered] tax re-evalua-
tion caused turmoil in county politics. Last election,
there were twenty county commission candidates for five
seats. The five who won were all against the incumbents.
It was an against vote. One is a liberal veterinarian, one
a rich farmer, two labor men, and the fifth a young non-
entity who just got out and worked hard. Now the trouble with them is that *they've had a lot of squabbling
over minor things.* They didn't run as a ticket. The
county board of education is the same way. The anti-vote
put them in and kicked out the old superintendent. At
their first meeting, they voted to consolidate two schools
without even bothering to talk to any of the community
leaders or anything. The communities took it to court.
There was a bond election and they lost it on the con-
solidation issue. And they've lost two subsequent ones.
They didn't explain the bond issues. A filling station
man doesn't understand about curriculum and all that.
And it would have meant a tax increase. So there's just
been turmoil these past two years. And two scandals in
the courthouse. [Very earnestly:] We are honest people
generally. It was mainly just bad bookkeeping.

Now the city is different. We had a long-time city manager, a fine man. A short man with thick glasses and so
on. He wasn't married. His family was the city. He ran
the city for twenty years. He was more powerful than the
commissioners. The Negroes loved him. He was straight
with them. The commissioners are businessmen. They
caucus before their meetings [this approvingly, meaning
that they make all the decisions in the caucus with no
public to hear the pros and cons, and announce the results at the public meeting, a common thing]. It's quieter
that way. They don't argue, and so on. The present city
manager was trained by the former one. He's dead now.
The new one's not the politician the old one was.
But I like him. He speaks his mind. The nine commissioners aren't as close-knit as they used to be. Things

may be changing. The city school board though still runs as a ticket. So it's quiet. They act in unison.

So you see, county politics is amateurish and open. City politics is stable, quiet, professional. But I want to be fair. The county has raised pay, put in a merit system, and paved more roads than any previous board of commissioners. But then they ruin it with things like the big squabble they're having now about some little jail additions.

There was never a thought in his mind that the more open, more democratic, squabbling county government might have proved itself effective precisely because it did the people's business out in the open, a rarity in the South —and who would say not in the rest of the nation? Here was the essential condition of the cities of America, shown frighteningly in the figure of Mayor Daley, shown clearly .. these small places of the South—places which one or a few men had in an iron grip, often like nothing so much as a child with a toy, running it by their lights as well as it could possibly be run, brooking no interference, detesting most of all any challenging, any unseemly public display of dissatisfaction, any demand for innovation. Hence, the fear of outsiders, the loathing of agitators.

Move a brand new electronics firm or some other sophisticated industry, sizable and of the enlightened turn of mind of modern business into such a city, and see its effects, and, yes, the temptation is strong to agree with the townspeople, it's a good thing. It will hire five thousand people. It has brought in modern-minded, young professionals, an influence in the many affairs of the small city, from church to PTA. It hires Negroes on somewhere near a fair basis; the personnel manager has a feeling of mission about it. And most of all, it shakes up the old power structure, the old power configurations, loosens the iron grip of men to whom a community has become a plaything. "It's not that the old regime is dislodged completely," said a liberal describing the effect of such a new plant in such a small city. "But it just can't keep things under control any more. There's too many people dissatisfied, and too many new elements responding to them."

Nothing was more fierce, more unyieldingly angry and loathe to compromise or even talk reasonably than the old power structures whose towns and little cities had not begun to budge on desegregation and suddenly in the early 1960s had the calamity of a series of Negro demonstrations come upon them. Much of the impression the nation gained of the South's hopelessly ingrained racism was the result of encounters of Northern reporters—who had never seen these little places before, in their tranquil times—with the angry, near to apoplectic power structures at their time of trial, seeing their prize possession tampered with, torn apart, besmirched. People who had known these places when they were humming along with all the controls manned came away shocked at the ugly reaction of men they knew to be in normal times pleasant and no worse even in their racism than the ordinary run of Southern white humanity. The possessiveness power structures have for the small cities and towns, the misplaced love for them, the anti-democratic, autocratic control that they feel is normal and necessary for governing them (no squabbling, no fuss)—only this would explain in retrospect their bad behavior, redeem them in the opinion of the rest of the nation. Even back then, too, when it was happening, there was the occasional flare-up of the same kind of exacerbated unreasoning anger in the rulers of cities of the North, when, for example, members of CORE chained themselves one day to the pillars of the New York city hall. And then such bad behavior on high became common over the nation as rioting broke out in the ghettos, showing to the world, as demonstrations had in the South, that all was not well, even if the men who ran the cities had pretended that it was, or really, in their proprietary pride, believed that it was. Finally, the same kind of anger could be expressed in the seat of the national government itself, as during the Poor People's Campaign in 1968. How much was different in the South, how much merely more clearly and earlier apparent?

VIII

One can begin to appreciate the impact of such a social institution as a decent, non-exploitative new plant in a small city by comparing it with the other institutions more often thought of as forces for social change and for the amelioration of differences between people. Several years after hot dog stands and bars had integrated, the governing body of one of the larger churches in one of the small cities enacted that sad Southern drama of trying to decide whether to admit Negroes, if they should so apply, to membership. One of the older pillars of the church got up and made an impassioned plea for allowing the Negroes in—not that he personally thought it was the wisest thing, but because of the new plant in town and the wishes of its management in these matters.

Surely there were motives better than this in the white Southern church, something out of the religious tradition of Western Civilization that mitigated racism in the Bible Belt? Some, at least. At that same meeting, another old man got up, an outspoken segregationist in his daily doings, and declared: "I know how I want to vote. But I look here at this church building, and I realize it's not mine. It's the Lord's House. And so we are going to have to do this thing. . . ."

The surface irony, the absurdity of such a meeting being held at all (considering the main tenets of the predominant religions), is too easy, too facile an explanation of the meaning, or lack of it, of religion in the South. More probably than in the rest of the nation, religion did have meaning for Southerners, white and black. The large cities were more into the mainstream of church as a social institution, one among many, or of an unwilled paganism founded in the desire and—considering the stresses of urban life—need to sleep late at least one morning of the week. But in the small cities and towns, the church was central not merely to the social but also—nearly the way it used to be in America—to the spiritual life of the people.

The laggardness of the white churches to desegregate, to formalize in their membership policies the brotherhood of man (essentially, one more Southern exercise in form and ritual, since few Negroes would anywhere, even in the large cities, wish to leave their own congregations), got to the very heart of the tragedy of Southern racism. It involved the proprietary autocracy of the rich and powerful who liked to run their churches with the same disregard for democracy with which they ran their towns.

The splendor of the white Baptist churches in all the little places of the South was a notable phenomenon: no hamlet was so debased as not to have on a prominent corner some cement and brick temple of imposing grandeur, largely endowed by one or a few wealthy old townspeople —though the pressure of the building fund committees, often employing professional fundraisers, upon the widows and the like for their mites were fierce and formidable. The Baptist edifices usually were most prominent, pretentious, for theirs was largest, most powerful, most reactionary among the denominations (indulging Southern propensities in the denomination's bylaws for each church's being autonomous to the point of anarchy). But the "first churches" of the other Protestant denominations were also splendidly housed on prominent corners and similarly financed and controlled. A description of one of the better situations in a small city suggests the tone of this leadership: "The downtown churches have made Negroes welcome on the rare occasions they have sought admittance. Even the First Baptist did this, deciding that if they should

come, there would be no issue made of it. Some of the
leading citizens are members. There are no Negro members of any white churches. The Presbyterian minister has
been very good on race, although he has a very conservative board. The board is always mad at the National Council of Churches over some outrage. But the preacher works
with them, despite his sympathies the other way. He is very
patient. . . ." In some of the towns and cities, large as well
as small, ushers have barred the church doors to demonstrating Negroes seeking to worship, this at the will of the
powerful, autocratic old men.

What of the memberships, the average worshipper?
They come to the churches in the self-deluding spirit that
their towns are Mayberry, regarding race and the other
realities of human existence with the hysteria of "nice
people." To confront them there with the race issue in a
sermon is not too much of an affront; many Southern
preachers have gently chided them for generations about
this (among their other more standard sins, which yet in
the exhortations may include drinking and smoking, card-
playing, dancing, the cardinal one, not coming to church) .
But to confront them with the race issue in its black flesh—
that is a terrible and cruel blow to the heart of their pretenses and self-delusions. Most pitifully, it exposes the
emptiness of all the years of Sunday sermons they have sat
through and destroys the welling up of warmth and good
feeling that on each of those Sundays the preacher's skilled
performance has given to them out of the good and truth
in their Bible. For the very most of them, out of conditioning, fear, shame, out of the sense of what everyone else
might say or feel, out of all the past fancifully elaborate
structuring of custom and etiquette, literally cannot welcome and worship with these black Christians as their
brothers and sisters. This is the terrible thing done to
them by their culture; it is a cruel knowledge to stamp
into the heart of a human being—that not merely his
paternalistic fondness for the colored, ever a source of good

feeling inside himself, is a sham, but the basic tenet of his religion, its whole meaning, is impossible for him. No wonder there is anger, savagery in the secular manifestations of the religious white Southerner's racism.

The sermons are bland, are banal, are filled with the showmanship and ancient thespian skills of which Billy Graham has become the grand champion and has held to ascendancy longer than any of a long line of notable predecessors. We may not say that the message of the religion the congregations professed escaped them, but it is worth noting that the means of conveying its message was a relic from another age of communication, before television, movies, radio, before reading even, with one man talking, many listening. (The only other institution which continued to use it as the predominant form of communication was—education.) The attention span of adults with none of the burning motivation of novitiates in a monastery, or geniuses in a medieval college, is small. The preachers must know this, as they know that the education and intellectual development of the average church-goer is little. Perhaps, like the mass media, they underestimate both. The people seem to have gotten from television far more than it was ever meant for them to get. But the churches were not for instruction or intellectuality; they were essentially for the emotions, for the spirit, and the people went right on, however crippled by the new self-knowledge from the race issue of the failure of their faith, singing every Sunday, "Praise Him all creatures here below . . ."

The talk was ever of change in the heart of man, and the preachers were in the forefront of those who were willing to see another generation or five or more of Negro degradation and needless suffering in the patient effort to will in the hearts of the dominant white majority a complete change in the fundamentals of the culture. The Negroes, some of their own preachers leading the battle, churches their headquarters and staging grounds, ended the debate

between the changers of hearts and those pragmatic souls
of complete faith in liberalism who said change the institutions, and the hearts will follow along. The Negroes forced
the change of the laws regarding the institutions; there was
no chance to see fully what the effect on the heart (though
the evidence was heaviest on the side that it would indeed
follow along). And the preachers, the good ones, went
right on with the patient and slow effort to change attitudes in the midst of institutional flux and indecisive administration of law. Few had the firm knowledge (the intellectual ability to translate ancient dogma into modern
relevancy) of Will Campbell and his followers that the
basic symbolism of the Christian myth was the only and
complete religious answer to racism. But they kept at it,
the good ones among the white preachers, and there were
many stories of their trials and tribulations, failures and
occasional successes.

"You have to appreciate what it does to a preacher to
have his board against him," one who had been through
the experience said sadly. It gets to where there is nobody
in the church he can turn to. This is the penalty for going
too far on race, this the dread thing of losing influence
with the powerful. Some preachers crack, the one who had
been through it said, and some run out. But most are men
of integrity, and see it through. The powerful men will
withdraw their large financial support from the church—
for good or for a period of pouting. Or they will just not
attend services for a month or so, never saying anything,
just not gracing the church with their presences.

In the smaller places, the preachers might be called
Communists. One rich old man, one of the powerful pillars of the church, was giving voice to his theories about
Negroes being infected with diseases unknown to the rest
of humankind when the preacher gently remonstrated
with him, saying, "Now I've heard that stuff all my life,
and I've about concluded that it's not so." The old fellow

told other pillars of the church to watch that preacher; he sounded "half-Communist." The preacher confronted him. "Now you've put me in an awkward position," he said to him. "I'm going to have to sue you. You have defamed my character. The church headquarters has a lawyer for just this kind of thing, and I'm going to turn this over to him. I just want to tell you, gentleman to gentleman." The old fellow apologized, and the preacher made him agree to go to the three other powerful old men to whom he had confided his suspicions and refute what he had said.

But there were more sad stories than happy ones. A poverty program official in a small city told of the efforts to obtain Sunday school buildings to house desegregated Head Start schools, and of the newly arrived Baptist preacher who went with great assurance to his board of deacons to get their permission. His deacons voted fourteen to two against it. "That preacher was just crushed," said the poverty program man. "I told him, hell, be thankful for those two."

Except in Louisiana, the Catholic Church was not the power for good and evil that it was in other areas of the nation. In the 1950s and to a lesser extent in the 1960s, it concentrated a great proselytizing effort among Negroes, with some success. But by and large, the Negroes were Protestant, too, with their own proud first churches on prominent corners, inordinate in splendor and investment to the resources of the congregations and, like the white edifices, sacrificial of human needs apparent all about.

But what went on in these churches and the more humble ones, in the Negro church and the religious heart of the Negro South since slavery times, was something sacred, something truly apart from the norm of psychic experience in America, and for the most part, in the white South. The religion and rites of the poor whites in their more frenzied and evangelical sects were closer than either they or Negroes would want to admit to the basic religious experience in the Negro churches. Mencken's cruel description of a Holy Roller service in full swing was indicative of the fear that such primitive religious instinct, such profound emotion in the human repertoire instills in the supercivilized breast. But the old white fervent religions were part of the vanishing rural scene, and had never been the dominant religious expression. The Negro version had ever been more dignified perhaps because Negroes were, their God was. The white fervent sects had ever, beyond the beauty of their foot-washing ceremonies, tended into twisted, cruel ways, the snake-handling cults, suicidal, the sects that forbade their members to be treated by modern medicine. (I once tried to interfere in the criminal cruelty of this in the case of a little girl with a diagnosed case of tuberculosis of the spine—she was in danger of becoming a hopeless cripple. Her mother, thin-faced and sweet in the way of mountain women, finally invoked her religion against me: "There's a great big God up yonder and He doesn't like you poking your nose into His business." A few weeks later, after the family had fled the area of my newspaper's reach, I came down with a near-fatal infection —on my nose.)

The Negro religion, in its old and modern forms, was not fanatical, and except in formal, ritualistic ways, as best a white observer might judge, was not piously puritanical. It was joyous and satisfying, and respectful of the humanity of the participants. Whites were privileged to participate in it during the direct-action days of the early 1960s, to discover the amazing beauty of music that welled up, often unaccompanied, in all kinds of complicated harmony and rhythms, out of the congregations, people's faces transfigured in the experience of the songs, and the sermons and prayers. The latter themselves were often more musical than expository, were often long, impromptu poems full of the sounds and repetitive patterns of poetry. And

the congregations were a part of the preacher's performance, responding in every nuance of agreement, assent, to
his strong points, reacting with groans to his telling of the
evil men do, with cries of joy to his assurances of eventual
justice, the sermons and prayers and their responses one
long symphony of shared emotional experience, religious
experience. Whites who were privileged to take part
learned that religion, against all the cynical scorn for the
namby-pamby and puritanical thing it had become in
America, could have deep meaning, could touch the core
of one's humanity, like great music or poetry or nature,
and could impart dignity in the doing of what had always
been considerd undignified, a sudden, completely natural,
uninhibited shouting out, and could hold forth hope and
comfort and solace. There has come fashionable scorn for
such uses of their religion by Negroes, from black power
sources mainly and in justifiable condemnation of the old
opiate-of-the-people tendencies to enduring the evils of
this world for the promise of a better one on high. But this
was not the message of that powerful religious surge of the
early 1960s. Indeed, the opposite was urged, the righteous
anger and demand for action of the Old Testament prophets, along with the always fervently assented to New Testament dictum to forgive your enemies and do good to
those who have done evil to you. Perhaps this, too, in an
age of despair and hostility, is worthy of scorn. But for a
time it was more than words, was a living thing in those
churches, and in the drama of the demonstrations that
poured out of those churches by the thousands across the
Southland, to change it so that it would never be the same
again.

Dr. Martin Luther King, Jr., had the genius to pull
together all the best of the religious tradition and the deep
religiosity of the Negro South to accomplish those secular
miracles with which he has been credited. But it may well
be that when time allows full judgment, his greatest ac-

complishment, his real meaning will be found to be spiritual. That a spiritual leader, in many ways a mystic, might rise in the materialistic and harsh America through which Dr. King moved, and might move that America in its own harsh and militaristic terms, remains the most tangible indication that something remains alive in the South that is missing elsewhere, the strongest threads of fact behind the myths of a superior new society evolving, some day to show America the way. To say that this was a phenomenon of the Negro South, a subculture in many ways out away from the main American culture, blocked from its main activity—business—and therefore moved into a different kind of self-expression, spiritual, mystical, is not to say it all. For there was that remnant of the old white South that had shed somehow the curse of racism, and had for years before Dr. King sought the same goals that he was to, and rejoiced to rally to him when he did come forth—and these, for the very most part, had religion as a large part of their motivation and responded to the religion that was the core of Dr. King's message.

A young Episcopalian priest, the Rev. Francis X. Walter, a white Southerner who worked in a ministry devoted to race relations and the Negro poor in Black Belt Alabama, one of the many who kept on in a hope forged out of hopelessness after the high promise of Dr. King's work and life came to so little in the late 1960s, summed up the feeling of those who followed not Dr. King as a man, but the human impulses of the Negro religion that he personified, in this about what happens in the churches:

> Today I leave to attend Dr. King's funeral . . . Yesterday I went to Greensboro to a memorial service. I had not wanted to say anything, but found myself standing again in the pulpit from which I had, three years earlier, struggled to speak of the murder of Jonathan Daniels. Hate had forced us together again to celebrate and memorialize Love. After the preacher was introduced a man came to the pulpit and stood. With many, I expected he was the speaker. But then he began to sing "Precious Lord."

I was seated directly behind him. The voice was high and it soared. It made the church, packed and now very hot in our southern spring, seem bigger, higher, cooler. Able to receive now our grief, tension, love, guilt, and wonder. The man's back quivered before me. I thought how his muscles must be working. Our tears could come now. There was release like breath held too long but something was given too. The voice and the flowing out allowed a flowing in. Since I am a Christian, I named it. To me it was the Spirit of God. The effect was to know, to be able to take, as if it were a material object, Love. The Love then was everything that is, bigger than hate or death, a force that binds, casts out fear, that sharpens, does not diminish, one's sense of tragedy, injustice and hypocrisy, that gives courage, not ease. The soul can begin to run from death and hate, hardly knowing the flight has begun. So death and hate enlarge themselves in that act of flight. To celebrate Dr. King, an emblem of love, stopped that for us. Our souls, infused with love, stand, turn on these demons, and see them diminished and without power.[9]

Maybe the South might force America to acknowledge that such words, once more, may be spoken, may have meaning. I attended services with a friend one bright spring Sunday morning in a remote Alabama sawmill town. There had been no civil rights movement in the little town; the presence of two whites in the church was an occasion, not impolitely made over, but evidenced by the nervous hurry of the preacher to get us inside and away from the eyes of any whites who might drive by and see us in the churchyard, and in the quick glances and polite lookings away of the congregation. The service had begun when an old Negro man came in and moved automatically into his regular seat, which happened to be beside me. He was seated before he saw that I was white. I introduced myself quickly, telling him my friend was to speak later about organizing a cooperative. He made me feel welcome with his smile, but he wasn't quite clear on what I was

[9] Selma Inter-Religious Project *Newsletter*, Selma, Alabama, April 8, 1968.

doing there. Some young people were being taken into
church membership that morning; once he leaned to me
and asked if they were some of my people, meaning did
they work for me. The preacher up on the pulpit, like God
Himself on high, a big man in black robes, had an idiom
common to the white evangelical sects as well as to Negro
preachers of the small places, a rhythmic gasp in his delivery every three or four words, the gasp becoming more
pronounced, more fervent as he preached, built to his
climax, a compelling, hypnotic use of the voice. At the
climax of the sermon, he came down from the pulpit, and
stood before the altar and held out his long arms and one
by one members of the congregation rose, in an exalted
state, and walked down to him and touched his hands,
receiving from him the touch, the grace of God. The old
man beside me stirred, turned and asked me politely if I
would come. I was too much an alienated American, not
able to do it in the spirit that was demanded, and so shook
my head, no. He moved down and touched the preacher's
hand, and then he came back to his seat, his face radiant,
aglow with all that he had felt in the experience, and when
he sat down, without looking at me, he reached his hand
over and touched mine, gently bestowing to me the touch
of God. And that way I could feel it, experience what he
had. Maybe, maybe . . . the best of what has survived in
the South, that is peculiarly its own, might reach out and
touch America, even as the worst has.

We started out seeking some explanation for the
voting patterns of the white South, which in its mood
and tone in the late 1960s was dominated by the mood and
tone of the small cities and towns, why it could vote for
the worst possible choices, all alone in its preference, in
two presidential races in a row. And we have ended up
in a Negro church of the South. The end of the quest
may not be as far off-mark as it might seem. There is no
avoiding, no denying in any examination of those small

urban units that white racism is shot through anything
they do, including making political choices. Indeed, reading their papers, listening to the men of power in them,
it can be understood how they might believe that a Goldwater, a Wallace, expresses a norm, not a dangerous devia-
tion, of American political and social belief and aspiration.
But beyond these sad facts, we sought whether there was
not also in the errant choices some hint of honesty, of
disapproval—expressed as the South has a way of doing
it in the worst possibly way—of all those evils in America
that deserve the disapproval of us all.

The Negro church we're sitting in is the same sort of
church where Dr. King stood many times and looked out
at black faces that were worn and frightened and scarred
by all the brutalities and deprivations that being a Negro
in the Black Belt of the South had meant, looked out at his
people there, and said to them, his voice choked with emotion: "You're good. I came over here to tell you you are
somebody. You may not know the difference between 'you
does' and 'you don't,' but you are as good as any white
person in this country." George Wallace stood before his
audiences in his campaign for President and looked into
their faces with the same kinds of marks of a harsh country's effect on the human personality, on the haggard faces
of the poor whites, and told them the same thing:

"They look down their noses at us and call us red-necks.
But I'll tell you, when they write against us and say those
things, that's just one person writing that. And you're one
person, too, just as good as he is. . . . I've never minded
saying that I was a Southerner, and I've never apologized
for it any place in the country. . . ." And in broadened,
national terms: "And so we see that the issue today in our
country is that pseudo-intellectuals . . . don't have any
confidence in the average man on the street—the taxicab
driver, the textile worker, the barber, the beautician, the
little businessman, the big businessman. . . ."

Maybe the most that the South, in all the bad and good

and beauty of its people, black and white, can tell America is what the whites through the evil of Wallace and the Negroes through the good of Dr. King have said—that they want and deserve dignity and respect, and that, moreover, all people do.

PART FOUR

The South and the Nation

CHAPTER 6

I

EVEN IN THEIR BEST LIGHT, the phenomena of the South in transition in the 1960s, wherever one looked—at the roadside, in the countryside, in the towns and in the cities —offered little hope for the fulfillment immediately, if ever, of the more hopeful mythology that had nurtured in it a will to change. The dream of a new Populism, government and the economic powers forced into responsiveness to the great needs of the people, had fallen upon the disappointment of the liberals that Negro enfranchisement did not immediately accomplish the great miracles it had been expected to, did not even much dent the racism of the old politics. The dream of a great new era in race relations wherein the South, freed of the law that demanded an unjust sharing of the land between white and black, would develop with them side by side a truly integrated, truly just interracial society, floundered on tokenism, ran afoul of faulty federal law and feeble enforcement, and disclosed that racism instilled in whites by childhood conditioning and the sanction of society does not die easily or fast.

But these have been myths, the holding out of promises and ideals and the highest of hopes. Their value has been and will continue to be that they exist, that in varying degrees of awareness they are embedded into consciousnesses and the culture, as the inspiration for greater effort, more change, the goad for dissatisfaction and criticism.

What of the reality? Might the South in its time of turning in the 1960s, the time of the most fundamental change in its history since slavery, have come closer to realizing its better dreams? Again, from what we have seen, the answer would seem to be that it has been amazing, maybe merely fortunate, that it achieved what it did. For the old profile of failure in the basics of a society's responsibility to its people continued almost unchanged; what was accomplished was by a people unprepared, ill-equipped for the job.

We have encountered these failures in their various forms and locales—in the ordering of the economy, in education, in health services and welfare and other functions of government, in the election and running of the governments, in law enforcement, in journalism and the other requisites for an informed citizenry, in the white churches most pitifully—a dismaying record of failure, but nothing new, lamented through the history of the South in the same particulars, reflections, all, as always of a most profound failure in leadership.

It is striking to see how racism has continued to run through so much of the failure. In education, where so much had to be done before there could be any reasonable expectation of prodigies of innovation or achievement among the people, the small resources of money and energy continued to be sapped by the stratagems and bureaucratic struggles over degrees of token desegregation. Racism had nakedly displayed the moral bankruptcy of educational leadership—college presidents, superintendents, boards of education, down to many in the ranks of professors and teachers—making it a serious question whether anything approaching real education could be hoped for any time soon.

The same sort of moral bankruptcy remained evident in quarters less vital to future generations, but not to the future condition of the society, in the dynamics of blockbusting and the exodus to the suburbs, in the machinations of business and government leaders to maintain and further housing segregation, in the cities to build ghettos.

Racism (the old ingrained kind and the newer, more chilling kind which calculated policies not on conviction but on perceptions of what effect racial aspects of a situation would have on immediate gain, self-interest) was shot through the failures of government at all levels, the failures of press and pulpit, and the larger failures of the economy in such particulars as the fall of the plantation system, the 1950s collapse of the effort at rational economic planning if not the inability to revive such efforts, the obliviousness of all leadership to the maxim that an adequate economy could come only with full development of the people. Racism remained the core of the notorious injustices of the Southern police, courts, and prisons, ameliorated slightly but not enough. This perversion of justice was capable of reaching out to other classes, as in speed traps, as in the persecutions of hippies, even as it had ever been a weapon against real labor organization.

This debilitation of leadership by racism (a debilitation overlaying all the other more common, nationally characteristic debilities) was a legacy of the tragically mistaken Southern past, the remnant and after-effect of the old order. A grim statement about race (part of a folklore of white and black commentary) of the kind encountered in virtually the same words in all parts of the South was the one usually spoken by a Negro, solemnly, in the face of some new atrocity or the death of some old rabid racist: "The undertaker is the only man who can solve a lot of these problems." A major problem was the possessive old men who held an iron grip on churches, culture centers, and other establishments in which racism was not too apparently a factor in policies. With racism shorn or at least disguised, Lyndon Johnson was of their tradition out of the South; his stewardship of the nation reflected more than one manifestation of their dogmatism and possessiveness. Theirs was a generation which had known the scarring, indeed, brutalizing effects of World War II, the Depression and, for many, World War I, and had close touch with an American past of more certainty in conviction, more sanctimonious, self-righteous—the America of Manifest Destiny. Understandably, the young of the Nuclear Age despised them universally, rose against them in a rebellion that was indeed not just generational but cultural, and certainly not confined to the South.

The fierceness of response of these old, powerful leaders to challenges of their order was a national phenomenon. In the South, it had been on display perhaps without anyone's knowing it in the ugly reactions of small places and large to the civil rights demonstrations. These, like the murderousness at Orangeburg in 1968, or more metaphorically in the murder that year of Dr. King, had been imbued with the old savage violence of racism. It was hard to know where one stopped, the other began. A frequent question to Orangeburg whites defending the firing into the students had been, "Suppose the students had been white?" But suppose, again, they had been hirsute, bearded, beaded white students?

The undertaker would, indeed, with geometric increases in the rate, be taking care of the old, dogmatic rulers, but not necessarily of the antagonisms they embodied. What of those coming up behind them, nurtured in the acceptance and tradition of their rule? Not their least comforting characteristic was the ability, indeed, conditioning to accept other rulers, other dogmatism: colleges moved from church to military-industrial control while Southern leaders in all spheres—educators, government officials, even some of the possessive old men themselves—accepted and administered desegregation decrees that were against their stated principles. Here, in Southern paradox, was the Eichmann phenomenon. The Southerners of real racist conviction who fought desegregation were surely less sinister. The most frightening thing of all was the failure of both to reconsider the issue, to come to terms with racism's moral issue, to realize racism's evil. Here, in one more form, was the South's oldest line of defense—never to consider first causes, but to harangue and maneuver and forever be embroiled in the complexities and legalisms of what to do about those first causes, either in holding on to them or in ending them.

In this, I have spoken of white leadership, for by and large it still held the instruments and most of the hidden resources of power. Liberal whites, in this context, had fallen into a new kind of failure: paradoxically, where once they lacked just about any power at all except the persuasive force of their conviction, now that they were gaining footholds of real power, their conviction seemed to falter. For the most part, theirs was the predicament of the tiny portion of the Southern press that might be called liberal, a holding to obsolete formulas. In politics, the few white liberals in practice tended to be what the National Committee for an Effective Congress has called "custodial liberals" in an analysis that declared the Democratic Party was splitting apart not on traditional conservative versus liberal dispute, but on philsophical and psychological antagonisms between the custodial liberals and ones termed "humanistic."[1]

The Southern custodial liberal was probably less trade-union oriented, but was otherwise in accord with his national counterparts in such things as simplistic acceptance of the Cold War and its costs, in interest in things over people, construction expenditure over self-help welfare, and enthusiasm for programs that seem to do something whether they do or not, and for statistics comfortingly suggesting they do. Like them, he was vindictive against allies

[1] Press Release, "Underlying Cause of Democrats' Agony Revealed by NCEC Survey of Profound Liberal Split in House," National Committee for an Effective Congress, Washington, D. C., September, 23, 1968. "Two groups are crystalizing: the classic, orthodox labor liberals and the emerging political modernists. What separates them is personal style, choice of priorities, understanding or rejection of the contemporary revolutionary scene."

not conforming to his views and contemptuous of agitation for such things as participation of the poor in programs supposed to be helping them, for civil liberties, and for such keys to a really open society as integrated housing. Few white Southern liberals in politics wholeheartedly espoused the humanist liberal positions for expansion of civil liberties and support of protest, insistence upon quality as well as quantity in education, conservation, urban design, and the like, "with prime interest," in the words of the analysis, "on the role and rights of the individual." Among Negro politicans and even among those black and white who might still be called the civil rights movement, including workers in the field, there was probably as much of a cleavage in the two styles as on the national scene. But of those who had been closest to direct action, the humanist style was preponderantly the natural one; indeed, the Southern civil rights movement of the early 1960s was surely the first thrust toward the humanist position. The figures of such men as Julian Bond of Georgia or John Cashin of Alabama, Negro leaders of challenge delegations to the 1968 Democratic Convention, were the most prominent Southern promise of political leadership, and they were as much in the fore of national affairs as the early movement had been.

The white South had ever wanted to show the nation a thing or two. But it was the persecuted black South that kept doing it. Ironic, too, was the fact that pragmatism was so central to the custodial liberalism that found itself with bewilderment often opposed to the main thrust of its old ally, the Negro leadership. For pragmatism had ever been the rationalization of moderate white leadership in its failures, its inability to move against racism. What you ask may be right, they would say. But it is politically impossible. The scorn that the conservative racists of the South held for the idealist, for the intellectual (the two words become epithets in their lexicon of abuse of integrationists), was matched on a national level by the contempt custodial liberals displayed for their humanist counterparts. The humanist liberals were obviously oriented to the field; the custodial ones were headquarters.

One more of those oversights of Negro achievement (such as America's failure to celebrate jazz fully) was that the most remarkable thing about the Southern civil rights movement—its assumption of responsible leadership and continuing a tradition of it in the South where none had ever been before—was largely ignored, mostly lost on America. The only hope that W. J. Cash could see for the South in 1941 was that somehow it might solve its many problems through a leadership "willing to face them fully and in all their implications, to arouse the people to them, and to try to evolve a comprehensive and adequate means for coping with them."[2] It was "the absence of that leadership" that he most lamented—as though he were predicting what was to come from Negroes.

If anything was clear from a study of the great achievements of Southern Negro leadership, it was what great odds it struggled against, what a frail framework it had within which to work. By the late 1960s this uneven battling had begun to take its toll—in despair and anger and black power's bitterest overtones among some leaders, in continuing inability despite the procedural political and legal reforms to consolidate gains against racism, to force effective administration of desegregation law.

The early triumphs of Negro leadership had been symbolized by the beautiful spirit of the early SNCC and the spiritual, indeed, mystical influence of Dr. King: they showed the world what the best of the Southern heritage, its beauty of belief and great braveness, could do, shaming and by contrast showing the shabbiness of the rest of Southern leadership, and most of the nation's. But Dr. King was slain by the spirit he fought. SNCC had known

[2] Cash, p. 428.

the worst of that spirit, but it was at the hands of the custodial liberals at Atlantic City in 1964 that they suffered the disillusionment that finally removed so much of black and young America as a constructive force in society, and raised for a generation and a race the ultimate question of whether destruction alone was the appropriate answer to what the nation had become.

By the late 1960s no one great organization or man spoke for, embodied the greatness of Southern people, black and white. Many of the most thoughtful and responsible Southern Negro leaders were creatively consolidating and building on the better instincts and intentions of the black power spirit which was influencing all the Southern Negro population, on its sane seeking of self-awareness, self-respect, cultural and historical pride, and enlightened self-interest. But there were enough indications in other Negro leaders—politicians especially, who were like their counterparts the world over—of that fearful attitude of the white leadership which shaped policies and postures on racial questions in terms of assessments of self-interest alone, at least to raise the fear that debilities of the white leadership, as well as its evils, might finally overcome and contain the promise and potential of black leadership. Many Negro leaders had become as fearful of the label "Tom" as white ones were of being named "niggerlover." There were practical reasons for this, obvious in political races, and not without the old white Southern desire to remain effective, to hold onto influence with the people, but once more the old Southern failure of white leadership to oppose irrationality in the masses of whites, even if it meant immediate defeat, in the interest of ultimate justice, at least in part applied.

No Negro Southerner of great stature had emerged to lend full prestige to a public rejection of those tendencies in black power which were undifferentiating in assessing white culture and white people, which were, in short and bluntly, prejudiced and racist.[3] Dr. King seemed to move toward the kind of difficult assessment of black power that likely would have allowed his kind of balanced sorting out of the good and evil of it, and then the assertion of his kind of leadership in terms of the good (even as he had ever a genius for drawing forth from not particularly prepossessing or gifted lieutenants and followers the very best in them). The warning against the fallacies and dangers of black power would have to come from Negro leadership, of course. No white, however good his credentials, had the right to make it. Negroes who were sensitive to pressures from the people and nevertheless maintained friendships or political relations with whites, showed a courage of the kind that had been required of those white friends previously in breaking racial custom. (That there were so few such Southern whites and that not always among them had courage held fast might account for some of the reluctance of black leadership to speak out.) But most of all this, beyond fearful opportunism, was merely a reflection that leadership had become fragmented, that none any longer spoke to all of the Negro South, could be heard by all of it.

This was not necessarily all to the bad. It was a part of the New Left stance of sticking to local issues, local problems, local leadership and was to some degree a realistic reaction to the temper of the times—a drawing-in out of realization that Negro ability to influence Southern (or national) affairs was reduced. It was, finally, an expression of that old Southern propensity for the specific, for

---

[3] Dr. Kenneth Clark had done so in a remarkable speech to the Southern Regional Council in 1967. But his constituency was Northern, was different, as were Northern and Southern experiences of black power. And he unfortunately only indicted, with no balancing assessment of positive strengths in the concept. Nevertheless, he offered the impeccable assessment that Negro leadership "must dare to say that the enemy was never to be understood in terms of color, but in the more difficult and abstract terms of human irrationality, ignorance, superstition, rigidity, and arbitrary cruelty. These are the common enemies which underlie all forms of tyranny."

solving one's own problems. Where it eschewed regional and national organizations and leaders, it was also expressing for much the same realistic reasons another old Southern aversion—for the outsider.

II

But the situation of the South of the 1960s, even the failures and the small signs of continuing new strength in the leadership, could no longer—if ever they really could—be explained entirely in Southern terms. The effect of all the change that had occurred since 1954 had been to make the South, more obviously than it had been before, part of America—systematically, inseparably, and inescapably. The shifts from rural to urban, from agrarian to industrial, changed more than the landscape. Life in cities meant ties of interdependence with the national economy and culture: as never before, most of the people were obliged to make a living like, to look like, to act like, to live like most other Americans.

Not merely economic ties were formed. The city has its own culture, its own ways of shaping people, transcending probably national cultures, certainly the subcultural idiosyncracies of even so insular a section as the South. The Southern changes were occurring at the very time that the standardizing forces of America's urban culture were most forcefully felt, attention and concern focused on the situation in the sociology and jargon ("gray-flannel suit," "lonely crowd") of the 1950s, television at the time only beginning its frighteningly tremendous standardizing and acculturating influence. Perhaps most forceful of all, the corporate and impersonal ethics and ethos of business came finally, fully upon the life and culture of the South.

In such a context of interdependence and unity with the rest of America, the figure of the Black Belt planter presiding over the collapse of the plantation system—with all its cruelty to the laboring people who had depended on the system and lived by its logic and values, however cruel they themselves were—becomes understandable. Most of the victims of the system's collapse were black, and the fact that planters had for more than a century most mercilessly subjugated and exploited these laborers, blurred the essential truth that the forces at work on the plantation system and its human factors were, in the 1950s and 1960s, no longer Southern—but national. They were the same blind, cold economic forces built out of the nation's past, out of its willing itself philosophically and politically far back in history to develop and exploit and use all the great resources of the continent in a certain way, that made small farmers outside the South one and two generations earlier move to the cities, or acted with similar cruelty on human beings outside the South wherever their skills or the particular manufacturing or selling system they had built their lives around became economically unfeasible. The death of a salesman can at the mercy of such blind forces occur to anyone.

Similarly, the old movement villain, the mystical demon, the power structure, had to be, in ultimate terms, seen in a national, no longer Southern, context. Part of the sit-in strategy (and it was not any concerted, conspiratorial thing) was to go after the national chains located with proud names on the main streets of simmering little Southern towns and shopping centers of bumptious Southern cities, the dime stores and drugstores and mail-order department stores, and later the motels and restaurants that were part of chains. This was out of knowledge that the Northern headquarters of such would be vulnerable to embarrassment nationally by exposure of their conformity to Southern segregationist custom, and out of knowledge, too, that they could exert influence on the local merchants. These, including most of the old possessive masters of the towns and cities, would have done almost anything to put the sit-ins down, to resist their threat, the oldest one haunting the South, the ultimate fear, the slave uprising. But another more powerful structure—the national one—spoke. It spoke in an idiom the Southern power structure was then only beginning to learn, the computable cost of national embarrassment, and with a shrug (after all, all the Negroes wanted to do was spend money at the lunch counters). It prevailed in the matter of lunch counters. Restaurants and motels were less easily toppled; it turned out a good number, Morrison's Cafeterias notable for resistance across the South, were Southern based. It took the 1964 civil rights law to bring many in line.

In like manner, big national money power sought for a while to avoid embarrassment and unpleasantness for branch-office transferees in Southern locales prominent for spectacular racial clashes. Big business, in this, was not making any moral pronouncement, not punishing the evildoers, not seeking to avoid evil. It was, by all accounts, doing what comes naturally (and what in most other cases is a detriment to the society's well-being): it was avoiding controversy. Though a state like Alabama, for all its luring and boasting, did continue to lag in development of industry (probably as much because of its general political instability as its racism), the national power structures were quite capable, especially as the racial antagonisms of the country became more exacerbated, of locating in the most notorious of towns, given proper inducement. Not often would the Southern power structures be at cross-purposes with national ones, as in the sit-ins.

We have noted that Southern racial experience would seem to bear out the New Left's generally undocumented but certainly plausible belief that whatever threatens or infringes on big money power's prerogatives, its real interests, is, in one way or another, ruthlessly and effectively squelched. In this, too, Southern and national power structures would think alike. The clutch of utilities and banks on Southern governments was no anomaly in the states of the union. Tax structures, regulatory functions, and the

encouragement of uses of public monies by the banks were
probably more blatantly favorable to these institutions
than elsewhere. Indeed one of the crying needs for objective study and reporting in the South was the simple one of
showing just how unfair in each state tax structures were.
Strangely, no one undertook such study; least of all would
universities. But the point is that this was a national problem, the Southern version of it only likely more extreme.
A further point would lie in the ownership of those utilities and banks and other businesses benefited at the expense of the Southern public, the great Southern needs.
Again, documentation was scant. Jack Minnis, a white
former member of SNCC who moved on to write for the
National Guardian, used to delight in drawing up complicated charts showing what he felt were sinister intercon-
nections between Southern and national business and political interests. He could trace the most remote act of
Black Belt racial barbarity to the highest and most respectable echelons of big business, the Chase Manhattan Bank
figuring nearly always large in his scheme. If sometimes his
lines of connection seemed tenuous and if he seemed to be
shouting aha! over something entirely in the nature of and
normal in an advanced capitalistic society, his insight was
correct. The vast and intricate system of American business did, indeed, involve the most respectable elements of
all the society of all sections, including individual liberals
and the most liberal of institutions, from great universities
to civil rights organizations themselves, in the racist atrocities of the South. It was in a way merely saying that no
man is an island. But when a plant of a giant corporation
supported the economy of a notoriously racist little city, or
when in every Southern city banks ruthlessly and effectively blocked public housing from areas of expensive
land, or, when a great corporation or small erected a manufacturing plant (or for that matter, the federal government erected some costly, land-enhancing, job-making installation) in the white part of town, never the Negro—in

all of this, certainly, all of American business was implicated. The economists had long ago understood it in their own terms. The growth and expansion that was occurring in the South was a phenomenon of the national economy, they had said, not of any prodigious ability at by-the-bootstraps lifting among Southern businessmen and developers. Their main point continued to be missed not merely by the South, but by the nation. The Southern economic growth had not been as great as it should have been, considering what was happening in the national economy, and the reason it had not was that the people were not adequate to the potential.

As in the Southern Gothic novels, the norms of the people are better understood and felt by consideration of abnormalities.

The six physicians who reported on conditions of starvation in Mississippi in 1967[4] gave terrible details of what starvation does to the brain, bone, and sinew of children:

> In child after child we saw: evidence of vitamin and mineral deficiencies; serious, untreated skin infections and ulcerations; eye and ear diseases, also unattended bone diseases secondary to poor food intake; the prevalence of bacterial and parasitic disease, as well as severe anemia, with resulting loss of energy and ability to live a normally active life; diseases of the heart and the lungs—requiring surgery—which have gone undiagnosed and untreated; epileptic and other neurological disorders; severe kidney ailments, that in other children would warrant immediate hospitalization; and finally, in boys and girls in every county we visited, obvious evidence of severe malnutrition, with injury to the body's tissues—its muscles, bones, and skin, as well as an associated psycho-

[4] "Hungry Children," by Dr. Joseph Brenner, Medical Department, Massachusetts Institute of Technology; Dr. Robert Coles, Harvard University Health Services; Dr. Alan Mermann, Department of Pediatrics, Yale University Medical School; Dr. Milton J. E. Senn, Sterling Professor of Pediatrics, Yale University; Dr. Cyril Walwyn, private practice, Yazoo City, Mississippi, medical adviser to Friends of the Children of Mississippi; Dr. Raymond Wheeler, private practice, Charlotte, North Carolina. Published by the Southern Regional Council in cooperation with the Field Foundation and other interested groups.

logical state of fatigue, listlessness, and exhaustion. . . . In sum, we saw children who are hungry and who are sick—children for whom hunger is a daily fact of life and sickness, in many forms, an inevitability. We do not want to quibble over words, but "malnutrition" is not quite what we found; the boys and girls we saw were hungry—weak, in pain, sick; their lives are being shortened; they are, in fact, visibly and predictably losing their health, their energy, their spirits. They are suffering from hunger and disease and directly or indirectly they are dying from them—which is exactly what "starvation" means.

It was not known how many starving children there were in the South of the late 1960s, or how many there had been in the recent past, or through Southern history. The House Appropriations Subcommittee on Agriculture and the U.S. Department of Agriculture responded to the disclosures of starvation not by making anguished emergency efforts to end it, but by defensively disputing the findings, quibbling over degrees of hunger, and quoting local health authorities (a culpable source) that anybody who wanted to grow a garden or fish the rivers could—one more incredible display of cold disregard for people, obliviousness to suffering. The Nixon Administration in its first year showed more willingness to confront the problem, at least acknowledge the existence of starvation, than had the liberals of previous Democratic administrations.

Pellagra, hookworm, malaria in the past had ravaged the population. Perhaps much of the stereotype of the lazy Southerner—all the jokes and comedy scenes of slow and stupid black and white Southerners—was based on the cruel physiological (not to mention emotional) effects on brain and body of hunger and disease. In general, more Southern babies were born without proper medical attention, more died at birth, even more died during the first year of life, more starved, and more went without medical care into adulthood than in any other part of the country.

We have noted the paralyzing effect of psychological schisms working on the white "nice" people, conflict between culturally approved racism and the American creed. Let us also consider the crippling physiological effects that combine with crazy patterns of acculturation in large numbers of the poor whites. A Southern white who went hungry as a child, saw his father defeated and mother degraded by economic forces over which they had no power at all, went to war in his early teens (he lied about his age and got adequate food for the first time in his life), learned to be a killer, came home to little more opportunity than his parents knew, and became an avid Klansman is not atypical at the extremes of Southern society. Neither is the element of truth in the rationalization of white employers that they could not find competent Negro workers. A woman, seeking employment in a textile mill, fails the skills test and protests, probably justifiably, that the white administrator made her so nervous she could not function normally. But then she fails, too, the required physical examination, which discloses a severe and long-neglected blood pressure condition. Too, without going into it deeply (for knowledge is not great on the subject), there must be considered purely psychological forces at work on Negro Southerners in the new milieu of procedural reforms and flux in racial custom. Consider a Negro man or Negro woman, maybe poor, more likely middle-class, who has all of a lifetime had as an ultimate, burningly angry reason and rationalization and excuse for every failure, the undeniable fact of systematized white discrimination. Then overnight tell that person that the system has been destroyed (and it has been), that all kinds of equal opportunity are now available, and that whites are even now disposed to social acceptance. Aside from all the knocking about of the psyche inherent in the uncertainty of what will happen in the various situations involved, there is also the loss of that crutch for the ego, part of the conditioning and personality of the Negro Southerner: when the person fails, he cannot with the same certainty he once had blame it all on the white world. More likely, facing the terror of life without the crutch, he may even more vehemently than before assert that everything wrong in life is the fault of the whites, all whites. White liberals, in their never-ending quest to understand the dynamics of white-Negro relationships, might look no further than this for the increasing abrasiveness of that relationship in polite and political society.

There were all the indices of failure whose flesh we encountered in the towns and cities and out across the countryside. There were no indications (no crash programs, no apparently innovative thinking) even of moderate improvement in education, let alone the kind of quantum leap needed to allow the economy similarly to leap to its full potential.

Racial violence continued as it had through Southern history, stamping the society with the mark of Cain, the stigma of savagery, haunting if only unconsciously the conscience and the sense of security of all the citizenry. The press, ever more expert in chronicling violence, weighing, comparing, scientifically categorizing, criticizing, sometimes seeming to celebrate it, invariably sought cause and effect in Southern violence of whites to Negroes. Was there an upsurge because of more widespread token desegregation of schools? The truth was that it was a constant, that no one calibrated fluctuations in it, and that it was usually as senseless as the random violence in an all-white slum any Saturday night in any Southern city, some of it the same kind of expression of personal, not racial animosity. Where there was purposefulness, it was as intimidation or as punishment, retaliation—as often as not, randomly against some misfortunate, innocuous Negro for the temerity of some other Negro daring to assert humanity—racism in its essence, violence against the race, not an individual. More than one observer sensed in the late 1960s a new wave of meanness among whites, new proneness to violence of the retaliatory kind, expressed as public policy in a new harshness in police treatment. Perhaps so. But it had been going on a long time. The Southern Regional Council's informal list of "race-related" deaths counted 15 racially motivated killings of Negroes by whites in 1968 (among the victims, Dr. King and the three Orangeburg students). In 1967, there were 16; in 1966, 14; in 1965, 25; in 1964, 14; 1963, 13. Non-lethal violence, of course, was commensurately greater in proportion, far less often reported.

The South had only by the late 1960s penetrated to the real meaning of integration, that it meant not the acceptance of token members of extraordinary Negroes into white institutions, nor even the destruction of Negro institutions for the purpose of integrating the white ones, but the integration, fully and without regard for race, of both kinds of institutions. This was most clear in schools and colleges. This was a feat of understanding that had eluded the rest of the nation, but it was not accompanied by any real achievement in practical application. The dual system of schools was not yet abolished; in 1968, only 20.3 percent (518,607) Negro children were in school with whites; 2,551,790 were in segregated schools; virtually no whites were in Negro schools. And the beginning of the Nixon Administration showed the most depressing signs of retreat from even the feeble previous enforcement efforts.

In all of these effects of failure, as in all of the failure of Southern white leadership, racism was the constant, common factor. How might this be, with all the federal legislation against discrimination, with all the new joining of the South to the nation? We have seen that the old white conditioning to racism, in "nice" people and "common" alike, was not that monolithically solid, that on the level of the ten-cent store and of the public schools and the biracial committees of power structures, there were fragile hints of something close to the dreams of a new racial order, a tiny, poignant potential in Southerners. But we also have seen that, most tragically, there was just not much everyday

integration of the races in any situation. Where it happened, it was imposed. Few white Southerners were capable
of it (as we saw sadly even in their churches) volun-
tarily. This should come as no great surprise; it was, indeed, the rationale for passing laws requiring integration.
The problem was of course the failure to enforce the
laws.

The failure of the federal government in both the
promulgation and enforcement of integration laws was
profound, surely one of the most irresponsible adventures
of a national government in all history. It was law capri-
ciously, dishonestly created (as in the self-canceling provisions applying to schools in the 1964 act), not to be obeyed
by those who disagreed with it. Beginning with the 1954
school decision and with each step of change in racial law
that ensued, the South might have gone either way—the
way of reasonably full compliance, or the way it actually
went. No ruthless, totalitarian force would have been required for real enforcement, merely the technical, intelligent skills and means by which income tax law is so uniformly and efficiently enforced, or by which other social
enterprise of the nation (selling automobiles, for example) is achieved. What was lacking was the firm will to
enforcement, first by those who made the laws, then by
those who administered them. All three branches of the
federal government were implicated, lacking the responsibility men must expect from a system of law, a government, if society is to have any stability at all. Even further
erosion of enforcement, especially school desegregation,
was among the most ominous developments of the first
year of the Nixon Administration.

The South before the advent of the federal racial law
had a functioning social order—an unjust one, true, and
hurtful to all its people, but functioning. The new laws
disrupted that old faulty but functioning order, but there
was not the will or responsibility of those who imposed
them to apply them so that a functioning new order

could emerge. The result was the hodgepodge of practice and custom we have encountered across the South, not by the late 1960s resolidified into any kind of coherent social order. When such an upheaval and resultant shambles has occurred to primitive tribes, the anthropologists have told us, the society dies, its people literally pass from existence.

The situation in the South of the 1960s was like nothing so much as an antbed which has been most thoroughly stirred by a stick. The antbed was full of frantic activity, much of it random, full of panic, some of it a-building back and restoring what had been, some of it a-building anew, whole new constructions, a bastion still standing bridged over to a restored wall, a little of the old superstructure still intact to be connected with a new one. Most of the damage was above ground. The deepest part was almost intact, would be changed only subtly and more slowly by what eventually took shape above.

The South could go back toward what it once had been or in the direction of its best traditions and the best instincts of its people. But it was no longer, if it ever was, a fate entirely in the hands of Southerners. If, in its first great failure to the people of the South in the aftermath of Reconstruction, the nation may be said for nearly a century to have allowed Southerners, uniquely in America, to have had exclusive control of their region, that time of separate self-determination, of distinction, was ended with the vast economic and attendant social changes beginning with World War II and the vast legal changes that began in 1954. What happened in the South, what will happen to it, have become on every level of national life, economic, social, governmental, spiritual, not merely a responsibliity but a part of the experience of the rest of the nation.

But of course this has always, in the deepest sense, been so. The new thing was that at last it had to be acknowledged—by the North as well as the South.

III

The federal failure to enforce the desegregation law was but the most spectacular of a long history of such failure of responsibility that has marked the relationship of the South and the nation. The watering down of TVA, the failure of will in the 1930s beginnings of land reform, the capitulation of federal force before private and state violence in such matters as union organization, the long years of non-interference with Southern law enforcement's ugly denials of the Bill of Rights—all of these helped prolong the sickness in Southern society.

The most charitable thing that might be made of the most glaring failure, desegregation, was that the federal government acted out of some mistaken notion of caution, a crippled and dwarfed ancestral memory of the problem of reconciliation of majorities and minorities. For throwing over institutional racism in the South was against the will of the majority of whites who were the majority of the population of the region. Delicacy of feeling about such a situation, timorousness, uncertainty must surely have been a part of the foolish passing of faulty laws and feeble enforcement of them. (There was law enough already, indicative of just how long the federal failure had been going on, in the Bill of Rights, modern and positive law as compared with the prohibitive, Old Testament dictums of the Fourteenth Amendment.) It was, for all intents and purposes, an all-white federal government that faced the task of imposing unpopular law on the white Southern majority: this, too, sadly, must have been part of the federal impotence. Perhaps it was thought that only totalitarian methods would suffice for firm enforcement, that a precedent would be set for demagogues to enforce other laws against the will of other majorities, repeal of the Bill of Rights, for example. If so, of course, the meaning of the Constitution and the Civil War's supposed reconciliation of the problem of minorities were ignored. We are close to no government when the majority is afraid of itself, afraid to exercise its will. The risk that freedoms might be lost is implicit in self-government. If totalitarianism should arise, it would not bother about whether there were precedents for whatever controls it would impose. And totalitarianism, as any Southerner who sensed the willingness of the white majority to go either way each time a new change in law came, would not have been needed.

A more valid fear concerns the way in which the will of the majority of Americans seemed moving, racism not the least of dangerous tendencies. Once more, the South reflected the nation in extreme. We delude ourselves if, in contemplation of the mass of the people of America, not merely the South, the state of their education, their awareness of new realities of the world environment, their ability to function as whole people, we think our democracy is healthy, the duties of citizenship in apt hands. The profile of failure of Southern leadership was precisely the profile of failure of national leadership, and it was that national failure, in the final analysis, which did the South the disservice of breaking up its old evil system without providing the necessary base for reformation on sane, orderly, cohesive lines.

Tracing more superficial similarities between the glaringly bad South and the (until recently) seemingly superior rest of America, it appears that economic conservatism, for example, of the Southern small towns and cities which so vehemently blamed the poor man for his impecunity was little different from the liberal-mentality poverty program designed to remodel poor people so that they might be fit to take advantage of economic opportunity, and not to give critical attention to the economy, the economic system. Perhaps there was not a great deal of difference in the social origins of objectless anger in the ghetto riots and the latter-day Klan. If we judge men and nations by what they do rather than what they say, was there any judgment of white America more just than that of the Black Belt whites, contemplating the hunting preserve plantations, that those Yankees were just the same as *they* were in their essential attitude toward Negroes?

But we may not stop there on the inference that yes, indeed, as the President's Commission on Civil Disorder assured us, all America (or as the black power apostles would have it, all of Western civilization) is racist. The term becomes meaningless in such blanket application, and where real racism yet exists, it is spared scrutiny and eradication by such assumption of an amorphous amount of it. The crucial difference between the South of the past and the rest of the nation was that the laws and the acculturation of the society of the South supported racism, were racist, and those of the rest of the country opposed it. After reform of the laws of the South and in the flux of incomplete reorganization of the society, the main differences remained between people who had been brought up to believe that racism was right, and those brought up to believe the opposite. So much of the new paradox of the South and the nation was bound up in the struggles of the Southerner to unlearn the lessons of his childhood, at the same time that the non-Southern American struggled within his conscience against the irrational seductions of racism as the simple answer to problems too complex for his degree of education and mental health to cope with rationally. The difference between the genuine non-Southern racist and the practicing Southern one was the difference between guilt and a certain surface innocence. The essential fact out of the South's having joined the nation at last was that the adult generation of the 1960s was the last that would ever have the claim to that innocence in evil which had ever been the white Southerner's excuse, had allowed him to escape the blanket condemnation and ostracism of the rest of mankind that his racial practices deserved. He had believed in the evil that he did, had thought it right, and had in his racism at least the acquiescence if not the agreement of the black people with whom he so unfairly shared the land. If we may say that the institutionalization of racism was ended with the thunder-clap will within Negroes, mustered finally, that it should end, we must also acknowledge that the seeming innocence of the white Southerner had not been very deep. We know that he was afflicted at least unconsciously by the torment of guilt that was come to the rest of white America wherever it trifled with the seduction of racism; he sensed that his racist society was against everything that his religion and his adherence to the American creed taught him. And as he became more of a modern American, he became more possessed of the knowledge of good and evil. His Eden was almost gone.

Maybe the deepest part of the honesty of the white Southerner in his still-lingering preference of racist politicians over hypocritical ones was based on the Black Belt belief that he had always had, that didn't require the Presidential Commission's confirmation, that all white men were as he was—racist. Maybe he felt that since they were, they ought to have a George Wallace to speak and act for them and be done with it. If things were that simple, if the racism threatening to beguile America were as strong a thing as the racism that had controlled the institutions of the South, Wallace might well have done as well as many Southerners thought he would. But he didn't, and on such evidence I would strongly question, out of understanding of Southern racism, that the rest of America has become similarly racist.

The Southerner's understanding of racism is so ingrained that both black and white have difficulty verbalizing what they know. As in the common occurrence of a Northern liberal's being taken in by a Southern moderate who claims great progress that has never been made in race relations, at the same time, in the subtle ways of it, mostly deprecating the intellectual or sanitary levels of

local Negroes, he excuses lack of progress, having it both
ways at once and saying it will take time, take time, the
Southerner who knows all the nuances of dishonesty in
such moderate rationalization of racism can only snort, and
scorn the Northern innocent. The Southerner is aware
that the innocent has responded to the genuine warmth of
that racist moderate, to his genuine sincerity, his ability to
believe all the lies he tells. Southerners, black and white
alike, who have fought the racism have known that they
were fighting insanity, and they have correspondingly
treated the enemy as one treats the insane—gingerly, cau-
tiously, indeed fearfully. You don't ordinarily need to respond to the hate stare of some old gentleman affronted in
his consumption of the blue-plate special by your white
appearance inside the restaurant with black companions.
You know how to avoid eyes on you and withal act normally.

You don't argue race with a racist or if you do, you don't
do it with any expectation of winning or even finding
common definitions of terms. You don't, unless you are
demonstrating somewhere for a purpose, provoke a confrontation with a racist. You don't carry a pistol into
backwoods racist territory with any delusions that bran-
dishing it might discourage attack; unless you are prepared
to use it first and ask questions later, you have merely
given your attackers the excuse they need to kill you rather
than merely assault you or arrest you or harass you. If you
are traveling interracially in the backwoods racist country,
you don't flaunt it; you don't break traffic laws, you make
yourself inconspicuous. If you are interviewing a racist on
his home ground, you might even (as I have sometimes
done) not discourage him in his assumption that you and
the rest of all white humankind agree with all his racist
rationale and rigmarole. Or if you are white and have the
accent, the Southern credentials, you might as the writer
George McMillan does, at the outset of your interview, say,

"Looka-here, I don't want to argue with you. I just want to know what you will tell me. And let's understand from the outset that I'm a Southerner and I hate segregation—"

The black Southerner fought the white racism with such insight into its insanity. That was the essence of Dr. King's strategy. You don't fight him with his own weapons; he'll kill you. You find new weapons to which he is vulnerable; you probe at his sense of guilt and the schizophrenia in his soul between Southern conditioning and the American creed. The most frightening thing about the ghetto riots has been that they seem without this knowledge of the insanity in racism. They fight it with its own weapons, and not the least of the effects of them was devastation in the South to whatever Dr. King's strategy and philosophy might have begun to achieve among racist whites. The fight of Southerners, black and white, against the insanity of Southern racism was not unsuccessful. It was in dealings with allies from outside the South that the movement met its great defeats, the 1964 Democratic National Convention symbolic of them, the use of the Meredith March as a sounding board for black power another example. Perhaps if the North were really racist, if Northern white liberals were (as they masochistically like to think they are), the Southern movement might better have been able to cope with its Northern allies.

Paul Goodman has suggested that rather than racist, the mainstream of white America (and this would include people of all races, including successful representatives of the Negro middle class) has been simply ruthlessly impatient, to the point of genocide as with the Indians, with anyone who did not conform, did not shape up, did not in point succeed. One thinks of the poor who resist the ministrations of the poverty program, of the white and black poor, North and South, who arouse so much ire in the economic conservatives by their revolution of negativism, their refusal to shape up, of the ghetto riots as expression of irrational rage at things, not men, as a revolution

against the material symbols of all that success the mainstream of America insists is good (the looting of television
sets eloquently suggesting that maybe it isn't) —one thinks
of all this and Goodman's diagnosis, and shudders. For our
purposes, his diagnosis is as deep into the subject of what
ails the rest of the country as we need to go. For we are
concerned with the South, and have reasonable basis for
belief that what ails America is not what has ailed the
South, racism.

One of America's ills, though, does have the hysterical
feel of Southern racism; this has to do with the hunting
preserve plantations and the kind of killing that occurs
in the Vietnam War and the willingness not merely to
acquiesce in the blind and impersonal forces of the economic system whichever way cold machines moved them,
but to be unable to apply any humanistic concern, any
effective help to those, like the victims of the collapse of
the plantation system, who happened to be victims—in
short, to let babies starve.

The South had ever been urged and cajoled by its best
leaders and thinkers to try to attain the national norms,
and in the 1960s, partly because it was much more a
part of the nation and partly because most of its leadership
had come to see the national norms as desirable, the South
at its best was wholeheartedly seeking them.

The irony was deepest, saddest in two of the most constructive, bravest of the organized efforts of Negro Southerners to improve their lot—political participation and the
cooperative movement among poor people. For all the
struggling and suffering and nobility of the voter-registra-
tion effort over the many years would be of little avail if,
in the end, all that it came to was a proliferation of black
versions of the standard American politician, black participation in politics as usual, the spoils system. Little
would have been gained from all the hope and human
values invested in the little cooperative movements if out
of them came only one more handful of hard-bitten Amer-

ican businessmen. Both these instances were like the effort to desegregate the non-union cotton mills. No one had the right to say desist. No one had the right to ask that the gains for Negro people that would ensue from both be weighed against the losses likely in spiritual and human values. But the clear duty of leadership and citizenship, North and South, was to try to find ways to imbue politics and business with some more humane and decent standards than was their norm in modern America.

Here then was the task of a real Southern leadership, old and new, white and black, in the crucial new patterning of society: to examine not merely regional deficiencies with a view to correcting them, but in the quest for cures to examine what the rest of the nation had already accomplished before accepting it as the South's goal—to examine national deficiencies with a view to avoiding them, helping to correct them, certainly not jumping blindly to them. If—as I have set out as a chief reason for trying to understand the South in its time of greatest change—the nation were only beginning in all its institutions and values the kind of painful experience of challenge and change that the South has known regarding racism, the South's position regarding national norms provides a gauge by which America might look at itself. In every misbegotten and misguided effort of the South to catch up to something that was essentially sorry and shabby in the rest of America, there was a standard by which America might measure its own failure. In everything that America had that the South with honor and dignity and true self-interest might still aspire to, America might assess its strength.

IV

In that terrible but necessary struggle that seemed inevitable, America had object lessons and wisdoms to learn from the South's smaller experience of it. Most of it has been obvious: that the institutionalization of an evil (racism only one among many that might be in the nation, greed another) has been the South's tragedy, making it a society of tormented people and much absurdity, making it insane; and that, as through all history, response with force cannot prevail ultimately when the challenge against the force is based on reality and sanity.

Beyond the obvious, there has been surely in what we have seen of the South's soul struggle with race an underlying truth that has ever eluded yet always tormented analysis of the South, has been clearer in the fiction about the South, most clear in Faulkner—a truth with terrible pertinence to the nation's coming ordeal. This is that there are no villains whose overthrow will assure the end of evils.

Simon Legree was the prototype, and through its history the South has provided villains whose overthrow, or whose human death could be thought to end the evil, solve the problems. "Only the undertaker," said the Southern folklore. What a disgrace—the Vardamans and Talmadges and Bilbos and Lester Maddoxes, the backwoods sheriffs, the state troopers, public embodiment of the savage ideal, Jim Clark, Bull Connor. They were flamboyant and they provided clear-cut targets for those who fought the racism, and they performed various kinds of symbolic functions, as extensions of the racist insanity in the white Southerner's breast, as scapegoat for the guilt of the North's long history of irresponsibility in the matter of Southern racism and its own Negro population, as devil incarnate properly to be hated by black Southerners resisting the normal-enough impulse to hate all whites.

We have examined lesser villains—the planters, the power structures of small cities and large, those possessive old men whose ugliness in a crisis reflected the anger and dismay and panic they felt at seeing their prized possession tampered with, the cotton mill owners, the faltering labor leaders, the ineffective liberals, the corrupt Negro leaders, the emasculated educational elite, the very policeman whose presence makes us shudder and say, "I hate cops." Time after time the Southern "and yet" has to be invoked about these villains. In the flesh, in the particularity of their own situation, in the things that their society has done to them, they are not evil men, or more exactly the evil that they do has its own unextraordinary rationale. They do what the society has fashioned them to do. Evil is indeed banal. Eichmann, not Simon Legree, is the villain.

This is not to deny the evil that they do, or to say as in the myth of the separation of the poor of the two races, which seems to hold the culpable poor white blameless, that they are not to be held responsible, accountable for their actions. It is merely to say that their demise will not end the evil. Sheriff Clark was toppled by the Negro vote that was won for all Negro Southerners by the alligator stupidity of the evil that he did in Selma. Bull Connor came to know the ignominy of standing in a Birmingham Negro church like those from which the demonstrators marched into his dogs and fire hoses, like the one whose bombing, with the murder of four little Sunday school girls, his police could never solve, and in a quest for votes singing in that church "We Shall Overcome" with those who had overcome him, who refused in the offing, his singing notwithstanding, to vote for him. The villains fell; the undertaker through Southern history performed his duty. But the evil lived on. Something else was wrong.

The Southern movement used the figure of such villains to gain sympathy and support from the rest of the nation, but it was never fooled about them, never thought that deposing the villains, putting them down, as joyful an experience as it might be, was the answer to the evil. The Southern movement sought and won basic changes in the institutions of the society which produced the villains, which tailored, conditioned, programmed them as agents of evil. The young Northerners who came to the South to work in the movement soon learned the human truth be-

hind this wisdom. Their reports, their talk was full of a
bemused fascination with the villains; the best came eventually to know real compassion for them even as they despised them out of experience of their evil. This was, out
of the South's history of the closeness of the two races, their
humanity transcending dehumanization, the rational background for the highest spiritual rationale of the Southern
movement.

In the coming attempts to change *institutions* of the
nation, in what has occurred already, the gravest danger
would seem to be an inability to make the distinction between villains and the institutions which create them.
Mayor Daley, even as Sheriff Clark, may well have been
the agent of his own destruction at the 1968 Democratic
Convention. But the institutions out of which he rose—in
Chicago, in national politics—would not be changed with
his political demise. The New Left, screaming "Pig" at
police, seemed little aware of this. Acrimony, vilification,
the breakdown of communication, violence that seemed
not strategic but simply vindictive on college campus or in
the ghetto—these were no marks of a revolution with any
assurance of succeeding. Or, if successful, it would be like
revolutions have so often been, a change of villains, not a
rearranging of the social order so as to eliminate them.
That bankruptcy of leadership which was such an appalling condition of the South through the 1960s was most
evident in its national manifestations in the willingness of
radicals, liberals, and intellectuals alike of the generation
old enough ordinarily to assume leadership of the move to
challenge and change basic values and institutions, to defer
so easily, so uncritically, to the young. It is the natural
propensity of the young to seek simplistic villains, superficial solutions; it is entirely understandable, but hardly
efficacious, that they spit in the eye of the cop who acts on
orders destructive of the Bill of Rights, instead of developing strategies to strengthen the Bill of Rights. (Negroes
and the whites who worked with them in the South had

the Southerner's knowledge of the insanity of racism, had
the manhood to control emotional response to the bestiality of the cops where it was suicidal to do otherwise, and
they had a strategy which, when they did goad cops into
doing them violence before TV cameras, made it purposeful. One feels a lack of such strategy in the New Left. It
was a mark of the perspicacity of the New Left that it was
aware that free speech had been perverted so that it was an
instrument for avoiding, rather than causing change. So
had courts, for example, among all the institutions of
Southern society, been perverted into instruments of denial of civil liberties, rather than protection of them. But
the Southern movement did not conclude that courts were
evil and had to be abolished or that they were irrelevant to
the better society they sought, as the New Left seemed to
have concluded about free speech.)

There were many other parallels. Those who fought
racism in the Southern movement—whites especially but
black people of wisdom as well—knew before they were
too far along in the struggle it was not race itself that was
important. Racism caused men and institutions in the
South to be bent toward the destruction of civil liberties
and human dignity. It was civil liberties and human
dignity that were ultimately important, not the racial context. The end of the struggle was not to destroy the human
agents of racism nor to replace white ones with black ones,
but to destroy racism and restore civil liberties and human
dignity for all people, black and white.

SNCC was one part of the strength of the Southern
movement at its best. SNCC was young people, probably
the bravest and, for a time, most visionary group of the
young ever organized in America. Most of SNCC's impact
on the revolutionary young people of the world (and it
was vast) was out of a Southern feel for the particular, a
grasp of the field's reality that overrode the cautions and
equivocations of headquarters. They knew that in the matter of a child's starving, a man's being beaten to death in a

Black Belt jail, for example, a situation existed which was not susceptible to the processes or compromise and conciliation ordinary to American self-government. They knew that in the manifestations they saw of blind economic forces at work, in the suffering of people left behind in cotton fields by a computerized, nuclear and electronic new reality, verbal conflict between concepts of nineteenth century capitalism and communism were as irrelevant as fine points of medieval theological dispute during the dawn of the Renaissance. "That's old stuff," they would sneer. They knew that in America language had become in many ways as corrupted as it had been in Nazi Germany, had practitioners of it with purposes, as in advertising, so unrelated to truth that it had more often than not ceased to reflect reality. Like the postwar German writers, they sought to bring language down to a level of concreteness that would impart to it once more a relationship with the real world. "Tell it like it is," they would say.

But the young, more than people who are more than thirty years old, have a tremendous energy of the emotions of childhood and adolescence, an urgency of the impulse to revolt against parental authority. Older Negro Southerners, the Southern movement of black and white together, were awed and inspired by SNCC's braveness and insights, but were not willing to follow SNCC blindly, not willing to say that, because it was so right in what it did and what it was against, that it was right in all things. Blind, adolescent rebellion against sterotyped villains as an end in itself never became the main thrust of the Southern movement. There was the danger that it would, if in the struggle for broader change in America, that struggle were not joined by older men and women of the same humanistic belief as the young, and if these older Americans had not the will to differentiate between the genius and damn foolishness of the youth movement, as the Southern movement had with SNCC.

Real change of the kind the nation so desperately

needed could not be achieved by the young alone, any more than by the poor, and would no more come with the elimination of villains than in the South. The forces involved—science and technology beyond most people's comprehension, economic and social organization and systems almost beyond control, problems like overpopulation too difficult for even a Solomon—were so vast and complex as to require the best of all elements of the society, and then might not yield. What was required would, as surely the South shows, mean compassion not only for the human victims of the gigantic forces at work, of the old evil order, but for the human agents of evil as well. Compassion would be of the kind the Negro South offered to whites. As in the Southern experience, one would fight the human agents, hold them responsible for the needless human suffering they caused, hold the poor white as much to blame as the Bourbon and know the difference between the skills of the two. But in the struggle one would not somehow cease to respect the humanity of the enemy, abandon all comity and civility of discourse. This would not be out of any misguided sentimentality, but out of the kind of knowledge the Southerner has of racism's insanity, that you are destroyed when you become what you fight. This would not mean further involvement in the kind of pragmatism that was the downfall of the custodial liberals, the weighing of chances of success as the only criterion for moving, the willingness to do business with the enemy and to do in the friend for the sake of some specific success. Above all, it would not mean compromising on matters of principle that cannot be compromised, as racism, as the Bill of Rights. What it would mean would be the kind of will and conviction and understanding of what one was doing that would allow, in the end, not punitive harshness toward those one had defeated, not radical reconstruction, but firm and just correction of evils at their source, the kind of enforcement, for example, of civil rights laws that was lacking in the South.

What was indeed required, what was appropriate to the national situation was intelligent, civilized, forthright adjustment of differences, not warfare. If out of all its sad history the South offered any truth to both sides of the conflicts confronting America, it was of the folly and tragedy of implacable enmity, of hatred, of dehumanization. If the South had any insights into the human flesh of the national conflicts, it was out of what we have seen of the modern South in its norms and extremities, that its people, black and white, are more like all other people than different, that its majority whites, for all their involvement in evil, for all the evil of the society which shaped them, are not in themselves evil people. We have seen failed leaders and incompetent citizens alike, woefully unequipped, by training or acculturation and even by inadequate supply of the basics of existence, for the great tasks of reorganization and consolidation facing their society: it was possible at least to doubt that they would be able to correct those very conditions which caused them to be so unequipped. The most that the people of the rest of the country might learn from the South was that these same things were true in some degree of all American society; perhaps, from such knowledge, they might find compassion for one another, even in their gravest conflicts.

V

Would the South, indeed, be able at last to find interracial harmony? Things were so chaotic in the 1960s that no one could really know. Prediction could be made least of all with social science's wistful renditions of the scientific method. From what we have seen through myth and old analyses, from the roadside and in the towns and cities, out of intuition and as much hope as realism allows me to muster, I would, if forced to answer the question pointblank (as Yankees are prone to demand), give a typical Southern answer. I would say well, yes—maybe—if . . .

The most important thing, and the most hopeful, was
that the South would never be the same again. This was
not because of the vast economic changes and attendant
social ones. It was because the civilization of the South was
no longer undergirded by law that, in its deepest meaning
—dehumanization of Negroes—was based on murder,
based on the antithesis of the meaning of law and civilization. That was crucial. Southerners were free at last. They
could struggle within the limit of law rather than against
it for a just society. No longer did the law make inevitable
that all endeavor would be absurd, the best in people used
to the worst purposes, and with the law changed, custom
was beginning to change, reducing further the absurdity.
The good little white child need no longer be racist; the
dutiful white citizen need no longer discriminate; "good"
Negroes need no longer demean themselves.

As ever, the greatest problems of the society—race and
poverty—were so clear-cut, so unambiguous that by comparison with the subtleties and complexities of those the
rest of the nation had come to, they seemed much more
amenable to the best efforts of the best and worst people,
seemed so promising of great tangible, unambiguous gains.
It is not, I hope, romanticism or wishful thinking to suggest that there was a feel, a spirit of realistic effort to meet
the challenge abroad in the South. Not all the people,
certainly not even the majority of the whites, were imbued
with it; it was fragile, wavery, needing of encouragement,
but there. We have encountered it in the large cities and
small, the towns even, and the rural areas, especially those
where solemn black men and women were imparting a
dignity and decency for the first time in many years to
political offices.

But there were all those debilities of leadership, of citizenship. How to break the circle of an adequate economy
that is possible only with enhancement of the people which
required an adequate economy? Racial attitudes, as we
have seen, were still the key to the development of respon-

sibility in leadership and citizenship necessary for real progress in solving the riddle. Elements of the "nice" people, the better off, older ones, with an economic stake, still real in towns and cities if not any longer on the land, in such effects of racism as surplus labor, would continue a negative influence. But others of the "nice" people, caught in the newer cultural and corporate ties to the nation, city creatures, professionals and the like, had evidenced in the 1960's moves toward real racial moderation, and would probably continue to do so. At worst, they would come to national norms on race; at best, they might out of complex motives, not excluding business interest and civic-image pride, exert the kind of influence they were capable of for integration, racial justice, and effective relief of poverty. The likelihood of continued and more just coalitions of "nice" white people and Negroes in the cities and in state elections was a larger likelihood than any kind of conscious coming together politically of the poor whites and Negroes.

The young of the "nice" people class, especially in the cities, showed the most hopeful promise of all: more of them than one might expect held strongly to the new values of the youth movement, motivating work toward real integration, real racial justice. Many of the white young, "common" and "nice," maybe a majority outside the Black Belt, just were not imbued with racism, were not much conscious of race, were capable of casual acceptance of black people where they found them, as in school. Only in Alabama, and to a lesser extent in Mississippi, was racism still an intact article of official faith, and even there, significant numbers resisted. The older poor whites would hold to their racism out of those old habits of pitiful pride which separated them from self-interest, had nothing to do with their economic situation or anything else rational. As long as there was a surplus of labor in the South—and despite the optimism of economists' statistics which resorted to shrinking definitions of labor supply, this would be for some time to come—there was the danger that self-interest would at last assert itself among the poor whites to fight Negroes, consciously competing again for jobs, as in the rest of the country. The poor whites would continue to be less amenable to organization, to being banded together into any kind of political-action coalition based on self-interest, if this depended on their trusting organizers or leaders other than those they regarded as loyal to their prejudices, the Wallace kind. We have not explored this distrust, examined it as we might have because it seems to be mostly a part of that bundle of irrationality, prejudice, superstition that expresses itself in racism. But insights into it out of all the history of the exploitation and degradation of poor whites are suggested in a finding by Robert Coles about hungry Negroes:

> In my experience with families in the Delta—some of whom I've known for many years—their kind of life can produce a chronic state of mind, a form of withdrawn, sullen behavior that the word "depression" only begins to describe. I have seen some of the families I know in the South go North and carry with them that state of mind; they get more food, more welfare money, and in the public hospitals of northern cities certain minimal medical services—but as one tape-records their expressed feelings and attitudes month after month, as I am now doing in a northern ghetto, one sees how persistently sickness and hunger in children live on in adults—who doubt any offer, mistrust any goodness or favorable turn of events as temporary and ultimately unreliable. I fear that we have among us hundreds of thousands of people who have literally grown up to be and learned to be tired, fearful, anxious, suspicious, and (as a physical fact of life) in a very basic, inflexible, and tragic sense, *unbelieving.*[5]

Such a development was probably the least encouraging of observations to be made about Negro Southerners, for

[5] "Hearings Before the Subcommittee on Employment, Manpower, and Poverty of the Committee on Labor and Public Welfare, United States Senate, Ninetieth Congress, First Session on Hunger and Malnutrition in America," July 11–12, 1967, p. 53.

their ability to believe had been one of the two or three salient, atypical attributes they had to sustain them and give to the South and the nation for a better society. Certainly, it was not all gone, even after the high expectations it had nurtured and then—partially for some, completely for others—seen disappointed. The churches, even in the desolation of the plantation lands, reduced there from services every Sunday to once a month, continued to give succor and energize courage, to help make possible those difficult personal assertions of selfhood in small situations, refusals of petty injustices in personal and public dealings with whites, that would eventually make the largest differences in the new ordering of society from the old. The Negro middle class seemed likely to continue for some time to combine its best traditions of moral rectitude and selflessness, with ability to resist becoming a replica of the white one, with its overbalancing to obsession with possessions and fear and fascination with disease, its overconcern with self, its greed. Not the least of the ability to resist that gray life consuming so much of the white middle class came from black power's better instincts, from the new understanding that integration did not mean going to the white man's place, but intermingling in both kinds of places, drawing them together toward some middle point containing the virtues of both.

The wavering delineations of race relations, what might come, could be seen in two kinds of reactions to the new familiarity of the races with one another: on the one hand a breeding of a kind of contempt, on the other, a building of new and real respect. Tape-recorded reactions of Negro children to token desegregation in Black Belt counties of Alabama revealed the new insights they were gaining:

> Well before I went to the white school I always did think that the white person was smarter than we were . . . But I found out this year that this isn't true. There were a lot of them who had more trouble than I had in getting their lesson. . . .

Some people think that white people are higher class than Negroes, but from the way the children did behave they are lower class people than Negro.

I think some Negroes just get excited when they are around a white and they laugh in his face, and at his little funny jokes, and at what he says. He can give you the twinkle in his eye so that it makes Negroes go crazy. Well I think you really find out when you go to a white school . . . So it really makes you mad when you find out about him. They really try to take advantage of you with their smiles and their funny words, they really try to take advantage of you.[6]

If these are harsh insights, they are human ones that end forever the old misconceptions, the real barriers between the races. There could be compassion, as in this description of other-directedness in the white children, revealing also of the difference in the white and black middle class:

They all seem to be afraid of what someone else might think. They can't seem to think for themselves. They can't even follow their own moral right . . . There are very few incidences of violence, killings, etc., but they are afraid to take me home after practice . . . They are just afraid. They are afraid of nothing; there's nothing left to be afraid of.[7]

Similarly hopeful were the kinds of insights on both sides described by a Negro teacher after her first year in a predominantly white school in a small city. She had, she said, never before been aware of how badly the "better-off" whites treated the poor whites. She spoke of white teachers' indifference and even mistreatment of children of cotton-mill workers in the school. "Why they treat them worse than they do us," she said. At first, predictably, the parents of these children resented her. But before the end of the year, she said, some of those poor white parents came to her and told her that they were glad she was there, glad of

6 Mark A. Chesler, "In Their Own Words: A Student Appraisal of What Happened After School Desegregation," published by the Southern Regional Council, 1967.
7 Chesler.

the change, because she was the first teacher their children
had ever had who took trouble with them, seemed to care
about them.

Here was the very exceptional kind of new understanding, new coming together of people of a shared land and
culture that hearkened to the myth of a new order of race
relations. There could be so much more of it if the integration laws were really enforced.

Another hopeful, if exceptional sign appeared when
white students at Berea College, themselves from poor
homes near the little foothills cooperative school, organized
their own self-help organization to work with the mountain poor whites. The following editorial from the student
paper indicates how thoroughly they had borrowed from
the better instincts of black power:

> The founding of this program indicates that mountain
> people are capable of the initiatives necessary to wage
> their own war against riches. It should demonstrate to
> middle-class Yankee "organizers" that mountain people
> have little faith and a great deal of distrust of those who
> spend their free time between their parents' wars "or-
> ganizing" a "Movement" in Appalachia. It should
> demonstrate to [them] that mountain college people
> have not been impressed by attempts to organize their
> parents for a revolution which exists only in the minds of
> a few misguided, politically naive escapees from the
> middle-class suburbs and the Ivy-League universities. It
> should demonstrate to those "organizers" that they can
> more profitably waste their time planning conferences
> for each other, talking social change to each other, shar-
> ing bed and pot with each other, and exchanging the
> latest hippie dress and records with each other in some
> other locale than Appalachia.[8]

But these were manifestations of strength in a general
population that seemed too weak for the responsibilities
forced upon it and in a society weakened by flux and uncertainty. If neo-Populism came, it would be mainly in the

[8] The *Pinnacle*, Berea College, Berea, Kentucky, February 17, 1968.

unconscious ways, the development of a politics more strongly on the lines of that begun in Tennessee, shorn of the irrationality of race as an issue, forced to rational appeals to needs which presumably would produce biracial support. If a political movement could be built by appealing to the dissatisfaction in all classes across America with the education of children and the tax structure, surely it would be irresistible—and since these situations were worst in the South, if there were any logic in politics and any rationality in the South, such a movement might most likely develop there first.

But politics and the South being what they were (no politicians were willing to lose at first for the sake of ultimate victory), they would more probably merely try to catch up with the rest of the nation. This would mean a continuation of a politics, minus the favorite issue of race, devoted to the interests of big money and better-off citizens, more sports stadiums and superhighways at the expense of the children and the poor, ever higher sales taxes, continued limitation of vision to the dubious benefits of lured industry exploitive of the labor force. Under such governments, ghettos would continue a-building, probably less and less as public policy but fortuitously, from forces beyond the ability of the governments to do anything about. By the time court orders demanding real integration became effective, they might in most of the large cities be up against the accurate answer readied for them by Atlanta's school superintendent John Letson: "There just aren't enough white children to go around."

Negroes, for the power to themselves in the situation, and racist whites outside the city limits of the larger cities were becoming a formidable coalition of the unconscious kind against consolidations and annexations that would, on the one hand, mitigate the likelihood of black takeovers of municipal governments and, on the other, allow real integration of schools. The possibility of a model city government imbued with the spiritual strain of Southern Negro politics, truly responsive to the people, capable of reforming the unjust tax structures, was a real one. But then, so was the specter of the all-black city government being only a replica of the all-white one, a new set of wheeling-and-dealing villains. So, too, with the dreams of a rational development of urban areas, with mini-metropolises serving humanly proportioned smaller cities imbued with the best of the nation's urban culture, a realizing of real advantage from the development of the superhighway community. If this came about, those seeking it would have to be the most skilled of professionals, able to make sense of all the maze of hidden government and blind forces at work in the modern city, and to wrench them into some rational pattern. There was little evidence of any desire to do so among the South's planners, architects, economists, no organizations of them, for example, as in some Northern cities, to give *ad hoc* help to neighborhoods beset by manifestation of the city's right of eminent domain.

The continuing strength of the racist white vote remained a real threat that in the South there might logically evolve from the old conservative order and the new right-wing, know-nothing tendencies (blaming the poor for being poor) America's first all-out fascist political movement. The Citizens' Councils in their full strength had come close to it; so had Wallace. This would seem more possible than the fear expressed often that these tendencies would reveal themselves once more in purely Southern, mainly racial terms, a return to the kind of oppression of Negroes and suppression of their white allies the South has known periodically, most notably before the Civil War, after Reconstruction, and during the late 1950s and early 1960s.

What would most effectively discourage this was the will of the Negro people. They were not going ever to return to what had been in the South. Their movement, proclaimed dead, was alive in every city and hamlet to the degree that small organizations were working away at what they deemed the important local interests, mostly political efforts, mostly economic self-help. And it was alive in another fundamental way: wherever whites became oppressive, usually in the smaller places in some indecency of violence or flagrant dishonesty of school desegregation policy, there was the tradition and the forms of organization for protest, and these sprang to life. Demonstrations, boycotts, the bringing down of federal pressure, and the recourse to the federal courts were a part of the repertoire of citizenship for Negro Southerners. And these methods were effective—seldom enough to bring complete victory, but quite enough to prevent ever again the clamp-down of the old-style closed society. Only if this kind of calamity came upon all the nation would it come again to the South.

The continued existence of the movement, as the best expression ever of the good things of the white and black Southern culture, was not merely a negative force. Indeed, the most hope that could be seen in surveying all the sorry scene of failure in the South of the late 1960s was contained in the incredible strength of the people who fought for the safety and dignity of all people.

On a warm spring day of 1968 under trees before a public building in St. George, South Carolina, with thick honeysuckle on a fence combining its tanged sweetness with the fainter, more mellow sweetness of the purple chinaberry tree blossoms, with bees sounding and dogs far-off barking, Mrs. Victoria DeLee stands, a tall, middle-aged woman with a broad tan face framed in big gold earrings, wearing a green tam, a pink cotton dress and flat shoes with stockings. "We will straighten this county out," she says, "from what it was." She has been the leader here in civil rights, voter registration, poverty work, since the early 1960s; her home has been bombed and burned, her family threatened more than once, children mistreated trying to desegregate schools. "If I don't do the work, who goin' to do it?" she says, some of her accent almost cockney, from the nearby coast. "Lots will follow, but they won't lead. If I don't call another meetin', no meetin' will be called. . . .

> And so much to be done. People, every day we go out, starvin'. Children purely naked. Shacks like goat shacks. People sick, down, on welfare, and get so little. Some are not even on. They're sick with poverty—all out in these woods. We have records of children have died of malnutrition. . . .
> What really got me started in this was that I was born into it. It was the way I was brought up. My grandmother raised me. We had to work in the fields. For twenty-five cents a day, we worked. They'd give us clabber and blue milk, grits, meal, the bones after the meat was cut off. If we ever got a piece of meat it would be full of maggots. We'd scald it to clean the maggots out. They'd feed us on the back steps. Many days I'd be sitting on the back steps eatin' with the dogs, hunting dogs, fox, coon, rabbit dogs. The dogs would pull the bread from our plates. We'd eat scraps. Grandmother would go in an' take scraps they left. We had three months school. Had to walk six miles both ways. Many a time I would be dressed for school and the white man would come and say he was sorry but you got to help me in the fields today. I'd go by the graveyard and say I ought to be dead soon. I got to the seventh grade and had to quit. This growed in me, and I said when I got grown I would kill all the white people before they could kill me. I was of a different mind then. But I never have since then been afraid for my life. After I was grown, I came to know God and the Holy Ghost. So I have tried it another way.
> I believe God is helping us change Dorchester County.

Here, the strength that transcends the statistics of deprivation, debilitation, here the miracle of the South's humanity triumphant over all the idiocies and evils of its ways. There is an innocence of good as well as of evil, an ability yet to believe in an age of unbelief, an ability to be individual in an age of programmed conformity, that special ability to laugh, a cosmic laughter, and nobility. All of this is most evident in Negro Southerners, perhaps only because the twists of history have given them a role in which these traits may be expressed positively. In a little Mississippi Delta place, Mr. William Franklin, a middle-aged Negro farmer who took in two white Northern civil rights workers when they came there in 1964 to help the people, who lost his land as a retaliatory result and who was, yet, in the late 1960s still enduring the enmity of local whites, explained why he did what he did: "They came wanting to help us. No gentleman could turn them away."

That tradition of noblesse oblige, of the lady and the gentleman, had real meaning in the culture of both races. So did the spirit of resistance, of rebellion, strong in the whites out of perversions of it in the past, the essence of the movement's stubborn negative force. There might come the dark time in the nation's history when it would be needed to resist insanities as terrible as those of the South's past from the rest of America, as it was needed in the late 1960s to resist the worst inanities. Southerners of the generation which saw racism brought into question and had their own certainty about it, if not destroyed, at least troubled, had that advantage the rest of America would have to come to—of being able to question all the rest of what they had accepted at face value, of being incapable ever again of accepting dogma and ideology without thought. It would serve them in the trials to come—in the South and the nation.

What the South had given the nation in the past had been mostly evil, most notably the taint of its racism and the human products of all its social and economic failure.

Prominent in what the South has given the nation is militarism, the extraordinary number of national policymakers bent on war through the twentieth century. They include Woodrow Wilson, Cordell Hull, James F. Byrnes; such U. S. Senators as Russell, Stennis, and Walter George; and Representative Mendel Rivers, Secretary of State Dean Rusk, and former President Lyndon Johnson.[9] This had, possibly as warning to the nation, a significance that seemed deeper than the celebrated bellicosity of the South, the pitiful paradox of its willingness, yea, eagerness to give more than its share of sons to all the wars. There was at least the suggestion that men reared in a society with racism's brand of murder at its base were more capable than most men of warfare's brand of it, that the ability to live with a system that declared a fourth of the population, people one grew up with and knew intimately, less than human has a direct connection with the ability to declare nations or races of men one has never seen inhuman, and to destroy them, inhumanly. The nation's increased militarism, like race in the South, was at the heart of most of its problems. The future of the South as the seedbed and support of that militarism was among the direst of the possibilities.

If SNCC's brand of anti-intellectualism was a black Southern import of destructive quality, this is against the record of unprecedented offering to the nation by black Southerners of much good. Most of this was summed up in the precept and philosophy of Dr. King as the personification of the best of the white and black Southern cultures. Here, out of all the South's humanism and mysticism and

[9] Harry Truman was from a border state. And of course the chief opponent in the Senate to the Vietnam War was William Fulbright of Arkansas. Fulbright's peace record and his equally great record of early civil libertarian opposition to McCarthyism might be explainable by the fact that he was a former college president (not a usual occupation for a Southern politician). His sad record of racism, on the other hand, was probably as much as anything else of the pattern of men who know better being afraid of losing their influence, or in his case, his office.

particularity and ability to believe, was what he held out
to the nation as antidote to its militarism a year before his
tragic death:

> The war in Vietnam is but a symptom of a far deeper
> malady within the American spirit, and if we ignore this
> sobering reality we will find ourselves organizing clergy
> and laymen-concerned committees for the next genera-
> tion. . . . We will be marching and attending rallies with-
> out end unless there is a significant and profound change
> in American life and policy. Such thoughts take us be-
> yond Vietnam, but not beyond our calling as sons of the
> living God. . . .
> This call for a world-wide fellowship that lifts neigh-
> borly concern beyond one's tribe, race, class, and nation
> is in reality a call for an all-embracing and uncondi-
> tional love of all men. This oft-misunderstood and mis-
> interpreted concept so readily dismissed by the Nietzsches
> of the world as a weak and cowardly force—has now
> become an absolute necessity for the survival of man.
> When I speak of love I am not speaking of some senti-
> mental and weak response. I am speaking of that force
> which all of the great religions have seen as the supreme
> unifying principle of life. Love is somehow the key that
> unlocks the door that leads to ultimate reality.[10]

In lesser ways too, the South might add distinctive flavoring and original thought to the national mainstream of
which it had become fully a part. This would be essentially
in terms of the traits of the people, their culture, not
unique ones but developed differently or more fully in the
South—such things as the ability to experience music in
the fabric of their life, to experience ritual violence, to
experience God, such things as politeness and manners.
(Politeness and manners were not lacking in the rest of the
country; they were merely more a point of pride in the
South where so often they were in their pitiful, hysterical
superficiality among "nice" whites about the only redeeming grace. Freed of hysteria among whites, a part of the

[10] Address given at Riverside Church, New York City, Tuesday, April
4, 1967, to Clergy and Laymen Concerned About Vietnam.

beauty newly prided of blacks, they might serve as a model for softening the nation's increasing mood of total incivility in disputes.) Out of their hard experience, Southerners might influence whatever transformation of the economic system of the nation that in some form seemed inevitable: by continued insistence on such values as the rural poor knew, of the right of a man to do what he loves to do, regardless of economic utility, or such values as the non-business South had always known, like the need of people to have some relationship with nature. Much of the elusive, ephemeral sense of the good of the South had to do with its knowledge of the value of humanity over economic and other abstract concerns. Maybe from this the nation might draw heavily for the value system of its new age. At any rate, these kinds of things were the sum of the strength the South would have to draw on in its own desperate struggle against the overwhelming problems of its society.

I have tried to understand the weaknesses of Southerners in full human context so that their predicament might be appreciated, so that the myths of villains and an evil people might be dispelled. I have not tried to excuse the weaknesses that are summed up in the failure through history of leadership and citizenship to act responsibly. These were white failures; the assertion in the 1960s by many Negroes of full responsibility of leadership and citizenship was the model of the best that might come to all the South's people, white and black. (The white Southerner certainly never needed anyone to make rationalizations for his failures; his whole history has been fabricated of them. All he has ever needed to do was to face and accept his humanity, its weaknesses and strengths. But he had ever preferred to see himself not as a villain but as a hero, not as all evil, but as all good. Perhaps at last he was ready for reality.)

Out of all the flux of the 1960s, from the midst of the upheaval of the South's society, I cannot say with certainty (nor do I think can anyone) what might come of the many possibilities we have glimpsed—their variety and contradictions summed up in the promise of a truly healthy society, and in the threat of a continuing festering and spreading of evil.

We do know that the South will never be the same again, the cohesion of its old distinctive racial, economic, governmental, societal structures forever disrupted. What it will become will be from a gradual forming, shaping into permanence of the trends, potentials, possibilities, patterns that we have observed. The vision of its becoming something better than the America it had always lagged behind, of its continuing from the days of the Negro movement to lead the nation has as the most important basis for hope of fulfillment the simple fact of its existence in the minds and hearts of a growing number of Southerners, white and black, myself included. But I think we have seen rather overwhelmingly that what the South does become will not be in fulfillment of all those grand expectations that it would develop models for national emulation of new political alignments or new kinds of cities or new economic prodigies or new never-equaled racial harmony.

The efforts at self-help cooperatives and the like have been innovative, the nearest thing to the grand expectations. But if they held out any meaning as a model for the nation, it was the same kind of meaning that the civil rights movement from which they grew had held out all along—spiritual, not practical or pragmatic. They will not likely develop any ingenious competitive ability to succeed in the business system of the nation, to beat the enemy with his own weapons; rather, they will continue to assert human values, spiritual qualities that transcend the business system—and maybe they will help install them into it.

It has been the same in politics. In our book on the great Negro voter registration effort of the early 1960s (*Climb-*

ing Jacob's Ladder, Harcourt, Brace, and World, 1967), Reese Cleghorn and I concluded that the important thing about the triumphant entry of Negroes into Southern politics had been spiritual, the influence of Negro voters themselves on the developing broad policies of the region, and the freeing of whites from the anti-democratic influences of the past policy of disenfranchisement. But in practical terms, we foresaw no millennium. Not much more than the ordinary performance, haphazard and not always wise, of American voting patterns could be expected of Negro Southerners, and not much more than the ordinary advantages from voting would accrue to them, specifically the consideration of their interests along with the many others competing for attention of government.

And yet . . . The bringing into consideration of Negro interests, proved in the instance of the need to feed the starving just how great a gain these ordinary advantages meant, and just what a powerful influence for the good of the whole society Negro political interests involve. The emergence of Senator Ernest F. Hollings of South Carolina in early 1969 as the first high-level elected official in the South to acknowledge the existence of widespread hunger, to admit his own past participation in efforts to hide its existence, and to seek relief for the situation, was precisely the kind of not really spectacular, but fundamentally important effect Negro voting was bound to have.

It was the spiritual forces abroad in the land that seemed likely to accomplish the most. Not the least of these was the feeling alive on almost every level of Southern life, as we have seen it in this book, that things men do, the efforts like self-help cooperatives or for that matter fighting integration, still matter, still are worth doing, worthy of one's humanity, in an increasingly mechanistic world where a feeling of futility and absurdity consumes more and more people.

So—development in the South in economic matters, in

politics, in all things, would not be in broad strokes of innovation and radical departure, but in subtle, intangible influences at work, motion inevitably toward the forms and shapes and patterns of the rest of the society, but with a hope, a chance of such special Southern forces at work on them as the spirituality of the Negro movement. The best that might develop in the South would be the kind of thing we encountered with the Regionalists and the writers, the adding of distinctive and even crucial Southern flavor, Southern influences to national and indeed international social, political, economic institutions and movements, the adapting of these to Southern ways and needs. In this and in that old desire of the South to work out its own destiny, solve its own problems, there was the likelihood that the South would continue a distinctive subculture, and in the process contribute substantially to the national welfare.

As never before in history, with the joining of the nation fully, with elimination of racism as the core of the civilization, the opportunity was there for the assertion of white responsibility, a joining of it with the Negro's. This would be the only lastingly real integration, this would be the South truly free at last—free of the neurotic paralysis of the "nice" white people, free of the brutalization of the racists, free of the self-destroying unrealism of the poor whites, free of the degradation of Negroes. Only with a better start toward the assertion of such responsibility than seemed evident in the late 1960s might the people be expected to succeed in the job of intelligently restructuring their civilization. This could come only with more responsibility from the rest of the country, for the matter of law was the real key to the future. Whether or not Southerners eventually developed the kind of society the best in them deserved, whether they were able to catch up with the best in America depended not merely on them alone. Any one of the dire or desirable possibilities we have just discussed depended on developments in the rest of the nation. The South could not do all that had to be done, alone. The South was not just of America; America was of it, their destinies inseparable.

Bibliography

Carmichael, Stokely and Charles V. Hamilton, *Black Power: The Politics of Liberation in America.* New York, Vantage Books, 1967.

Cash, W. J., *The Mind of the South.* New York, Alfred A. Knopf, 1941.

Caudill, Harry, *Night Comes to the Cumberlands.* Boston, Atlantic Little-Brown, 1962.

Clark, Thomas D., *The Emerging South.* New York, Oxford University Press, 1961.

Coles, Robert, *Children of Crisis.* Boston, Atlantic Little-Brown, 1967.

Good, Paul, *The American Serfs.* New York, G. P. Putnam's Sons, 1968.

Greenhut, Melvin L. and W. Tate Whitman, editors, *Essays in Southern Economic Development.* Chapel Hill, N. C., University of North Carolina Press, 1964.

Hunter, Floyd. *Community Power Structure.* Chapel Hill, N. C., University of North Carolina Press, 1953.

Key, V. O., Jr., *Southern Politics in State and Nation.* New York, Alfred A. Knopf, 1949.

Killian, Lewis and Charles Grigg, *Racial Crisis in America: Leadership in Conflict.* Englewood Cliffs, N. J., Prentice Hall, Inc., 1964.

Lester, Julius, *Look Out Whitey! Black Power's Gon' Get Your Mama!* New York, Grove Press, Inc., 1968.

Maddox, James G. *et al., The Advancing South: Manpower Prospects and Problems.* New York, The Twentieth Century Fund, 1967.

Matthews, Donald R. and James W. Prothro, *Negroes and the New Southern Politics.* New York, Harcourt, Brace and World, 1966.

Myrdal, Gunnar, *An American Dilemma,* revised edition. New York and Evanston, Harper & Row, Publishers, Inc., 1962.

Silberman, Charles E., *Crisis in Black and White.* New York, Random House, 1964.

Smith, Frank E., *Look Away from Dixie.* Baton Rouge, Louisiana State University Press, 1965.

Sutherland, Elizabeth, editor. *Letters from Mississippi.* New York, McGraw-Hill Book Company, 1965.

Tindall, George B., *The Emergence of the New South, 1913–1945.* Baton Rouge, La., Louisiana State University Press, 1967.

Trillin, Calvin, *An Education in Georgia*. New York, Viking Press, 1963.

Watters, Pat and Reese Cleghorn, *Climbing Jacob's Ladder*. New York, Harcourt, Brace and World, 1967.

Woodward, C. Vann, *The Burden of Southern History*. New York, Vintage Books, 1961.

Zinn, Howard, *The Southern Mystique*. New York, Alfred A. Knopf, 1964.

The following list of writers and books is offered not, by any means, as complete or fully representative of the literature. They are additional works that I have found useful over the years for their fidelity and lasting insights.

The works of the following writers where they are concerned with the South: James Agee, Dr. Robert Coles, James McBride Dabbs, W. E. Burghardt DuBois, Leslie W. Dunbar, Dr. Martin Luther King, Jr., Benjamin Muse, Howard Odum, Saunders Redding, Lillian Smith, Robert Penn Warren, C. Vann Woodward.

Of Southern fiction, the works of Erskine Caldwell, William Faulkner, Eudora Welty, Thomas Wolfe have been most useful to me.

And the following individual books among many recently published stand out in my mind: *Race and the Renewal of the Church*, by Will D. Campbell, Philadelphia, The Westminster Press, 1962; *A Time to Speak*, by Charles Morgan, Jr., New York, Harper & Row, Publishers, 1964; *Black Power—White Resistance*, by Fred Powledge, Cleveland and New York, The World Publishing Company, 1967; *Gothic Politics in the Deep South*, by Robert Sherrill, New York, Grossman Publishers, 1968; *Mississippi: The Closed Society*, by James W. Silver, New York, Harcourt, Brace & World, 1963.

Index

PAT WATTERS has lived in and studied the South, first as a staff writer on the Atlanta JOURNAL, then as a contributor to major journals, and, since 1963, as information director for the Southern Regional Council. His major concern has been with race relations; he has covered most of the major civil rights events in the South since 1960, has traveled throughout the area, studying its variety and complexity, and becoming deeply concerned with the poverty and tensions found there.

VINTAGE HISTORY—AMERICAN

V-623   KRADITOR, AILEEN S.   *Means and Ends in American Abolitionism*

V-367   LASCH, CHRISTOPHER   *The New Radicalism in America*

V-560   LASCH, CHRISTOPHER   *The Agony of the American Left*

V-488   LYND, STAUGHTON   *Intellectual Origins of American Radicalism*

V-502   MATTHEWS, DONALD R.   *U. S. Senators and Their World*

V-552   MAYER, ARNO J.   *Politics and Diplomacy of Peacemaking*

V-386   MCPHERSON, JAMES   *The Negro's Civil War*

V-318   MERK, FREDERICK   *Manifest Destiny and Mission in American History*

V-84   PARKES, HENRY B.   *The American Experience*

V-371   ROSE, WILLIE LEE   *Rehearsal for Reconstruction*

V-212   ROSSITER, CLINTON   *Conservatism in America*

V-285   RUDOLPH, FREDERICK   *The American College and University: A History*

V-394   SEABURY, PAUL   *Power, Freedom and Diplomacy*

V-279   SILBERMAN, CHARLES E.   *Crisis in Black and White*

V-52   SMITH, HENRY NASH   *Virgin Land*

V-345   SMITH, PAGE   *The Historian and History*

V-432   SPARROW, JOHN   *After the Assassination: A Positive Appraisal of the Warren Report*

V-388   STAMPP, KENNETH M.   *The Era of Reconstruction 1865-1877*

V-253   STAMPP, KENNETH M.   *The Peculiar Institution*

V-110   TOCQUEVILLE, ALEXIS DE   *Democracy in America*, Vol. I

V-111   TOCQUEVILLE, ALEXIS DE   *Democracy in America*, Vol. II

V-103   TROLLOPE, MRS. FRANCES   *Domestic Manners of the Americans*

V-516   ULAM, ADAM B.   *The Unfinished Revolution*

V-540   VER STEEG, CLARENCE L. and RICHARD HOFSTADTER (eds.)   *Great Issues in American History, 1584-1776*

V-265   WARREN, ROBERT PENN   *The Legacy of the Civil War*

V-605   WILLIAMS, JOHN A. and CHARLES F. HARRIS (eds.)   *Amistad 1*

V-660   WILLIAMS, JOHN A. and CHARLES F. HARRIS (eds.)   *Amistad 2*

V-362   WILLIAMS, T. HARRY   *Lincoln and His Generals*

V-208   WOODWARD, C. VANN   *Burden of Southern History*

76

77

83

88

93